MW01195153

"The Troubled Roar of the Waters"

Revisiting New England: The New Regionalism

SERIES EDITORS

Siobhan Senier, University of New Hampshire
Darren Ranco, Dartmouth College
Adam Sweeting, Boston University
David H. Watters, University of New Hampshire

This series presents fresh discussions of the distinctiveness of New England culture. The editors seek manuscripts examining the history of New England regionalism; the way its culture came to represent American national culture as a whole; the interaction between that "official" New England culture and the people who lived in the region; and local, subregional, or even biographical subjects as microcosms that explicitly open up and consider larger issues. The series welcomes new theoretical and historical perspectives and is designed to cross disciplinary boundaries and appeal to a wide audience.

For a complete list of titles in this series, please visit
WWW.UPNE.COM and WWW.UPNE.COM/SERIES/RVNE.HTML.

Deborah Pickman Clifford and Nicholas R. Clifford, *"The Troubled Roar of the Waters": Vermont in Flood and Recovery, 1927–1931*

JerriAnne Boggis, Eve Allegra Raimon, and Barbara A. White, editors, *Harriet Wilson's New England: Race, Writing, and Region*

Kimberly A. Jarvis, *Nature and Identity in the Creation of Franconia Notch*

Christopher Johnson, *This Grand and Magnificent Place: The Wilderness Heritage of the White Mountains*

Denis R. Caron, *A Century in Captivity: The Life and Trials of Prince Mortimer, a Connecticut Slave*

Paul M. Searls, *Two Vermonts: Geography and Identity, 1865–1910*

Judith Bookbinder, *Boston Modern: Figurative Expressionism as Alternative Modernism*

Donna M. Cassidy, *Marsden Hartley: Race, Region, and Nation*

Joseph A. Conforti, editor, *Creating Portland: History and Place in Northern New England*

Maureen Elgersman Lee, *Black Bangor: African Americans in a Maine Community, 1880–1950*

T. A. Milford, *The Gardiners of Massachusetts: Provincial Ambition and British-American Career*

David L. Richards, *Poland Spring: A Tale of the Gilded Age, 1860–1900*

Donald W. Linebaugh, *The Man Who Found Thoreau: Roland W. Robbins and the Rise of Historical Archaeology in America*

Pauleena MacDougall, *The Penobscot Dance of Resistance: Tradition in the History of a People*

"The Troubled Roar of the Waters"

Vermont in Flood and Recovery, 1927–1931

Deborah Pickman Clifford
and Nicholas R. Clifford

University of New Hampshire Press
Durham, New Hampshire

PUBLISHED BY UNIVERSITY PRESS OF NEW ENGLAND
HANOVER AND LONDON

University of New Hampshire Press
Published by University Press of New England,
One Court Street, Lebanon, NH 03766
www.upne.com
© 2007 by Deborah Pickman Clifford and Nicholas R. Clifford
Printed in the United States of America

5 4 3 2 1

Library of Congress Cataloging-in-Publication Data
Clifford, Deborah Pickman.
The troubled roar of the waters : Vermont in flood and recovery, 1927-1931 /
Deborah Pickman Clifford and Nicholas R. Clifford.
    p. cm. — (Revisiting New England)
Includes bibliographical references and index.
ISBN-13: 978-1-58465-654-8 (cloth : alk. paper)
ISBN-10: 1-58465-654-9 (cloth : alk. paper)
1. Floods—Vermont—History—20th century.
2. Vermont—History—20th century.
3. Vermont—History, Local.
4. Rivers—Vermont—History—20th century.
5. Disaster relief—Vermont—History—20th century.
6. Disaster victims—Vermont—Biography.
7. Vermont—Biography. I. Clifford, Nicholas Rowland. II. Title.
F54.C58 2007
974.3'042—dc22   2007016403

To Samuel Hand and Michael Sherman
in gratitude for their contributions to the history of Vermont
and its place in the world.

God is our refuge and strength, a very present help in trouble. Therefore will we not fear, though the earth be removed, and though the mountains be carried into the midst of the sea; though the waters thereof roar and be troubled, though the mountains shake with the swelling thereof.

—Psalm 46, spoken by Governor John E. Weeks to open the emergency session of the Vermont legislature, 30 November 1927

Contents

Preface xi

List of People xvii

1. Rising Waters 1
2. "Her Great Product Is Character": Vermont in 1927 30
3. "Sympathy Flowed in from the Hills": The Provision of Emergency Relief 59
4. "New Experiences in Disaster Relief": Reconstruction Begins 88
5. "Squeezed Through After Many Hairbreadth Escapes": Flood Politics in Washington and Montpelier 119
6. "Any Great Catastrophe Brings a Good Many Changes in Its Wake": The Flood and Vermont's Future 143
7. Conclusion: The Flood of 1927 in History and Memory 166

Notes 179
Select Bibliography 203
Index 217

Preface

By any reckoning, 1927 was an extraordinary year in American history. The flight of Charles Lindbergh—the Lone Eagle—across the Atlantic to Paris that spring demonstrated, as did no other event, the triumph of both American technology and American character. In August, Calvin Coolidge, the Vermont-born president, climbed to the top of Mount Rushmore, wearing cowboy boots and Mexican spurs as he covered the last four miles on horseback, there to dedicate the memorial about to be carved by Gutzon Borglum honoring four of America's greatest presidents. A month later, Babe Ruth finished the New York Yankees' season after hitting sixty home runs, and setting a record in America's national game that would stand for thirty-four years.

This book takes a slice—a small, some might say even microscopic slice—of that striking year. Catastrophes, however, have a way of laying bare issues and tensions that in normal times might be blurred or hidden, enabling us to focus on them, and in so doing to learn something about the larger society and nation in which such events take place. We try to show this by considering various aspects of the story as (to change the metaphor) a set of three concentric circles. First, we examine the flood as a story of disaster and recovery, worthy of telling for itself; meanwhile, we also consider the episode as it fits within the larger compass of Vermont's history; and finally, we ask how that story can illuminate some of the larger themes of the national history of the 1920s.

In those years, as Americans enjoyed an unprecedented freedom of movement thanks to the automobile, the stock market continued to rise, and prophets foretold that the specters of want and poverty presently would be driven from the land. Secretary of State Frank Kellogg was at work with his French colleague Aristide Briand on an international pact that would finally outlaw all war forever. It was an era in which, as Gerald Leinwand has written, Americans thought they "could do anything, go anywhere, make a fortune, lose it, and start all over again." Coolidge's speech that day on Mount Rushmore was an encomium to the American spirit, and that summer, similar professions of faith and pride in the past, speeches and parades, pageants and church services, marked the celebrations of the hundred and fiftieth anniversary of the birth of his natal state.

Yet even as Americans rejoiced in their past and congratulated themselves on their present as a new Chosen People, an undertow of deep uneasiness was abroad in the land. Rejecting the common image of the roaring twenties, recent historians have pointed to anxieties evident in many circles, particularly about the shape of a future that would challenge common conceptions of what it meant to be American. For all the optimism of the time, farmers, particularly in the South and the West, might be forgiven for making out little of the American promise of prosperity. The execution of Sacco and Vanzetti in August, far from being a triumph of law, order, and stability, seemed to many a serious miscarriage of justice. The dispatch of American troops in Nicaragua, bolstering a conservative government against the rebel Augusto Sandino, was roundly condemned by many, as was the landing of American forces that spring in Shanghai, sent to protect that city's foreign establishment against the surging Nationalist (and, for a while, Communist) revolution.

Above all, the fury of nature that year exposed the limits of American technology, American inventiveness, and America's capacity for coping. In the late winter and spring of 1927, the worst floods in history swept through the lands lying along the Mississippi River, bringing about the greatest relief effort the country had ever seen, and ultimately changing the balance of power between the states, the federal government, and private charity, particularly in the form of the National Red Cross, the most influential nongovernmental organization (NGO) of the day.

Then, in early November, after a wet summer and autumn in the Northeast, the heavens opened once more. Rain poured down on the already sodden ground, drenching a region stretching from central Connecticut to southern Quebec, bringing disruption, destruction, and death. Newspapers were filled with stories of drownings, of heroic rescues and attempts to save those who were caught by the water's sudden rise and unable to flee to higher ground. Photographs showed rivers coursing through the streets of towns and villages, houses carried away, automobiles awash or sunk in mud, and locomotives and railway cars lying on their sides, overthrown by the force of the water.

It was above all a Vermont story that the press of the day told. There, the flood was at its worst, and the tales were the most dramatic. Cities and towns like Rutland, Waterbury, and Johnson, and the state capital of Montpelier itself, were overwhelmed, suddenly cut off from the world, the subject of wild rumors about destruction accomplished or threatened. Highways vanished, rail lines were torn up, food, water, and other necessities ran short, while the specter of disease as well as winter's onset threatened even more hardships ahead. The flood story, which occupies our first chapter, was dramatic enough. But it was the flood's aftermath, the slow and painful process of digging out and rebuilding, that tested even more the character of the state, and of its septuagenarian governor, John Eliakim Weeks, who worked tirelessly to rally Vermonters for the effort needed.

It was this Vermont character that became the focus of the story as it was told then, and which we retell here. For Vermont's placement at the center of the flood story was not simply because this state—small in area and in population, less economically developed than its neighbors—was by far the hardest hit by the storm, but because Vermont occupied a very particular place in the imagination of many Americans at the time. To them, Vermont appeared to be set off from the rest of the nation as a place apart, even while Vermonters often reflected the deepest and most enduring traits and values on which Americans prided themselves. To both those living within the state and those from beyond its borders, Vermont was seen (and perhaps is still so seen) to possess a distinctive kind of psychic and social coherence, a commonly shared sense of itself and its place, less apt to be found even in neighboring states such as New Hampshire and Maine, with their divisions between industrial south and rural north, or between seacoast and hinterland.

Nor was this view entirely a figment of the imagination. Even in ordinary times, a blow inflicted on one part of Vermont might be felt by all those who, by birth or adoption, were fellow Vermonters. The misfortunes of November 1927 were distributed so widely that they genuinely became part of a shared statewide experience, and had an enormous, even traumatic, effect on all its citizens. From Bennington, just north of the Massachusetts line, to Newport and Richford, lying only a few miles south of the Canadian border, from Rutland in the west to the towns along the Connecticut River in the east, virtually every stream overflowed its banks, pouring its waters into villages and towns, covering once-fertile farmlands with silt and gravel, and wrecking much of the state's still rather primitive highway system, and its well-developed rail network.

In absolute terms, the number of casualties and damage to property and infrastructure might not be huge, when set against such references as the great Florida hurricanes of 1926 and 1928, or the Mississippi's spring flooding of 1927. Given Vermont's size, and its wealth (or lack of it), the damage was enormous, however, and this in an age that neither expected nor received the kind of disaster relief that has now become common.

Today, eighty years later, the flood occupies an important place in Vermont's historical and cultural memory, seemingly marking a divide between an antediluvian era and the years that were to follow. On this ground, the November flood is worth studying as an important part of state and regional history. But there are at least two wider reasons to examine it as well, and particularly to ask where it fits in the broader context of American history of the day. First, as this book argues, an examination of the disaster and the response it provoked can illuminate larger aspects of the nation and society of which Vermont was a part, helping us better to understand America as it passed through the great changes of the 1920s. Though many Americans might see Vermont as small and backward, and though many Vermonters might celebrate the qualities setting their state off from others, it remained subject to the same forces that affected those others at the time. In particular, as the United States underwent its often difficult transition to modernity, Vermont also had to come to terms with such changes as the decline of an older localism and communitarianism in the face of growing state and federal influence, and the rise of a new professionalism that changed the ways in which individuals and communities sought to meet their problems. Thus, while this is undeniably a local story and few of its characters are of national importance, there is nothing local about the kind of challenges that Vermont and Vermonters faced in dealing either with disaster or with the transformations that were part of the larger backdrop of the times.

Finally, like any work of history, this examination of an event now eighty years behind us tries to be useful, not so much to see where we've come from (important though that may be), but to enlarge the horizons of our own understanding, limited as they are by the times in which we live. For however similar these Vermont people and places may seem to those we know today, they are in fact alien, set apart from us not only by chronology, but by different ways of living and different approaches to their physical and social environments. It is the historian's task to bring such differences within our intellectual reach, translating them into terms that, while making them comprehensible to the present, allow them to maintain their own historical integrity. They remain different from us, these Americans and these Vermonters of eighty years ago.

Their response to catastrophe was not the same as ours would be today, and as our concluding chapter suggests, the difference tells us a great deal about the changes that have taken place in American society since the 1920s.

There are many people and many institutions to thank for help in having made this book possible. The Vermont Historical Society, in its new headquarters in Barre, provides a splendid place to work, and Marjorie Strong and Paul Carnahan were ever helpful and imaginative. Gregory Sanford, Christie Carter, and others of the staff of the Vermont State Archives in Montpelier have done much to unearth photographs and documents relative to our search, as have Peggy Powell and others of the staff of Special Collections in the Bailey-Howe Library of the University of Vermont, and the staff of the Division of Public Records in Middlesex. The Middlebury College Library's Vermont Collection has a rich collection of holdings, and Andrew Wentink, the college archivist, uncovered for us an apparently unknown cache of papers of the "Flood Governor," John E. Weeks, a man who otherwise left an unfortunately light paper trail. The Aldrich Public Library in Barre has many holdings on the flood, and we were helped here not only by Karen Lane, the librarian, but also by Pat Belding, whose own work on Barre history includes much about the flood. We also have benefited from the records held by the Henry Sheldon Museum of Vermont History in Middlebury, as well as the Vermont Folklife Center, the Bixby Library of Vergennes, and the Woodstock Public Library.

Further help came from the Library of Congress in Washington and the National Archives, particularly in chasing down the American Red Cross's records of flood relief. Professor Kendrick Clements of the University of South Carolina helped us to clarify our ideas about Herbert Hoover and his role in Mississippi. In addition, we are grateful to a long list of people to whom we have talked in individual towns and at local historical societies, some of whom have contributed copies of documents to us or made suggestions of other places to look. Particular thanks are due to Caleb Pitkin, who shared Flora Carpenter's contemporary account of the flood in Waterbury, and Barbara Carpenter, who shared the memories of Arecca Urban about the flood in Johnson. Jack Hall, of the Norwich University Library, helped us with records of the work done by the cadets in Northfield. Mary Fitzgerald of the Winooski Historical Society provided a tape of flood recollections in that town, while Marcus Blair and Herb Campbell of Rochester helped us with photographs of the White River and its railway. For the map, we are grateful to Natalie Guarin for her careful work in its preparation.

Kristin Peterson-Ishaq at the Center for Research on Vermont gave us a chance to make some of our findings public, thereby trying them out on an audience. Michael Sherman and Gene Sessions, two of the authors of *Freedom and Unity,* very kindly allowed us to read part of that work before its publication. Gene Sessions later read the entire manuscript and offered many helpful suggestions, as did Upton Brady, while James Ralph of Middlebury College and Nancy Gallagher graciously agreed to read and to comment on individual chapters. Finally, we owe our thanks for the suggestions made by two anonymous readers through the University Press of New England, and particularly to Paul Searls, the third reader, who was very helpful to us in clarifying our ideas. We are most grateful to all of them. And finally, we thank Ellen Wicklum, our editor at the Press, for her help and encouragement in this project.

D. P. C. and N. R. C.

People

The following list, consisting largely of Vermonters, identifies those who are referred to with some frequency, and who probably will not be familiar to many readers. Their positions, for the most part, are those held during the years from 1927 to 1931.

Adams, Charles B.: Disaster chairman, Waterbury

Adams, the Rev. Chauncey A.: Pastor, Waterbury Congregational Church

Aiken, George: Elected to Vermont House in 1930, later governor (1937–1941) and senator (1940–1975)

Bailey, Guy: President of the University of Vermont (1919–1940)

Baker, Henry: Red Cross expert on disaster relief, in charge of New England relief operations, 1928

Barrows, H. W.: Member, Advisory Committee of Engineers (studying flood control)

Bates, Stoddard: Vermont State Highway Commissioner

Billings, Franklin: Predecessor of John Weeks as governor of Vermont (1925–1927)

Brigham, Elbert: With Ernest Gibson, one of Vermont's two congressmen in Washington (1925–1931)

Bullard, F. Lauriston: Journalist, *New York Times*

Carpenter, Flora: Waterbury schoolteacher

Coates, Walter: Founder and editor of *Driftwind*

Comings, Herbert: Democratic challenger to Weeks in 1926; vice-president, Vermont Flood Credit Corporation

Crockett, Walter: Historian and Vermont state senator

Dale, Porter: Senator from Vermont (1923–1933)

Deavitt, Edward: Mayor of Montpelier, and unsuccessful challenger to Weeks in 1928

Demeritt, B. R.: Chairman, executive committee of Vermont Flood Credit Corporation

Dempsey, Clarence: Vermont Commissioner of Education

Ferrin, Charles: Army captain, Fort Ethan Allen

Fieser, James: Vice-chairman, National Red Cross

Field, Frederick: Chairman, Rutland Emergency Committee

French, E. S.: Vice-president, White River Railway

Fuller, Alvin: Governor of Massachusetts

Gates, Benjamin: Vermont state auditor

Gay, Leon: Chairman, Cavendish Red Cross chapter

Gibson, Ernest: With Elbert Brigham, one of Vermont's two congressmen in Washington (1923–1933)

Greene, Frank: Senator from Vermont (1923–1930)

Harris, William: National Red Cross official; first director of New England relief

Hartness, James: Former governor of Vermont, 1921–1923; exponent of governmental efficiency

Herrle, Colin: National Red Cross official in northern Vermont

Hindley, Howard: Editor, *Rutland Herald*

Howe, Frank: Editor, *Bennington Banner*

Howland, Fred: President of National Life, and state emergency finance commissioner after the flood

Jackson, S. Hollister: Lieutenant-Governor, drowned in flood

Johnson, Herbert: Vermont Adjutant-General

Johnson, Luther: Journalist, editor of *Randolph Herald and News*

Jones, Edward H.: Vermont Commissioner of Agriculture

Lovecraft, H. P.: Writer of supernatural stories, and Vermont visitor

Lyons, Louis: Journalist, *Boston Globe*

Mayer, William: Army captain from Fort Ethan Allen

Moody, Paul: President of Middlebury College (1921–1943)

Nolen, John: Urban planner and critic of Vermont's lack of planning

Noyes, Mrs. Harry: Chairman, Lamoille County Red Cross chapter

Nutting, Wallace: Author and protagonist of Colonial Revival movement

Orton, Vrest: Vermont writer

Partridge, Frank: President of Vermont Marble Co.; President, Vermont Flood Credit Corporation

Payne, John Barton: Chairman, National Red Cross

Peach, Arthur: Chairman, Committee on Conservation of Vermont Traditions and Ideals

Perkins, Henry: Zoologist, and motive force behind Eugenics Commission

Plumley, Charles: President of Norwich University (1920–1934)

Powell, Max: Unsuccessful candidate for governor, 1926

Proctor, Redfield: Former governor of Vermont (1923–1925)

Ratshesky, A. C.: Boston banker, heading Red Cross activities in Boston

Robsion, John: Kentucky congressman; member House Roads Committee

Rockwood, Arthur Edward: Journalist, editor of *Vermont Review*

Saleeby, A. J.: Johnson storekeeper

Sargent, John Garibaldi: United States Attorney-General

Small, Frank: Mayor of Barre

Smith, E. C.: Former governor of Vermont (1898–1900); president, Central Vermont Railway

Smith, Al: Governor of New York

Southwick, John: Managing editor, *Burlington Free Press*

Spargo, John: English-born chairman of Vermont Sesquicentennial Commission, 1927

Squier, Lloyd: Reporter and later editor of *Waterbury Record*

Taylor, Henry: General Director of the Comprehensive Rural Survey

Thompson, Clara: Bolton schoolteacher

Thompson, George: Chairman, Vermont State Highway Board

Thornton, Sir Henry: Head of Canadian National Railway

Votey, J. W.: Dean of University of Vermont Engineering School; chairman, Advisory Committee of Engineers (studying flood control)

Walter, Charles: Journalist; editor of St. Johnsbury *Republican*

Weeks, John Eliakim: Governor of Vermont (1927–1931)

Wilson, Stanley: Successor to John Weeks as governor of Vermont (1931–1935)

"The Troubled Roar of the Waters"

Vermont, 1927: Main Towns, Railroads, and River Valleys. *Cartography by Natalie Guarin.*

~~∿∼~~

Rising Waters

Near Moretown, in Vermont's Mad River Valley, the air is unnaturally warm this Wednesday, more like June than November, and from her house, Myrtie Redmond looks up to a sky "as blue as an amethyst and flecked with soft, fleecy white clouds." In Rutland, the temperature reaches 73 degrees, and even up at St. Johnsbury, only forty miles from the Quebec border, at four in the afternoon the thermometer stands at 67, tempting Charles Walter, the editor of the *St. Johnsbury Republican,* to take some friends along on a picnic in the countryside. To the west, where St. Albans stands among gentle hills rolling down to the broad reach of Lake Champlain, the Central Vermont Railway's publicity department gathers together several well-dressed employees, tells them to pretend they're passengers, and has them photographed seated in the observation car of the line's crack Ambassador. Each conspicuously wears a headset, for the train, put into service three years ago to make the daytime run between Boston and Montreal in only nine and a half hours, is the first in the United States to be equipped with radio reception for the entertainment of its riders.[1]

"The autumn of 1927 was one of marvelous beauty," Ernest Gibson will tell his colleagues in the House of Representatives a few months later. "The weather was perfect and the verdure fresh beyond the normal period . . . Over our roads, winding here and there among the hills, passed thousands of tourists contemplating with amazement scenes of rare beauty in this Switzerland of America."[2] Yet there's something strange, almost uncanny, about this late appearance of Indian summer and the damp heaviness of the air, mingling now with the faintly dusty smell of dead leaves, fallen after their brief autumn glory from the oaks and maples of the woodlands, and from the great rounded elms arching over meadows and village greens.

After a dry spring and a rainy summer, October has been the mildest and wettest such month here in a dozen years, the average temperature some three degrees above normal, the rainfall in places two or even three times heavier than usual. Yet welcome as it is, no one expects such warmth to last very long at this time of year. "Fair today," reads the *Rutland Herald*'s weather report this morning of 2 November. "Showers tonight; Thursday fair and colder."

What happens, of course, is quite different. The showers arrive as expected on Wednesday evening, gentle at first, and coming late enough not to spoil Walter's picnic near St. Johnsbury. By Thursday morning, instead of stopping as predicted, the rain becomes unexpectedly heavy and, as the rivers begin to rise, so does a sense of apprehension. The little school in Moretown closes early, as do many others, and people living near the streams begin to make their way to higher ground, as they are accustomed to do when the spring thaws bring sudden freshets. As the storm quickens, up in Lyndonville, nine miles north of St. Johnsbury, a fast Packard touring car lies wrecked against a telephone pole, apparently spun out of control on the slick roads. Police, arriving on the scene, find bloodstains and evidence of liquor, presumably being carried down from Canada along the bootleg route that runs the length of Vermont. Of the owner, a Charles Nyman of Ashburnham, Massachusetts, there is no sign.[3]

That afternoon, as the downpour continues, washouts along the Central Vermont Railroad's main line halt the Ambassador on its way to Montreal, at White River Junction, forcing its passengers to seek refuge in the Hotel Coolidge. Its southbound sister makes it no farther than Roxbury—the high point on the line—on its passage to Boston. No one realizes it now, of course, only a day after that carefully staged photograph in St. Albans, but it will be fully seven months before this train, the Central Vermont's pride, once more resumes its regular run.

⎯⎯⎯⎯

What happened?

At first, there seemed nothing unusual about the showers that began to fall that Wednesday evening of 2 November, borne in on a cold front, and moving north to cross into Canada around midnight. Then, however, the weather map began to change radically. A late-season tropical storm, barrelling northeast over the waters well offshore, found its way blocked south of Newfoundland, and instead of playing itself out in the Atlantic, sent a mass of warm wet air westward over New England. This, in turn, was absorbed by a secondary low-pressure center, which drove the tropical air further inland yet. There it met the mountain ranges of the interior—the Whites, the Berkshires, the Taconics, and the Greens— these last rising over four thousand feet. The lighter air, still warm and wet, rode up over the cold mass arriving from the middle west, and as it became cooled itself, its Caribbean moisture was condensed rapidly. Within twenty-four hours, a heavy rain was inundating much of western New England, eastern New York, and southern Quebec.

Off in the north Atlantic, several inbound liners arrived late in New York, among them the *Leviathan,* the *George Washington,* and the *Mauretania,* whose captain described the weather as the worst he had seen in his service aboard the ship, the Thursday night rain off Nantucket Light cutting visibility as badly as a heavy fog. At Hartford, Connecticut, anxious residents watched the river rise twenty-nine feet over low water, reaching heights unseen since 1854, tearing boats loose from their moorings, sweeping freight into the water, and bringing river traffic to a standstill. Connecticut's low-lying farmlands were flooded, highways were cut, and riverside textile mills had to shut down, while thousands sought refuge on high ground. The bursting of dams along the Hoosick River in Vermont poured water down into the Hudson Valley, raising the river's level ten feet above normal at Albany. High water in the Lebanon Valley cut the railway, the Champlain Canal was shut, and the New York State barge canal was closed east of Amsterdam. At Whitehall, streets were under water, and the Champlain Silk Mill suffered $150,000 in damage. Even Rhode Island, though spared the brunt of the storm, had a small area of extremely heavy rain, with more than nine inches coming down in Westerly, while swollen rivers threatened Pawtucket and Woonsocket, closing mills and throwing five thousand people out of work.

More serious was the damage in western Massachusetts, particularly in towns near the swollen Connecticut River. At the Holyoke Dam, the river reached record heights, flooding the lower section of the city, and crippling local industries. Every available man in Springfield was drafted into service in an unsuccessful attempt to hold back the river, while five square miles of nearby Chicopee were under water. All told, about fifteen thousand families in the region had to abandon their homes, finding safety where they could, often in makeshift shelters set up by the Red Cross, the American Legion, and other such groups. Students from Williams College appear to have rescued almost the entire population of the little town of Braytonsville, while Smith College women worked with the Red Cross and other agencies succoring the refugees. Elsewhere, rescuers set out in boats to carry to safety those who had been marooned, and after reports of looting in Springfield, armed police carried on their patrols in rowboats.

Near Westfield in the Connecticut Valley, the waters caught twenty-year-old Helen Moore and nineteen-year-old Harold Dewey in their automobile, and their bodies were not recovered until a few days later. The most spectacular event, however, was the near destruction of the little hill village of Becket, after the failure of a dam sent a wall of water down on the town, carrying away many buildings. Though there was only one drowning, the casualty toll would have been far higher, had it not been for the reservoir's owner, William Ballou, who drove through the village telling people to leave at the first signs of failure. (The papers called him the Paul Revere of the Berkshires.)

Farther north, the heaviest rains of all—perhaps as much as fifteen inches—may have fallen in New Hampshire's White Mountains, sending that state's rivers on a rampage, destroying highways and bridges, and sweeping away miles of railroad track. Nearly four-fifths of the state reportedly was cut off from the outside world, highway and rail traffic came to a standstill, and farms were under water, while the Merrimac River roared through the mill towns of the south. At Manchester, the passage of water over the Amoskeag Dam rose from a normal 3,000 cubic feet per second to 80,000, and water flowed into the streets of Nashua, as well as of Lowell, Lawrence, and Haverhill just over the border in Massachusetts, shutting down paper and textile mills, and throwing tens of thousands out of work.

Meanwhile, southeastern Quebec and western New Brunswick found themselves hard hit. Both Sherbrooke and Drummondville saw over five inches of rain, and the former city, where the water was ten feet deep, was isolated. Rail traffic between Montreal and Quebec City was cut, one bridge going down shortly after Governor-General Lord George Willingdon and Lady Willingdon had passed over it. Other bridges and highways were washed out, farms flooded, cattle killed, and all told, the province saw about $2 million in damage, and as many as nine dead.[4]

It was not simply a Vermont flood, or even only a New England flood. But Vermont, at the heart of the storm, was its chief victim. In the dramatic image of two meteorologists at Clark University, for the next two days the state found itself under a "cube of water more than a mile high, a mile long, and a mile broad."[5]

Mrs. Marin's house and barn (the old Dr. Crandall place), were slowly swept away, and in succession the big Safford saw mill, their house and barns; Mrs. Waldo Perkins's house and barn and soon after Emma Nye's house and barn and a small house, once a school, about half way up the big hill. This was owned by W. H. Ketchum, the "snow-shoe man," used as a storehouse, and in it when it went were thirty pairs of finished snow-shoes, and a quantity of dry lumber, besides much household furniture, some belonging to Mr. Ketchum, and some put there for safety from the houses below. No one supposed that house was in any danger as it stood so far up the hill but the mad river cut under the bank and it began to slide, till the house went, and all the road to the top of the long hill.[6]

Lawrence Mills's account of what happened to his tiny village of Gaysville in the White River Valley echoes many such records of the time. Written less than a year after the disaster, its immediacy and tangibility come from the references to people and places that mean little to anyone unfamiliar with that local topographical or chronological landscape. Yet despite such intimately local details, tying the events to a very particular place and time, the universal themes that emerge from stories like this make it possible to reconstruct a record of Vermont's experience as it appeared to the men and women who lived through those November days now more than eighty years ago.

What was striking at the time was how fast and how far the waters rose, the height of the rivers in many places far exceeding all previous records. Anyone who had followed the accounts of the massive spring floods on the Mississippi that year would remember how long that disaster had been in the making, how slowly the great river had prepared itself, how much warning had been given, as the crests—ten of them, all told, in the winter and spring—took days to travel down the rivers, from western Pennsylvania, Ohio, and Illinois, to St. Louis, and then south to New Orleans and the delta. Vermont's experience was entirely different. But then so too was its topography. Steep valleys, and rivers like the White and the Winooski, the Lamoille and the Otter, flowing through narrows on their course, brought hazards of a different kind from those seen in the flat lands of Arkansas, Louisiana, and Mississippi, where levees sought to keep the river in its man-made bed. Here in Vermont, the waters rose and fell in fewer than forty-eight hours. "The Mississippi Valley floods of last spring and previously were majestic demonstrations of vast volume and wide disaster," wrote the postmaster at Bennington. "The New England flood was all over in a few hours of darkness and terror."

But when the rivers subsided, they left behind them a changed land-scape and a changed people. Accidents of topography and of greater and lesser amounts of rain meant that the destruction and damage were not shared equally. Burlington, for example, had 5.1 inches of rain in those two days, while Somerset, in the Connecticut Valley, reported 9.45, Northfield 8.40, and Rutland just over 8 inches.[7] Some regions and some towns—Manchester in the south, for instance, or St. Albans, on the shores of northern Lake Champlain—escaped almost unscathed, suf-fering no more than inconvenience from temporary losses of power or the cutting of transportation and communication lines. Up on the steep slopes of the Green Mountains, hill towns—Stowe was an example, as was Weston and Underhill—saw little damage. Even in the same valleys, the experiences of different towns—Rutland and Middlebury, for ex-ample, both lying along Otter Creek, or Waterbury and Burlington, on the banks of the Winooski—could be quite distinct.

What everyone shared was fear: fear of the incessant driving rain, fear of the rising streams and rivers, fear of what was happening to oth-ers, as rumors spread of enormous damage and loss of life. Early news reports told of more than two hundred dead in Montpelier, after the supposed breaking of the new Molly's Falls dam in Marshfield, near the headwaters of the Winooski. Though that story was soon corrected, at Greensboro, the actual collapse of a small dam at Caspian Lake led to alarm that the whole eastern shore might give way, releasing the lake's waters in a sudden rush down into the Lamoille Valley five hundred feet below. In Rutland, where nerves were already on edge from the heavy damage caused by the flooding of Otter Creek and its tributaries, ru-mors of the impending failure of the great Chittenden dam, ten miles away and a thousand feet above the city, led to the attempted flight of two or three thousand people, jamming muddy roads already devas-tated by the storm.

Even those places that were largely spared could see the evidence of destruction elsewhere. Years later, Shuffy Tamer, who lived on Canal Street in the industrial town of Winooski, remembered the sight of cat-tle and horses being swept down the river. Children, let out of school early and ordered to go home at once, instead joined the crowds watch-ing the iron bridge linking Burlington to Winooski survive repeated batterings until it finally gave way, struck by a barn borne along by the water. To Consuelo Northrup Bailey, a rising politician, the bridge seemed an "animated being," almost like a stout old Vermonter, "as it resisted, held on, stood firm and for a while appeared equal to the destructive demon attacking it," quivering and shuddering as its foundations were destroyed. "Then slowly and reluctantly, with its frame proudly but momentarily raised above the ferocious torrent, it fell into oblivion. Pathetically, it seemed to gasp: 'I did my best.'"[8]

Though the rain that started falling on Wednesday evening would continue for thirty-six hours, in many places it was not until mid-afternoon on Thursday that the danger became clear. That evening, as power systems failed, the darkness added immeasurably to the fears of those who lived through that terrifying night, with no electric light, gas, or safe water supplies to help them cope with the disaster. So did the incessant roar of flooded rivers like the White and the Winooski, their noise drowning out everything except the horrifying sounds of buildings being wrenched from their foundations, and the cries for help from those caught inside. At Royalton, in the White River Valley, Charles Keay, a railway worker, managed to reach the house of a Mr. and Mrs. Hicks near the river, but the inhabitants were already beyond rescue. The lights within, Mary Whitney wrote later, "remained as a beacon of hope until about four in the morning when amid the awful screams of its occupants it was swept away. Some heard the screams and saw the lights as far as the iron railroad bridge . . ." The bodies of Mrs. Hicks and Keay were never found, but in a macabre ending to the tale, Hicks himself survived the night, hanging on to the branches of an overturned tree until the next morning, when he too fell into the flood. "One can hardly imagine anything more ghastly, gruesome, and agonizing," wrote the journalist Luther Johnson. In nearby Sharon, the river swept away the house of Mrs. Reynolds and her two children, "the light of the little kerosene lamp in the chamber where the mother sat with her children being visible and their cries of terror being heard above the roar of the torrent for a considerable distance on the terrible ride to a watery grave."[9]

Thirty-five miles away, the Dog River rose fifteen feet above normal, flooding much of the town of Northfield, destroying highways, and bringing down the great stone bridge that had carried the Central Vermont's tracks for seventy-five years. There, the Norwich University cadets went into action, some putting out in canoes in the pitch dark to rescue people from flooded houses, others helping to stem the river's flow with sand and gravel, still others patrolling the streets. Thanks to their actions, though property damage was considerable, no lives were lost, and as early as Friday some of the students made their way on horseback into Barre and Montpelier.[10]

Miles to the north, on the banks of the swollen Winooski, emergency workers at Waterbury were stunned to see a two-story house being carried down the river, "twinkling and bowing in the rush of water," as the journalist Lloyd Squier described it, "and every window lighted as if a family was about its ordinary living inside."[11] In nearby Bolton, Will Agan watched helplessly as two houses, one with the Fortune family, the other with the May family, went by on the flood, John May calling out to him as he swept past, "Well, we're gone. Good bye!" Both houses, with nine people inside, appear to have crashed into the railway bridge, throwing their inhabitants into the water.[12] The Agans themselves were rescued on Friday afternoon, though by then their cattle and horses were drowned.

"It was a night to leave scars on our souls," wrote Flora Chase from Gaysville, "to haunt our dreams, to recur to us with startling vividness, and even now, after ten months are past, to bring a cold, creeping dread with the thought of it."[13] Tales like these, with their juxtaposition of the roaring waters bearing away eerily lighted houses, the inhabitants still visible within them, appeared in the press at the time, and in the accounts published later in papers such as the *Vermonter*. So too did stories of those who risked their lives in rescuing others in the cold darkness of that November night. At White River Junction, on the Connecticut River, where the water rose thirty feet in twelve hours, Henry Leavitt, a policeman, saved many lives by repeatedly jumping into the icy water to bring people to safety. When the collapse of two dams brought a rush of water down Bennington's Main Street, plunging the town into darkness, Edward Adams, an African-American handyman and hunting guide, worked with a horse and wagon under almost impossible conditions to pull people from danger, narrowly escaping death himself. Other would-be rescuers were less fortunate. Andrew Shepard was swept away in Bennington, while far to the north in Troy, Philbert Chicoine and his nineteen-year-old son drowned in the waters of Mineral Spring Brook as they attempted to take their wagon to reach the children at the Hitchcock School.[14]

Everywhere that the waters rose, there were similar stories of heroism and tragedy, even humor, like that of the young man singing Venetian songs as he guided his boat through the streets of downtown Bennington.

Some of the tales, it must be added, owed a good deal to the imagination of the tellers. A spectacular eyewitness account appearing in several papers, of a wall of water looking like "a huge gray monster" as it rushed through Proctorsville on the Black River, was said to come from Sarah Pollard, President Calvin Coolidge's eighty-seven-year-old aunt. Mrs. Pollard unfortunately denied later that she'd said anything of the sort; she had gone to bed at her usual hour and learned nothing of the flood till the next day. The story in fact seems to have been dreamed up by an ambitious reporter, perhaps for the *Boston Post*.[15]

What made matters even worse in the darkness and fury of the storm was the sense of isolation. Many of Vermont's still primitive highways, often unsatisfactory at the best of times, were no match for the downpour and soon became impassable, while fallen bridges left even undamaged communities suddenly cut off from one another, making it difficult to bring or get help. Because telephone and telegraph lines went down as well, it was often impossible to find out what was happening elsewhere, who was hurt and who survived, magnifying the fears of those unable to reach friends or family. In Middlebury, for example, though townspeople could watch the badly swollen Otter Creek crashing over the falls that had powered the town's mills, no one gave the matter much thought until the failure of the afternoon train to arrive signaled that something was wrong, and gave rise to the wildest rumors. And a few days after the flood, a reporter who made his way into the Mad River Valley claimed to have discovered some in Waitsfield who believed that Boston itself had vanished in the waters. ("The natives of the isolated hamlet . . . were not as dumb as he pictured them, but never mind that," commented E. H. Jones, the commissioner of agriculture, and one of the natives himself.)[16]

Railways, though more solidly built than the roads, fared little better. From western Massachusetts to Quebec, trains were halted if they were fortunate, wrecked if they were not, their cargoes lost or their passengers stranded. On Thursday afternoon, the eastbound Green Mountain Flyer to Boston took a full two hours to travel the thirteen miles from Rutland to East Wallingford, before stopping for good at Cuttingsville. Its westbound sister was halted at Mount Holly, near the pass through the mountains, after a brakeman, sent to walk ahead of the locomotive, sank up to his shoulders in a washout. There, thirty-five passengers spent two wretchedly cold and wet nights on the train, subsisting on what they could procure from nearby farms, before being evacuated to

Rutland on Saturday.[17] John Newton, engineer of the Central Vermont's southbound Ambassador, stopped his train at Roxbury when he felt the tracks "soften" under him, presently learning that in any case a freight blocked the main line to the north, and that bridges were out in both directions. Roughly a hundred of his riders had to spend Thursday night in the coaches (that particular train, fortunately, carried a diner with a day's supply of food, as well as a ukelele-playing passenger who provided entertainment). The refugees presently found shelter in the town, and though on Saturday some made their way out by handcar, it was five days before the rest could be brought out on foot and horseback.[18]

When his train was stalled at Bethel, Fred Tuttle, a Central Vermont brakeman, managed to walk, wade, and swim the fifty miles to Essex Junction, where he was able to report the extent of the damage he had seen.[19] Fred Stevens, a railway mail clerk whose Newport-bound train was stranded in Lyndonville on Thursday night, set off on foot on Saturday, picking his way along the wrecked track, sometimes having to cross gullies or washouts on ties, wobbling "like logs in a mill pond." At South Barton, he came across a Canadian Pacific express unable to move, with a large number of passengers aboard. Meanwhile, the line's president, Edward W. Beatty, whose private car was attached to the Red Wing, northbound from Boston to Montreal, found himself caught at Wells River when the train stopped. He managed to get back down to White River Junction, then made his way to St. Johnsbury and Lyndonville by car on Sunday, and the next day reached Sherbrooke by handcar, on foot, and by automobile, where he could arrange for the rescue of his line's stranded passengers.[20]

Beatty's Canadian Pacific was only one of the main trunk lines that suffered heavy damage in the region. "The chaos of railroad transportation caused by the storm and floods was probably unparalleled," wrote the New York Times on 5 November, as the main arteries connecting New York, New England, and Canada were blocked. At Williamstown, Massachusetts, the Boston and Maine's Chicago Flyer came to a stop, unable either to proceed or to return to its starting point, while the damage at Becket blocked the Boston and Albany's tracks. Shortages of milk were reported in the towns, and in Boston, a railway spokesman predicted on Friday that only ten percent of the city's normal supply (well over half of which came from Vermont) would get through the next day. Governor Alvin Fuller ordered that it be conserved for children.[21]

Fig. 1. The swollen Otter Creek pouring through central Rutland. *Courtesy of Special Collections, Bailey/Howe Library, University of Vermont.*

A closer look at several of the cities and towns hardest hit gives a sense of the flood's effects on the lives of local people and their communities. If Burlington, for example, got off relatively lightly, that was not true of Rutland. The state's second-largest city, with its flourishing industry and its rich marble quarries nearby, was an important center of highway and rail traffic. Otter Creek, flowing through its southwest quadrant, is generally a placid stream as it makes its way north from the hills of Dorset to Lake Champlain, but by Thursday morning, its waters as well as those of its tributaries were already invading the streets, making some impassable. Volunteers turned out to help the rescue work of the fire and police departments, while at the West Street armory, local Red Cross and National Guard workers set up cots to prepare a refugee center. By nightfall, the power distribution station at Cleveland Avenue was under six feet of water, while the collapse of a dam killed the generators at Mill Village, leaving people to do their best with kerosene lamps and candles. "For the first time in history," the *Herald* reported the next day, "Rutland industries . . . failed to turn a wheel."

"FLOODS SWEEP CITY" cried the headline in the greatly abbreviated Friday issue of the paper. Three people had already died, one of them, John Cebula of the Vermont Marble Company, in a wagon that overturned as he tried to reach householders on the south bank of Otter Creek. By

Saturday morning, nearly twenty bridges were down, the rail lines cut, and only one road out of the city remained open. Rutland was now under martial law, its streets deserted, and householders ordered to boil their water, though with no gas supply, not only they but also hotels and restaurants had to find other ways to cook food. Meanwhile, the authorities tried to stem the panic arising from reports of an endangered Chittenden dam. "Ignore wild rumors," the *Herald* counseled its readers, its large print telling them to wait for "four long blasts of the fire whistle, which will be given as a flood signal if any trouble is anticipated. REMEMBER: FOUR BLASTS OF THE WHISTLE IS THE ONLY SIGNAL THAT MEANS FLOOD CONDITIONS. STAND BY FOR OFFICIAL NOTICE."[22]

Down in the railway yards below Strongs Avenue, a cargo of milk bound for New York was hastily converted to butter at a local processing plant, in the hope of saving it from total loss. Far more serious was the plight of the Thursday afternoon milk train from Alburg, hauling twenty-two cars south to the Boston and New York markets. Shortly after four, it reached the quarrying town of Proctor just north of Rutland, running only fifteen minutes late despite the blinding rains and high winds through which it had steamed. There, where the Otter Valley narrows, it was run onto a siding, ordered to wait for the northbound Green Mountain Flier, though that train, of course, was already stranded in the hills some thirty miles away. Rescuers managed to take off the brakeman and conductor, but the surging waters kept them from reaching the locomotive. There, Samuel Langill, the fireman, and engineer Henry La Parle had to scramble to safety on the roof of their cab, spending a cold and miserable night in the open, as the river roared through the station nearby, until a boat could reach them the next day and take them to the Proctor hospital (La Parle died shortly thereafter). The abandoned train's cargo—nearly 40,000 gallons, worth some $10,000—had to be dumped.[23]

By then, the Proctor village square itself was under ten feet of water. The Vermont Marble Company—not only one of the state's chief industries, but the largest enterprise of its kind in the world—was badly hurt, as the river swept tons of mud and gravel into its power plant, and threatened to undermine the mill. "I hope I never live to see another flood," wrote E. E. Sears a week later.

> We live up high so it could not reach us . . . Mr. Geo. Davis came near death. Had to pull him out of station with a rope. 2 men are in hospital

that were on top of engine all night. With all not a live (sic) was lost. we had a lot of extra to do . . . As you would know I was near wild about my own home. They moved out of one barn & the water was up to the house. Etta wrote me that it was quite scarey Sat & Sunday. She said Will worked day and night too . . .

Leon Turner's wife and three children were at Salisbury he lost everything even his money which he said was $40. Could not even get his car. Some of the people have moved back in houses. They have been living in school house & Parish house & old Catholic church. They say the houses are damp and cold. Miss Emily Proctor had to leave her house as the water undermined it. She came over to Cavendish house near us & how she did work. She keeps the house for sick & needy a wonderful woman. . .[24]

Thirty miles east of Rutland, the White River rises high on the eastern slopes of the main range of the Green Mountains, flowing south through rocky Granville Gulf and the narrow valley below, joined by some six or seven steep tributaries before reaching the Connecticut River at White River Junction. High up on its course, the failure of a dam near Hancock brought a rush of water through town, tearing up the highway, while a few miles downstream the inhabitants of Rochester—as one of them put it—"stood spellbound as we saw the wayside brooks become raging torrents and the rivers assume Styx-like proportions." In little Gaysville, clinging to the slopes of Vulture and Hunger Mountains, the surging river led anxious householders to carry their belongings on Thursday afternoon up to the large Methodist church, which stood on higher ground. By early dusk, the rising waters had covered the track of the narrow-gauge railway, and were beginning to invade the station itself. A few hours later, the depot tipped over onto its side and was carried off.

At midnight, with the river now only three feet from their house, Frank Arnold and his family quickly managed to hitch a team of horses to their automobile, and pull it uphill. From its shelter, fifteen minutes later, they watched their house swept down the current. After a seemingly endless night, daybreak on Friday showed the river tearing away the sandbanks on which Gaysville was built. The villagers watched helplessly as the church to which they had entrusted their goods now fell into the river, its steeple crashing down, before it too was borne away. "We never saw it again, except as a mass of kindling wood," Lawrence Miller later wrote.

In all, some fifty-six of the little village's buildings were lost—houses, farms, sheds, as well as the station and the church, and many people were left homeless. It was a huge toll for so small a settlement, and to make matters worse, when the waters finally subsided, Gaysville found itself cut in half by the river's new channel. Though its power plant still stood, there was no longer any water to turn the generators, and where once there had been meadows beyond the town, there was only a wilderness of gravel, stones, and ledge. "There is absolutely not one foot of anything left resembling soil," said Flora Chase, "not a sign that any building ever stood there, not a stone that looks like a foundation wall. There are absolutely no words with which to paint the picture. We who knew it so well and loved it can hardly convince ourselves that on that wild waste once stood houses, shade trees, green lawns, fertile gardens."[25]

Farther downstream, at Royalton and Sharon, more drownings occurred that Thursday night, before the stream reached White River Junction. There it added its flow to the swollen Connecticut, which was already spilling over into the streets of towns downstream: North Walpole in New Hampshire, Bellows Falls and Brattleboro in Vermont , and the mill towns of western Massachusetts and Connecticut.

A few miles to the south, near the head of the Black River in the hills above Plymouth, the birthplace of President Coolidge, a lake embankment gave way, inundating several woolen mills in Ludlow, and taking down the town's main highway bridge. On Thursday night, when a power dam collapsed in Cavendish Gorge, the rush of water dug an enormous gulch where Cavendish's main street had run, swallowing automobiles and buildings whose owners had fled, and not until the waters reached a ledge did the destruction stop. "A canyon over 50 feet deep and half a mile long, *made in one night,*" as a Boston geologist later described it, explaining that the water of the Black River had rediscovered its old preglacial bed. "One day there was a pleasant street dotted with comfortable homes," wrote Leon Gay, "and the next morning found a yawning canyon with seven homes gone and others tottering on the brink."[26]

Farther north, near a narrows along the Lamoille River, a stream notorious for its rapid rises, the little town of Johnson was one of the worst hit. Here too, rumors of broken dams upstream led some to abandon their houses for the hills above town, where they spent the night under a drenching cold rain. The rumors proved false, but the quantity of trees, shattered buildings, bridges, and livestock, cascading down the swelling river created its own dam at a narrows just to the south, sending the water back on the town. A. J. Saleeby, a Syrian and former country peddler, who now ran the largest dry goods store in town, later remembered watching the water rise three feet in less than half an hour. As his basement filled, he tried, too late, to save his store's records, narrowly escaping drowning himself when falling counters and display racks blocked his escape. Warren Annis worked from one in the morning until dawn, maneuvering a shallow boat through the waters to carry more than twenty-five people to safety in the Hotel Everett (one family had barely seated themselves in his boat when they saw their house tip over, and the attic window from which they had escaped disappear in the river). Less fortunate was the Shangraw family. Newcomers to the valley, they ignored the warnings of trouble, and three of their four members drowned as their house and farm, two miles south of town, were swept away.[27]

At four in the morning on Friday, the Lamoille River crested, and the coming of daylight a few hours later showed the extent of damage. The town was utterly cut off, with no way to bring in supplies of medicine, food, or fuel. Some twenty-four houses had been swept from their foundations, and every store but one was filled with water. The Johnson Woolen Mill was badly damaged, the bank under water, and only the ridgepole of the library was visible above the gray expanse of the river. A mile and a half away, a barn and and its outbuildings were carried off, and twenty-three cows, collared to their stanchions, were left hanging by their heads when the floor gave way. From another farm, Philip French wrote a few days later to his uncle that "[w]e are all safe, thank God. But financially I am ruined. Barn gone. Saved most of my stock. House about ruined. Everything gone down the river," and he described having to spend the night with his family in a sugar house up in the hills, surviving the long hours of cold and rain.[28]

Disastrous as were the effects of the storm in the White River and Lamoille valleys, they were even more terrible along the Winooski and its tributaries. In Barre, whose thriving granite industry had drawn an ethnically mixed and fractious work force unusual in Vermont, the Stevens and Jail branches (which, as one writer put it, usually held hardly enough water to float a rowboat) turned into torrents by Thursday afternoon. That morning, George Mosher, a Boston businessman, drove to the nearby quarries through two feet of water on Main Street, and found it risen to six when he returned. Depot Square was now a lake, the city's granite plants were shut down, and Goddard Seminary, a local high school set on a hill, became a place of refuge, serving also as a temporary hospital for an expectant mother, whose child chose that time to arrive. Two shopkeepers, trying to move goods to the upper floors of their buildings, became the town's first victims when they were caught and drowned. By that evening, much of the electricity had been cut off, the phone lines were going, and that night the gas plant failed as well. In the railway station, a group of marooned passengers boarded a stalled train, hoping to escape the rising water. The engineer tried to haul his cars to a higher point, but just south of the Harrison Granite Company, his locomotive began to tip, and he could go no farther.[29]

Down on Webster Avenue, near the confluence of the Stevens and Jail branches, the collapse of a dam at a woolen mill brought a sudden torrent through the street, and though some had already fled, others took to their attics, waving lighted newspapers in the night to show rescuers—police, firemen, and National Guardsmen—where they were. Two men, Helge Carlson and Sarsfield McNulty—the latter a mail carrier and sergeant in the National Guard—succeeded in getting a boat to the house of Fred Thomas and his family. They were able to take off four small boys, but then to the horror of the onlookers, the boat overturned and the boys were lost. McNulty and Carlson managed to swim to safety, though the latter was swept down over a dam, saving himself by reaching a stoneshed and hauling himself onto the roof.[30] The exact sequence of events remains unclear, and the accounts of McNulty and Carlson, set down many years later, contradict one another. Memories differ of course, and it is impossible to reconstruct the precise order of events, or even to speculate on whether the Thomas family might have survived if the rescue had not been attempted. It was the worst tragedy in Barre that night, and many years later, a marble memorial to the four boys was erected in the Hope Cemetery.[31]

The most notable of the casualties, however, was S. Hollister Jackson, the state's lieutenant-governor, and putative successor to Governor John Weeks. Born and raised in Canada, he had lived in Barre for some thirty years, and was a popular figure. "Handsome, well-groomed and cultured," the *Vermont Review* had called him that spring, praising his unceasing efforts to persuade young men and women not to leave the state to seek their fortunes elsewhere. Early Thursday afternoon, Jackson left his law office for his house at Tremont and Nelson streets, which, though on relatively high ground, was only three hundred feet from Potash Brook. According to a guard on duty nearby, he accidentally ran his car into a washout. Seemingly dazed, he asked the guard to retrieve his glasses, which had fallen to the floor. Then, ignoring the warnings, he started the car again, and began to drive up the street toward his house, only two hundred yards away. The guard followed on foot until stopped by the water, saw Jackson leave the car, step into the water, lose his footing, recover it briefly, and then disappear.[32]

That, at least, was the account given at the time. Many years later, Eldon Heath, who had been a teenager, remembered that he and several friends had seen Jackson in his car, with the water already coming in. Jackson asked them for help in reaching his house, but when they tried to guide him over the torrent, he walked right into it, taking with him Heath, who was able to grasp a bush and hold on. Jackson, however, was swept away, and not until the following afternoon was his body found. A few days later, he was buried in the Elmwood Cemetery; his brother, Major Horatio Nelson Jackson (the proprietor of the Burlington *Daily News,* and the first man to drive a car from coast to coast in 1903) had to walk the last fifteen miles to Barre for the funeral as he made his way from Burlington.[33]

At 11:30 Thursday evening, the flood's crest reached Barre, and though the rain fell steadily through the night, by the next morning, the water was beginning to recede. Here, as elsewhere, it left behind a sea of mud, sticky, gray, and foul-smelling, filling the basements of houses and stores, and burying cars on the streets. By the time a call went out for volunteers, many men, idled by the closing of the granite works, had already set to work to dig out. George Mosher, the Boston businessman, was full of praise for the energy and efficiency of Mayor Frank Small during the emergency. Finding a small group of merchants overcharging for supplies, he called the police, only to be told there was no law under which they could act. " 'We'll make a law,' said the mayor, and he did."[34]

Seven people died in Barre Thursday night, and property losses, especially to the granite works, were huge. Five miles away in the state capital of Montpelier, sirens in the fire station sounded the flood alarm at half past two, but by then merchants were already carrying stock from their basements up to the street level, a precaution they were used to, for the capital was no stranger to high water, whether from spring snow melt and ice jams, summer cloudbursts, or autumn storms. By five, in the early darkness and pelting rain, it was impossible to move through the streets, leaving those who hadn't already fled the business district trapped in the upper floors of their buildings. "The McEuen Store Inc.," read a later report, as was the case with every other store in the business district, received the full force of the flood waters for a period of eighteen hours. After the plate glass windows were broken, pulp wood and other debris practically destroyed the interior of the store, swept most of the merchandise entirely away and left a thick deposit of mineralized mud upon the small remnant of merchandise which did not go down the river. The average height of the water through the business district was fifteen feet, and the McEuen Store Inc., along with the others was practically wiped out.[35]

Another account spoke of a raging torrent twelve feet deep in the business section, "carrying in it everything from a baby carriage to a Grand piano and that is a fact." Three visitors from Massachusetts, taking refuge on the second floor of Miller's Inn, described Montpelier that night as "a place of horror," and told of listening to gunshots coming from a nearby house where an eighty-year-old-man, alone in a small room on the third floor, was trying to attract attention.[36]

Among those trapped by the water that night was Governor John Weeks, recently arrived from his home in Middlebury for what he supposed would be a three- or four-day stay in the capital. Instead, he and his wife Hattie found themselves caught up in their own adventure. Since neither then nor today has Vermont favored its chief executive with a governor's mansion, when the flood came they were staying in the Pavilion Hotel, an elegant five-story building near the State House. "I hope we will never have to spend another night like that," wrote Hattie Weeks to her niece at Middlebury College two weeks later. "It certainly was way beyond anything you can imagine," and she described the water "rushing and roaring with waves like a big mad Ocean," as they sat up all night with no light other than three short candles, and no heat, wrapping themselves in blankets.

It did seem it would never come morning and then Oh! when it did dawn the terrible things that came to our view first a building going past then a tree and the last time I looked out there came a Refrigerator up on the steps It was full of Fruit I presume somebodies' breakfast no doubt Well we left here the next morning by walking up stairs going out of a high window and then jumping down on the ruff then walking a board put out from one building to another and in a high window jumping down into a Garage and when my feet were on the ground I was some glad and thankful I dont think they thought I would do the stunt but I said if you Men can go I can and I did but I know you have to get some nerve to do these things I kept geting stronger every step as I went the long hall way

Fig. 2. Hattie Weeks, who left a description of her dramatic escape from Montpelier's Pavilion Hotel. *Courtesy of the Vermont State Archives.*

which is narrow and has many turns I presume you would have been pleased to have seen me climbing on ruffs When I came out I was most to the state House directly in front of the Convent. I hope the "Sisters" did not see me and yet one of the road men said he was watching me and I went through very gracefully.[37]

Fig. 3. State Street, Montpelier, afternoon of 4 November 1927. *Courtesy of Special Collections, Bailey/Howe Library, University of Vermont.*

Fortunately the governor and his wife found refuge with Adjutant-General Herbert Johnson, whom Weeks put in charge when martial law was declared on Friday, while the city council asked H. F. M. Jones to be responsible for the distribution of food. Though by Friday morning the water had slowly begun to subside, it was still eight feet deep in the business district, while a lake had formed where the land was lower, separating the eastern and western sides of the city. Mayor E. A. Deavitt had managed to put in an emergency call for boats before the phone lines went down, but by the time they were loaded on a train at Burlington, it was too late to reach the capital. Not till Friday afternoon did boats begin to appear in the streets, managing to take some people from downtown to higher land on Seminary Hill. Frank Hawley, a former mayor, had to be pulled from the second floor of his store with a rope made of twisted sheets; he was luckier than Frank Bailey, the janitor of the First National Bank, who was found alive after thirty hours of standing in knee-deep waters, clinging to a casing.[38] "Edwin Steele walked up from Waterbury, he was so anxious about his people & could get no word," Clara Harvey wrote her daughter. "His wife is expecting—they remained in their rooms until the water came to the window sill of their sleeping room—then they took a boat—said boat being two coffins nailed together."[39]

With telephone and telegraph lines down, the capital maintained a tenuous link to the outside world through one or two amateur radio operators. "Power off all day—electric plant under water . . . Am using door bell batteries," reported one, and it was thus that the press first learned of the conditions there. A message telling of Jackson's death, and of the havoc in the streets, but also putting at rest the original fears of a great loss of life, was relayed through Binghamton, New York, and then broadcast to others. Meanwhile, two amateurs working with the Army Signal Corps in Washington managed to stay in touch with Montpelier, passing on its pleas for aid; one of the early requests was for yeast, for although on Friday the town's bakery was at work, they were running short of supplies.[40]

On Saturday morning, under a cloudless blue sky, three visitors from Massachusetts, knowing nothing of the destruction beyond the city, and still thinking they might be able to drive to Burlington, went to the garage behind the Pavilion Hotel, where they had left their car. There, as they told the press later,

> a man drove up . . . and, when he learned that they desired to get to Burlington, he said: "You will not be able to get over the railroad or highway out of the city for two weeks."
> "Do you live here?' one of the men asked him.
> "I guess I do. I am the Governor," was the reply.
> The men said the governor looked very downcast.
> That was when they decided to walk.

Which they did, and by the time they reached Burlington were able to describe the devastation they had seen, with dead bodies in the railway station at Waterbury, and dead cattle littering the fields along the Winooski.[41]

It was at Waterbury and in the neighboring towns such as Bolton and Jonesville that the greatest loss of life took place. By the time the Mad River joins the Winooski, just below Middlesex, some seven or eight miles downstream from Montpelier, the hills have begun to rise more steeply, and the valley draws in more narrowly. A few miles further on, Waterbury and Duxbury lie on opposite sides of the valley, and, joined by the flow of the Little River, the Winooski begins its rapid passage through the main range of the Green Mountains. Just south of Bolton, five miles farther on, Camel's Hump rises over four thousand feet, while to the north lies Bolton Mountain, thirty-six hundred feet high, on the ridge leading up to Mount Mansfield, the highest point in the state. It is a region of forests clinging to steep, sometimes rocky slopes, of rushing streams, and a narrow strip of farm land in the valley that the river must share with the Central Vermont Railway and the highway leading from Burlington to Bolton—a highway that, in late 1927, was being newly paved in concrete.

Waterbury's story was the familiar one: A lovely Indian summer Wednesday; by Thursday the rain pouring down, and the river threatening, for Waterbury's mile-long main street, shaded in summer by trees, lies on flat ground near the river. "You know, the water always rises like that up there, every spring and fall, seems as though," Minnie Nelson wrote to her sister two weeks later, "so that's what we thought it was."[42] At six, the sirens sounded the flood warning, and within an hour all the town's lights were out. Some two hundred people took refuge in higher buildings such as the Village Tavern and the Waterbury Inn (a favorite of travelers since Civil War days), while others fled to the high school or the annex of the State Hospital for the Insane, on the outskirts of town. By that time, the first deaths had come, as the fire department's efforts to rescue the Sargent family from their house failed, and the building, with seven people inside, was "lost with its screaming occupants in the blackness," as one of the would-be rescuers said (Sargent himself apparently had been distracted by his efforts to get the family cow upstairs).[43] In some places, rescuers managed to lash coffins together into a makeshift boat that was able to take off several families. Others were less fortunate. Robert Cutting, trying to save his wife and three children with a raft he'd made, lost control of it. His family was drowned, and though he himself was pulled from the branches of a tree several hours later, his mind was said to be gone. Nine more people died at Duxbury Corner across the river, either on unsuccessful rescue missions, or simply because their buildings were swept away.[44]

One of the most valuable contemporary accounts of the flood comes from Lloyd Squier, who had held various positions, including office boy, reporter, and printer, for the *Waterbury Record,* the town's small weekly paper. Though his book makes no mention of it, he became one of the flood's heroes that night, hitching a team to a wagon to drive and swim through the water, rescuing several people, among whom was his mother. He stayed on the job, as he put it later "because there was nothing to do at the *Record* office," though shortly thereafter he ran a belt from a gasoline engine through a broken window in the office, managing to power a small emergency press. The State Hospital for the Insane, a group of brick buildings set well back from South Main Street on spacious grounds, was normally almost entirely self-sufficient, producing much of its own food. Now, however, it was without light or power, as the staff helped move almost nine hundred patients from the first floor wards up to the higher floors. Two workers in the power plant, who had stayed on duty to cool the boilers and lessen the chance of an explosion, had to climb to the tops of the boilers, watching the water rise toward them until, when it was only five feet away, it stopped. The hospital itself suffered significant damage, and its dairy herd of 121 Holsteins was drowned.[45]

"The mins. just dragged and of course no one could sleep, that is we didn't dare let them," Minnie Nelson wrote, explaining how she had kept her children awake in case they had to take to the roof. "The night seemed just about a month long . . . Well, finally after hrs. seems as though, we saw the dawn through the slits in the roof and felt just as though our prayers had at last been ans. Then came a horrible wind & we felt that help would never come before we froze. We all had coats, hats and blankets but the wind was so cold and we thought it would finish doing what the water had started blowing us away from the foundation."[46]

Twenty-eight-year-old Flora Carpenter, who taught in the elementary school on Stowe Street, took little notice of the downpour at first, but that evening, back in her lodgings in the Teacup Inn, heard the wail of the firehouse siren, with its "gruesome high water call." Outside, she and a fellow boarder watched women being carried from the Waterbury Café, and though by now warned themselves to leave the Inn, they joined the proprietor in an attempt to move vegetables, some of them stored against the coming winter, from the cellar, first up to the kitchen, and then to the second floor as the water kept rising. Exhausted, they stopped work at about midnight, listening to the roar of the water, and the cries for help. Occasionally a rescue boat, a canvas canoe, passed by, a man shouting out "Anyone want to be rescued this trip?" By the time the water was spilling into Flora's bedroom, she and her companions finally decided to leave, clambering into the boat, and carried through "the inky darkness and pouring rain among telephone wires and tree branches," until they were put ashore safely near the heated schoolhouse, where hundreds of other refugees by now were managing as best they could.[47]

Fig. 4. Main Street, Waterbury, 4 November 1927. Note the rowboat over the onlooker's left shoulder. *Courtesy of Special Collections, Bailey/Howe Library, University of Vermont.*

By Friday morning, Waterbury was a lake, submerged save for the higher land around the business district. Though the Catholic and Methodist churches were flooded—the latter losing, among other things, its brand-new organ—the Congregational church stood on higher ground, at the north end of Main Street. Here it was, in this century-old white clapboard Gothic Revival structure, that a community mess was set up to feed the refugees. A local lumber company began building emergency scows, not only for rescue work, but to carry food and drink to the many unable to leave their houses (Minnie Nelson and her family were finally rescued at one that afternoon). From Stowe, high in the hills and relatively undamaged, a truck arrived that afternoon bringing six boats, having taken half a day to cover the ten miles between the towns, in part because of the need to put up six temporary bridges. "The people of Stowe," said one of those caught in the inn, "pushed through to our relief. Coffee, sandwiches, and doughnuts were brought to us in rowboats."[48]

All told, twenty people died in Waterbury and Duxbury. In Waterbury's railway station, a large Italianate Victorian building, an emergency morgue was set up. Property damage was enormous: houses torn from their foundations, barns and outbuildings carried away, poultry and horses drowned, and photographs of the time show rows of dead cattle lying near the banks of the receding river. Thirty nearby railway and highway bridges were either destroyed or badly damaged, as debris, swept down by the river, piled up against them until they collapsed. At Slip Hill, three miles south of Waterbury, two thousand feet of the Central Vermont's roadbed and embankment was washed into the river, and though a milk train, caught at Waterbury, was forced to spill much of its cargo into the Winooski, it also provided milk and cream for the town and the hospital at a time when no other freight was moving (the engineer and conductor managed to scramble to safety up a nearby watertower).[49]

Terrible as was the calamity that hit Waterbury, even worse came a few miles downstream at Bolton. Water, streaming down from the steep hills above town, surged over the railway embankment that had acted as a levee in the past. By Thursday night, the Winooski River poured through the town, carrying away many buildings, including a boarding house, run by a Mrs. Hayes, in which roughly twenty men lived, part of the crew working on the new highway in the valley. Even today it is uncertain how many were lost, since some of the bodies were never recovered, but a later list speaks of a dozen. Days later, a reporter found the seventy-two-year-old Mr. Hayes and his son, a navy petty officer, wandering about the meadows, now snow covered, near

Fig. 5. Dead cattle lie in a field near Bolton. *Courtesy of Special Collections, Bailey/Howe Library, University of Vermont.*

the river, looking for the bodies of their family members. "People here saw the house go," the son told the reporter. "It came down the stream whirling around with the lights on and crashed against an iron bridge. It went all to pieces; you can see part of it in that pile of river refuse jammed against the bridge." His father added that the body of his little granddaughter was found half a mile farther down, as was his wife's dress, caught in a tree.[50] All told, twenty-five people died in Bolton—thirteen residents and the twelve highway workers. No other town—not even Waterbury—suffered as badly.

Two miles downstream, in the little settlement of Jonesville, R. W. Germain, who lived with his ninety-year-old mother, was at first unworried by the river's rising, until he found it too late to escape.

> . . . about half past two Friday morning I heard someone calling in the wood back of the house. They said the bridge was gone and three houses and if I would get my mother out of the chamber window onto the shed roof they would get us out. They put up long planks to the roof and my mother slid down the planks to where the men could wade in and get her. They carried her up through the woods back of the house. Then they held her up until one of the men could cut a big pine tree and fell it across the brook. Then they took her across on the tree. She never complained or said a word. She has the grit. She was all in when she got there.[51]

At the nearby dairy center of Richmond, where the Winooski River flows out of the mountains toward the lowlands approaching Lake Champlain, William O'Kane, a McGill University student trying to make his way home to New Hampshire by car, found his way blocked on Thursday afternoon, and spent the night there, "doing just what everybody else was—helping the other guy and yourself, anything, everything to keep out of the rushing waters."

> Cattle were going down in the middle of the stream, some of them drowned, others swimming. Houses were swept from their foundations and occasionally we saw one go floating by. Then you would see other animals going down. One pair I recall particularly, a hen and a rooster on a barrel, doing what people call "logrolling." They were walking as the barrel turned and kept at it until we lost sight of them.
>
> Another rooster went down on what might have been a surf board. It would strike an eddy and pitch, the rooster would squat and then stand upright again. Then a pig came down swimming like a porpoise, head under water, pushing up his snout for air. Down would go its head, then up with its nose, then even the busy people along the shore would cheer.

The next day, O'Kane set out again, on foot this time, walking to Waterbury, where a National Guardsman accosted him, and then took him to the church, where he was fed beans and bread. Then, after finally making it to White River Junction with no money left, he was able to cadge a ride on a milk truck to Concord, and at last reach Durham.[52]

Many, many such accounts emerge out of those terrible forty-eight hours, from places like St. Johnsbury, cut off from the outside world when the Passumpsic was in full flood, and Newport, where press reports warned of the specter of starvation, and Northfield, where the bravery of the Norwich University cadets in saving sixty-seven people later was cited by the Red Cross as one of the outstanding features of the rescue work.[53]

Fear, isolation, the impossibility of seeing or knowing anything of the world beyond the storm, the sudden prospect, or even reality, of death, much of it happening on a cold black night on the edge of winter—these are common features of all such stories. So are the sounds, sounds quite unexpected in these otherwise peaceful towns, the sounds of the waters in flood, and the sounds of their victims as well. "The roar of the monster was terrifying, never to be forgotten, incessant, so deafening that people unavailingly tried to close their ears to it," wrote Luther Johnson. "All that was *seen* was the flashing of lights in the doomed Hicks house," Mary Whitney recalled of that night in Royalton, "but the *sounds* of the roaring torrent and splintering of houses and tearing up of trees will never be forgotten."[54]

From one of the few houses that survived in Bolton, twenty-year-old Clara Thompson watched and heard the flood as it struck, carrying away houses, as well as the new school where she had begun teaching that year, down on Pinneo Flats.

> Rain was beating a continuous tattoo upon the house and ocean waves seemed to be driving against it. Struggling sounds of choking cattle perishing in the tide came plainly to our ears and it is not a sound to lend encouragement to one who is forced to believe he will soon be in the same position.

Yet almost as unnerving in its own way was the sudden silence that descended after the noise and destruction of the storm had passed. "Light disclosed a now unfamiliar valley," Thompson wrote of looking out over Bolton the next day. "Not a sign of a neighbor's house remained. We were absolutely alone in a vast waste of water. What would become of us, next?

"But listen! Voices! Never in my life had I heard a sound more welcome than the sound of voices that cold, bleak, dismal, watery day of November 4th."[55]

To Minnie Metcalf, fifty miles away in South Royalton,

> [t]he quiet that reigned in the valley that Saturday was oppressive in the extreme. No trains were passing, roads were washed out, bridges and culverts gone, communication cut off from outside towns, and a general fear filled all hearts as to the extent of damage and loss of life that would be reported later. Suddenly in the awful silence of the valley there came the sound of a whirring motor and out of the south appeared an airplane, flying low over the river, and turning toward the north. Oh, the joy of it that there *was* connection with the outside world, and that kind brave hearts had turned toward our flood-ravaged state to spy our need! Oh, the satisfaction of knowing there *was yet* an outside world to send us a token.[56]

There is a biblical resonance to Clara Thompson's voices, heard near Bolton's "waste of water," and Minnie Metcalf's airplane, high over the unaccustomed stillness of the White River Valley, these sounds breaking the sudden silence, and recalling Noah's dove returning to the ark at evening, a fresh olive twig in its beak. Yet though President Paul Moody assured his student congregation in the Middlebury College chapel on Sunday that the flood was no act of God, but that "such disasters are accounted for by the natural laws of science," for some, as they faced their changed world, the parallels with the greatest of all flood legends might have been more comforting than disquieting.[57] "Breed, multiply, and fill the earth," God told Noah, after he emerged from the ark with his family and his animals, had built an altar, and made his sacrifice.

Genesis does not record how the earth looked to Noah and his family after the waters went down. But for many who lived through the flood that November, the changed landscape and the destruction of everything familiar could be almost as shattering as the experience of the storm itself. By Friday morning, Luther Johnson wrote, "Waterbury was a town almost without homes." "Montpelier is mostly still there," the attorney Wade Keyes commented in a letter to Fred Howland, the president of the National Life Insurance Company. "Cavendish is not. Canyon 3/4 mile long 150 deep at one point 300 feet wide." Leon Gay mourned the losses in that town, recalling the vanished street, "with its carefully cared for over-arching maples," and the ruin of all those houses of "typical, thrifty Vermonters, attractive places that had represented the savings of a lifetime."[58]

"[T]he beautiful embowered banks, for which the White River was noted were stripped bare," wrote Lawrence Mills of Gaysville. "No graceful, over-arching trees now, no trailing vines, no banks of ferns and clumps of brilliant wild flowers reflected in the rippling water. The once lovely, mirror-like pond is now a spot of desolation, the river flows in the midst of a wide waste of gravel and stones, unshaded, unsoftened, its beauty but a memory." Farther north, from Hardwick to Cambridge, silt and mud covered ground, houses, and trees, while miles of highway lay destroyed, stretches of railway had become no more than twisted steel, and the once-peaceful countryside now become "a scene of desolation and death."[59]

Even when the rain stopped and the skies cleared, the shortening of the days and the increasing cold were constant reminders of the long winter lying ahead. Many of the provisions so carefully made for that difficult season—food, coal, firewood, feed for livestock—had been washed away or spoiled beyond recovery, and the barns and cellars that had held them were now covered with a with a deep, filthy, stinking mud.

Vermonters came out of that terrible week faced with a task of recovery on a scale of which they could hardly have dreamed. How well equipped was their state to do the job, and above all, where would they find the resources?

~~~⌇⌇~~~

"Her Great Product Is Character"

Vermont in 1927

"The people of Vermont are fortunate in that they have a state in which it is comparatively safe for us to live," wrote the *Burlington Free Press* in the summer of 1927. "Cyclone and flood and earthquake help to counteract some of the attractions of other States, but . . . [w]e are not only in a region 'beautiful for situation,' and scenic framing, but also in a land with which the natural elements have continued to deal kindly."[1]

Comparatively speaking, that is, for Vermont, not surprisingly, had a long history of severe storms, and not only those bringing winter blizzards. Given the state's mountainous terrain, local freshets and floods were a common enough occurrence, and some were widespread enough to damage substantial portions of the state. The first serious one recorded by settlers came in January 1770, when heavy rains flooded most of New England's river valleys, including that of the Connecticut. Sixty years later, the Torrent of 1830, as it was called, arrived on the heels of a late July heat wave, and became the most devastating flood of the nineteenth century. The Rev. Lemuel Eldredge left a graphic account of its catastrophic effects along the New Haven River, falling down the steep western slope of the Green Mountains, sweeping away mills and houses, leaving an entire settlement a barren island, and drowning fourteen people, one of whom was Eldredge's own son.

Early October 1869 brought another New England–wide storm, which dropped more than six inches of rain on Castleton and Woodstock, doing severe damage to several parts of the state. Then, after a heavy rainfall drenched soil already saturated in March 1913, came what was called—until fourteen years later—the Great Flood, causing heavy damage particularly to the Connecticut and White River valleys.[2]

As disasters go, it's arguable that the New England flood of 1927 does not rank particularly high on any common scale of destruction and human misery. The half-century from 1880 to 1930, Ted Steinberg has pointed out, saw an unprecedented rise in the numbers killed by natural disasters, and even a cursory look at the news of that day suggests how close death could lie.[3] Just over a year earlier, for example, a September hurricane in Miami killed roughly 370 people and left some 18,000 homeless. In May 1927, over 200 died as lines of tornadoes and other storms ripped through the middle west, and flash flooding in Kentucky a month later took 100 victims. In the spring of 1928, over 500 people drowned after the bursting of the St. Francis dam near Los Angeles. That autumn, a massive Caribbean hurricane left 300 dead in Puerto Rico before making landfall near Palm Beach, and moving in over Lake Okeechobee, where it killed probably another 2,500 or more. Closer to home, in January 1927 a fire in a Montreal movie theater took 77 lives, and that summer a gale carried off 100 Nova Scotia fishermen, helping to drive the province into depression.[4]

Above all were the enormous floods that engulfed so much of the Mississippi Valley in the spring of 1927, the floods that "changed America," as John Barry has put it, and that, by showing the limits of state and private action, brought massive federal intervention and helped prepare the way for the New Deal. There, the great river burst through its levees, spilling out over seven states, and causing damage variously estimated at anywhere from $246 million to $1 billion. Even today, no accurate count exists of those killed, for though the official death toll was put at 256, in fact probably well over a thousand lost their lives and over a million were made homeless. Vermonters, like Americans everywhere, contributed to the $17 million fund drive to support the Red Cross's rehabilitation effort in what that agency called the "most destructive catastrophe this country has ever suffered."[5]

The November flood in the northeast was far smaller. Still, as the waters receded, and people began to take stock, it became clear that the cost in lives and property was enormous, and that Vermont, lying at the storm's center, was by far hardest hit. Though a year after its occurrence a Red Cross report listed only 45 dead in all of New England, a 1929 study from the Department of the Interior talked of 85 deaths, only one of them—a woman near Westerly, Rhode Island—outside Vermont. These figures are certainly too low. William Minsinger's recent work speaks of 111 fatalities throughout New England and Canada, and newspaper accounts of the day suggest that the figure might have been even higher, possibly over 120.[6]

The extent of physical damage to buildings, to land, and above all, perhaps, to transport systems, is even harder to gauge. Though the U.S. Weather Bureau at the time estimated $45 million in damage to all of New England, only Vermont made a comprehensive study of the storm's effects, and even that was incomplete. A report presented to the governor at the end of 1928, but drawn up earlier by the Public Service Commission, set forth a preliminary estimate of $24,743,755 in damages, in nine separate categories (see table).[7]

Damages from the Flood of 1927 in Vermont

Agriculture (690 farms)	$1,350,156
Highways: Roadways	$2,483,916
Highways: Bridges (1,258)	$7,062,998
Railroads, steam and electric (12)	$3,901,200
Industry (125 plants)	$5,558,800
City, town, and village property	$6,121,151
State Hospital, Waterbury	$400,000
Telephone and telegraph companies	$319,650
Gas companies	$30,400
Total	$24,743,755

These, of course, were only preliminary figures, and were incomplete. (For instance, there was no mention of electric companies or dams). In the spring of 1928, E. H. Jones, the state commissioner of agriculture, put farm losses closer to $2 million, and, as the Public Service report itself pointed out, an appraisal by the American Railway Engineering Association set New England's rail damage at $8,668,000, to which should be added $4,131,000 for operating and miscellaneous losses (even then, not all lines were included). By way of comparison, the same group set the railway losses due to the Mississippi flood at $22,462,262 (including almost $8 million in operating losses).[8]

All in all, a figure of somewhat more than $30 million in Vermont probably would be more accurate than the preliminary estimate. That was already Herbert Hoover's guess when he visited the state a fortnight after the flood, and in the spring of 1928, Congressman Elbert Brigham, arguing Vermont's case to the House of Representatives, used the figure of $30,435,299, while the press was reporting $33 million. Though it's uncertain where he got the information, in May 1928 Ernest Gibson told the House of over $100 million in business and indirect losses.[9] It's notoriously tricky to convert such figures into present values, of course, though an economist at the University of Vermont has suggested that, given changes in material and labor costs over the last eighty years, a total of about $3.9 billion in today's values for physical damage generally would be accurate.[10] Whatever the final figure, the November flood was the greatest natural catastrophe that had ever struck Vermont (Gibson in fact suggested that it was one of the greatest disasters to overtake the people of any state in the nation's history), and indeed, eighty years later, it remains unparalleled in the extent of damage done and in the costs to the state in life and property.[11] If not a flood that changed America, it certainly was a disaster that changed the state.

In 1927, how well equipped was Vermont to meet such a disaster?

Not well at all, if one looks at the kinds of resources revealed by ordinary indices of population, wealth, income, and the like. Although the irrational exuberance of the Coolidge bull market might reflect boom times enjoyed in some other parts of the country, Vermont had some excuse for feeling itself left on the sidelines. A small state in every sense of the word, it had seen its population stagnate since the mid-nineteenth century, and indeed the census of 1920 counted 352,428 people, fewer than had lived there ten years earlier. In the fifty years after the Civil War, the nation as a whole grew by 197 percent, and New England by 112 percent. Even neighboring Maine and New Hampshire were up 22 percent and 39 percent, but Vermont had increased by only 6.6 percent. Vermont remained very much a rural state as well. In 1930, only 31 percent of the population lived in the ten leading towns, the largest of which—Burlington—had yet to reach thirty thousand. It was not true, as people liked to joke, that there were more cows than people, but the figures were close—in 1928 there were roughly 332,000 cows, and the total number of cattle of all sorts, at some 404,000, did indeed surpass the human figure.[12]

In 1929, the per capita income of Vermonters stood at $699, below the national average of $715.[13] There was relatively little large scale industry. Of course, there were a few exceptions, particularly in the production of stone. The huge Vermont Marble Company, with its headquarters in Proctor, had interests extending well beyond the state's borders, and Barre was the center of a thriving granite industry. Rutland and St. Johnsbury produced scales, and though there were no textile mills as large as those of New Hampshire or southern New England, the American Woolen Company's establishment in Winooski and others in Burlington, Bennington, and the Black River Valley were important for their regions. Springfield was known for its machine tools, and when Charles Lindbergh landed his *Spirit of St. Louis* there in July 1927, before a crowd of twenty thousand rapturous welcomers, the *Rutland Herald* boasted that the Wright radial engine that had carried him to Paris could never have been built without "the Bryant grinder, the Fellows gear shaper and the Hartness turret lathe, all products of Springfield."[14]

While the Great War brought a brief stimulus, in the decade of the 1920s, seven of the state's ten major industries declined, sometimes steeply. Though James Hartness, the Springfield manufacturer elected governor in 1920, had set forth a "Blueprint for Progress," foreseeing a greater role for Vermont's industry, it drew little support. In 1926, after a strike lasting four and a half years, the International Paper Company pulled out of Bellows Falls, moving its operations to Three Rivers, Quebec, and leaving much of the town crippled. As the historian Gene Sessions has concluded, Vermont's enterprises remained marginal to a national economy then largely being driven by steel, the automobile, and petroleum.[15] Not surprisingly, many Vermont leaders concluded that the state's future lay with its farms.

In the later nineteenth century, growing competition from the west had encouraged Vermont agriculture to change, and by the early twentieth century, the spread of dairying, and more particularly, of fluid milk production, gave hope for the future. Appointed to head the state's agriculture department in 1913, Elbert Brigham (a Phi Beta Kappa graduate of Middlebury College) worked hard for years to modernize dairy farming, doing much not only to encourage new marketing methods and cooperative associations, but also to improve the quality of herds through better breeding, better feeding, and the control of diseases such as bovine tuberculosis and contagious abortion (Brigham himself had developed a famous Jersey herd on his St. Albans farm). He also negotiated favorable freight rates, helping to open up the Boston milk market. After he went to Washington as one of the state's two congressmen, his successor as commissioner of agriculture, Edward H. Jones, helped to form the New England Dairy Conference Board, hoping to stabilize what he called the "deplorable and chaotic condition" of the Boston milk market. All this allowed farmers to take advantage of better transportation and lower costs to dominate the Boston milk shed and to make inroads

Fig. 6. Both as commissioner of agriculture and as congressman, Elbert Brigham was a constant champion of Vermont's interest. *Courtesy of the Vermont Historical Society.*

into that of New York.[16] Boasting that Vermont supplied some 65 percent of Boston's fluid milk, Governor John Weeks (himself raised on a Salisbury dairy farm) predicted to an audience in Bellows Falls in 1928 that it would never become an industrial state. Vermont's dairy receipts, at $30 million, more than matched the first five industries in the state, an official of the New England Milk Producers' Association claimed that same year, and these revenues were also the most important single item keeping Vermont's banks, businesses, and railroads operating.[17]

For Vermont's agricultural and industrial production (to say nothing of its people), the railroads remained the most important means of transportation.[18] Two major lines served the state: the Rutland on the western side, running from Bennington and Bellows Falls up to Rutland, north through the Champlain Valley, and thence west to Ogdensburg, New York, and its outlet on the Great Lakes. A southern branch to Chatham, New York, provided a connection with the New York Central. Reaching down to New London, Connecticut, the other great line was the Central Vermont, much of it owned by the Canadian National. This followed the Connecticut River Valley to White River Junction, where it turned northwest toward Montpelier and Burlington, and on to St. Albans (which served as the line's headquarters), and north to Quebec. In addition, the Delaware and Hudson ran down the western shores of Lake Champlain, and its spur from Whitehall into Rutland gave Vermont access to New York traffic as well. Such lines, and others like the Boston and Maine and the Canadian Pacific, depended heavily on "pass over" traffic, as it was called, hauling both freight and passengers from the coast through Vermont to the interior of the United States and Canada.

Many smaller lines served towns or whole districts by providing connections to the larger railways. Some were tiny, like the White River Railway, known familiarly as the "Peavine," which twisted some nineteen miles along the stream between Rochester and Bethel, or the Mount Mansfield Electric Railway, which ran between Waterbury and Stowe. Others were larger, such as the Montpelier and Wells River and the St. Johnsbury and Lake Champlain, whose tracks spanned 118 miles across northern Vermont from Swanton to St. Johnsbury. Unimportant they may have seemed compared to the larger roads, but the dairy farmers of the Lamoille Valley and the quarriers of Hardwick depended heavily on the St.J. & L.C. for access to the main lines of the Central Vermont, the Canadian Pacific, and the Maine Central, and for all the difficulties attendant upon the birth and early operation of the White River

Railway, its quarter century of service carrying marble, talc, and lumber from the local industries to the Central Vermont at Bethel had helped to bring a measure of prosperity to the upper White River Valley.[19]

Trains were thus vital to the state's transportation system, and indeed, in the view of one railway executive, Vermont, in proportion to its commercial significance, was better served than any other region in the world. In 1926, for instance, some fifty-five trains a day passed through the new Union Station in Burlington.[20] The Rutland, for the past several years, had done much to upgrade its equipment, the milk traffic remained profitable, passenger traffic was doing well, and after two years of falling revenue, 1926 was the best year the line had seen in a decade.[21] The Central Vermont's uneven fortunes began to rise after it became part of the new Canadian National empire in 1922, and though it continued to run deficits, there was optimism about the Canadian link. In 1924, the luxurious Montrealer and Washingtonian inaugurated a nightly service between those cities, and two years later, the Ambassador and the New Englander began their daily and nightly express runs between Boston and Montreal. That year saw a dramatic improvement in revenues, with the deficit cut to just over a quarter of a million dollars, and at the time of the flood, prospects were bright.[22]

Even without the flood, however, such hopeful signs promised little more than an Indian summer, for the lines faced a highly uncertain future. Very little new track was laid in the state after the 1870s, and in 1915 a new law forced the Rutland to give up its profitable shipping line on the Great Lakes, prompting the New York Central, which owned half the railway's stock, to become less interested in it. Above all, by the middle and late twenties, the inroads made by automobiles and trucks, earlier seen as ancillaries to feed rather than to compete with the rail system, were becoming obvious. "God speed in your highway program," Sir Henry Thornton, the American-born head of the Canadian National, bravely told the Vermont Chamber of Commerce in June 1927, but his assurance that no well-run railway had anything to fear from such competition already sounded dated.[23]

The highway program to which Thornton referred was that inaugurated by Governor John Weeks, elected in 1926 after a campaign that saw the construction of modern roads as one of the chief issues. Though in 1922, Wallace Nutting began his *Vermont Beautiful* with praise for Vermont's highways, others found them primitive even by the standards of the day. In 1924, the state had only 20 miles of hard-surfaced roads (neighboring New Hampshire had 31, and Massachusetts 902), and though for the next five years Vermont would add another 29 miles a year, it remained well behind its neighbors.[24] Some roads were graveled, but others were not, and spring thaws in particular turned dirt roads from passable frozen ruts into impassable quagmires, where automobiles might sink into the mire until a tractor or team of oxen arrived to haul them out. At such times, traffic came to a standstill, and even the larger towns found themselves virtually isolated. "The road to Montpelier," wrote the *Free Press* the spring before the flood, "one of the most traveled thoroughfares of the State, is impassable unless one knows every inch . . . From Vergennes to Brandon, the roads are impassable, and the going is bad from Brandon into Rutland . . . All traffic into New York through Rutland has ceased."[25]

Still, the number of automobiles grew rapidly, helped by the easy availability of the Model T, and bringing new problems of traffic congestion and road mishaps. Back in 1921, Benjamin Gates, who presently would become state auditor, wrote that in that year alone, motor vehicles had come in contact with 51 cows, 269 teams of horses, 139 dogs, 15 hogs, 1 sheep, 27 trains, 27 trolley cars, and 184 pedestrians. Among the human victims of these encounters, 132 were men and only 52 women, reflecting, the author suggested, "the sprightliness of the fair sex."[26]

"For twenty years or more the rational Vermonter has been of the opinion that hard roads would ruin the state," complained Putney Haight of the *Chicago Tribune* in 1928. "If they were to be built lengthwise of the commonwealth they would attract a motley gathering of picknickers. If built across, the travelers pop in at one border and out on the other side, and never buy a gallon of 3 cent taxed gasoline nor spend a cent for lodging." Look at New Hampshire, he said: Vermonters trooped across the border to drive up and down the concrete main street of neighboring Keene, "just to get the sensation of an automobile jaunt."[27]

On the other hand, whatever its distrust of Washington's intervention and paternalism, Vermont was quick to see the possibilities of the Federal Aid Roads Act of 1916, organizing a state highway system, and thus qualifying for one of the first new grants made for federal highway assistance in 1917. Yet for all the changes brought by the automobile to the quality of rural life, to say nothing of local landscapes and townscapes, the roads improved only slowly. Then the 1926 gubernatorial campaign brought the issue of modern roads very much to the fore, and

Fig. 7. John E. Weeks, Governor of Vermont, 1927–1931. *Courtesy of the Vermont State Archives.*

it would play a large role not only in Vermont's response to the flood, but also in shaping its future.

"The single positive program of a social nature advocated by the Coolidge administration was road construction," writes the president's biographer, Robert Ferrell, and Vermont made the most of it.[28] John Eliakim Weeks, the seventy-two-year-old victor of the 1926 gubernatorial campaign, had grown up on a dairy farm in Salisbury, just south of Middlebury, and had devoted a large part of his life to public service. One term in the state senate and two in the house—where he served as speaker in 1916—confirmed his stature in the Vermont Republican Party. Before becoming governor, his reputation was based less on his political accomplishments than on his management of state institutions. He had held a variety of positions, and most recently, as commissioner of public welfare since 1923, had overseen the state prisons, the State Hospital in Waterbury, and various schools for troubled students. "Never seeking, yet always sought," as an admiring Lois Greer later put it, "this man progressed step by step, from farm to county, from county to state, in one official capacity and then another."[29] Neither a professional politician, nor a full-time businessman or lawyer like so many of his predecessors, Weeks has been called the first bureaucrat to rise to the governorship. The term is an apt one, as long as it is not used in denigration. Weeks knew state government from the inside, understood its capabilities and limitations. Though a man without higher education (his father's illness kept him from going to college), his career nevertheless reflected a Vermont version of the kind of expert professionalism and managerial competence that grew out of the Progressive movement to become so important a characteristic of the twenties.

In 1926, both he and Herbert Comings, his Democratic opponent, made improved roads a priority of their campaigns. Promising forty miles of hard-surfaced highway a year, avoiding any state indebtedness by relying on a pay-as-you-go basis, Weeks's cautious and prudent program was less ambitious than those found in other New England states. Still, winning the support of the state legislature for even this limited undertaking proved to be an uphill battle during the legislative session of early 1927. The Vermont House had, as one observer noted at the time, as many minds as it had members. "The most typically democratic legislative organization in America, and therefore in all the world," Teddy Roosevelt once called it, but with some two hundred and fifty representatives—one from each town, regardless of size—the lower chamber suffered from a chronic incapacity for decision making. That was particularly true if the decision meant spending the towns' money (though some complained that it was more than willing to spend the state's money). But Weeks's farming background meant that he understood, better than many of his predecessors, the mindset of the rural legislator. Above all, he knew the importance of remaining calm, of maintaining a quiet, steady, and purposeful course, of leading lawmakers rather than driving them toward his goal. "I know of no session in recent years when there has been better feeling between the executive and the Legislative Departments," wrote Elbert Brigham at the time, "and when there has been more constructive work accomplished for the good of the State."[30]

In the end, his program passed. "Governor Weeks is not a spectacular man," John Southwick of the *Burlington Free Press* commented, summing up Weeks's accomplishment in the spring of 1927. "He will never be heard proclaiming to the housetops what he has done, nor boasting of what he intends to do. But what he has done speaks for itself." What made his victory all the more remarkable was that it was carried through without antagonizing anyone, so that, Southwick remarked, Weeks emerged from the session even stronger than he entered it, a record few governors could equal. "If the next two years are not years of unrivaled prosperity and unusual progress in the Green Mountain State," he concluded, "the fault will not be that of John E. Weeks."[31]

As the campaign was fought out in the summer of 1926, the state cooperated with the Federal Bureau of Roads in a traffic survey, and the discovery of how many "foreign" cars and trucks used Vermont's roads helped the conviction that hard roads were needed. As the *Free Press* commented some years later, it was not only fortunate that so few improvements existed by 1927, for the waters might have washed them away, but perhaps even more fortunate that the traffic survey had been made, so that much of the planning for reconstruction had in a sense already been done before the flood.[32]

In sum, if antediluvian Vermont was by no means entirely behind the times, neither was it particularly well endowed with the means to recover from the catastrophe. Though the Mississippi River's flooding that spring brought far greater losses than did the rivers of the Green Mountains, in the eyes of many Vermonters, their state, comparatively speaking, suffered far greater damage than did its sisters along the Mississippi. As Congressman Ernest Gibson told the House in March 1928, while Arkansas and Louisiana reported roughly $38 million in flood damage each, and Mississippi almost $50 million, Vermont had by far the highest per capita damage—some $86.35, he said, its closest rival being Mississippi at $25.85, and its flood damage, reckoned per million dollars of state wealth, was more than twice that of Arkansas and three times that of Louisiana.

Of course Gibson—together with his colleague, Elbert Brigham—was trying to make a point in his own state's favor, as he argued for Washington's help.

> Suffering from one of the greatest calamities that ever befell the people of a State in the history of the Nation, we are undertaking the problem of rehabilitation with courage. We are not faltering. Filled with the same spirit that actuated our forbears when they entered a trackless wilderness and with resolution and courage carved out a State and maintained its independence for years, and [sic] we are coming back.[33]

Gibson's moral was clear. Bad as might be the figures of loss of life and destruction of property, they were not the whole story. For beyond the quantifiable damages their state had suffered from the rising water, many Vermonters liked to believe that it had at least one great qualitative advantage. That was to be found in the character of its people, endowed as they were with a spirit of independence, self-reliance, and a kind of fortitude that set them apart from others.

Vermont in the Public Mind

"The year 1927 has been a glorious one for Vermont and Vermonters," Governor Weeks told an audience at Bennington in mid-August that year. "With commendable feeling and thankful hearts, we have paused during the rush of a busy age to recall the splendid traditions surrounding the early years of our existence, and to pay tribute to the patriots of old." Eight months earlier, in January, the state had opened the observance of the sesquicentennial of its founding by commemorating the drafting of the original constitution of 1777 in Windsor. In July, a crowd at Hubbardton, near Rutland, heard Governor Weeks recall that the battle fought there "furnished Burgoyne his first taste of the plucky resistance that was finally to dash to pieces his fond dreams of invasion and culminate in his capitulation."[34] Now in August, the celebrations, carefully planned by a commission under John Spargo (founder and director of the Bennington Museum, and a former British socialist now turned Coolidge Republican) reached their climax. Though unfortunately the actual fighting had taken place just across the line in neighboring New York, the celebration of the hundred and fiftieth anniversary of the Battle of Bennington, where the lovely Federalist church rose above elm-shaded Monument Circle, brought to town four days and nights of speeches, historical pageants, poems, fireworks, church services, military reviews, and band concerts.

Such patriotic celebrations, of course, commonly provided Americans with occasions to reaffirm the traditional virtues hallowed by public memory, and were especially popular in the years between the wars.[35] Yet in Vermont that summer, they had a very particular kind of resonance that set them apart from similar gatherings, such as the sesquicentennial of the Declaration's signing, held a year earlier in Philadelphia, or the huge bicentennial celebrations of Washington's birth, a few years later. For what they marked was not so much Vermont's role in the creation of a new nation, but rather the genesis of Vermont itself, brought into being not as part of the Union, but as an independent republic (though in fact the founders did not use the term, referring to Vermont as a "state" from its inception). Now, a century and a half later, there were still ways in which Vermont, though now certainly *in* the United States, was not entirely *of* it, and both Vermonters and outsiders marked the difference.

"Even as a boy," observed the writer Christopher Morley in 1930, "I intuitively felt [Vermont] to be different from other states," and he was not alone.[36] The claim to exceptionalism within the broader history of the American nation had several roots. One of the most important sprang from this early history of independent existence that Vermont had enjoyed for some thirteen years prior to joining the Union in 1791. Granted, Texas also entered as an independent republic; but the Lone Star State was not even a gleam in the eagle's eye when the Green Mountain Boys stood shoulder to shoulder with the colonists against the tyranny of George III.

Such themes were echoed at the Bennington festivities. For months, John Spargo had importuned President Coolidge to attend, and though ultimately he failed, his efforts may have helped nudge a reluctant Post Office to issue a stamp commemorating the Green Mountain Boys. From the Black Hills of South Dakota where he was summering, the president did send a letter to be read at the ceremonies, stating solemnly that no single engagement of the great war just finished "was more far-reaching in its effect, more potent in the determination of final victory" than had been the Battle of Bennington for the Revolution (a slight exaggeration, suggested the *New York Herald-Tribune,* reminding its readers that another engagement of some moment had been fought a little while later, at a nearby place known as Saratoga).[37]

Nor had George III's redcoats been the only enemy in those early years. To win its independence, Vermont battled not only England, but New York and the Continental Congress as well. "'Vermont was never anything but free,'" Herbert Corey, quoting an earlier writer, reminded the readers of the *National Geographic* in early 1927. "'Never a crown colony, never yielding allegiance to any province, State, or kingdom.' When she was admitted as the fourteenth State to the American Union, after the Revolution had been won by her loyal aid, it was upon her own terms. Bully little Vermont!" "Our forefathers fought long and hard for our civic entity," said the *Rutland Herald*, "not only against savages and foreigners, but against their own fellow-countrymen who sought to absorb our boundaries within their own." Vermont's relations with Washington, claimed the *Vermont Review*, writing of the federal government as if it were a foreign power, "have always been friendly, but never selfish."[38]

The Switzerland of America, Vermont's publicists often liked to call it, with its mountains and lakes, and its people marked by the same spirit of independence that had led William Tell to take up arms against Habsburg tyranny. Perhaps, though, the more apt comparison would be not with that Alpine republic, but with another, almost imaginary mountain kingdom in distant Asia. The name "Shangri-la" was yet to be invented, but the myth of Tibet was already well over a century old in the Western imagination. There, high in the clouds, guarded by its towering peaks and glaciers from the contaminations of civilization, an island of stability and constancy had been preserved, secure in its ancient traditions, and impervious to the uncertain imperatives of change and progress.[39] Of course, it would be a bit far-fetched to suggest that Vermont played the same role in the American imagination that Tibet played in that of the West at large — the Green Mountains are hardly the Himalayas, after all. Yet to certain kinds of Americans in those days, Vermont remained (and perhaps still remains) an evocation of what their country once was. If by the twentieth century the nation seemed in danger of losing its soul as it lurched towards an uncertain future, they took comfort from the knowledge that the old ways lived on in that still, small Shangri-la of the northern hills, "the repository," as Michael Sherman and Jennie Versteeg put it, "of some archetype of a lost and longed-for American character: rural, homogeneous, frugal, resourceful, stubborn, vigilant in protecting individualism and independence."[40] Seventy-seven years after the flood, former governor Howard Dean echoed these ideas as he campaigned for the presidency, telling his audiences that rather than seeing Vermont become more like the rest of America, the rest of America should be more like Vermont.

It's a commonplace that travelers, before they arrive, have often decided what they will find. In his *Vermont Beautiful* (1922), Wallace Nutting, the former Congregationalist minister from Massachusetts, now turned successful promoter of colonial revival, pictured for his readers a region of almost magical serenity, largely devoid of people, except for the few who, in their old-fashioned dress, seemed as much part of the natural landscape as the trees and hills. Instead of sprawling cities and suburbs, here was a country where dusty roads led along cool rivers, where scythed hay lay drying in the meadows under a July sun, and where white-spired churches rose above small village greens (only a few snowscapes or other reminders of winter's cold reality disturb Nutting's three hundred photographs). Never mind that a few years after the flood, John Nolen, an urban planner from Massachusetts, told the state Chamber of Commerce that he could "find in Vermont, easily in a short distance, an ugly picture for every attractive picture in Nutting's book, or in your admirable state folders."[41] Such criticisms were best avoided. "The Vermont character," wrote the Irish editor and critic Shane Leslie in the London *Observer* in late 1927 (his wife, Marjorie Ide, came from a notable St. Johnsbury family),

> has remained very much what it was, though there has been a great influx of French-Canadian labor, and each New England village has its plank-built ghetto round a wooden Catholic Church. But the main streets and the big farms are habited by the old sturdy stock, Congregational in religion, thrifty and hard-working in habit, but not without an intense interest in books and lectures. Vermont towns, with their little white porticoed churches and secular elm trees, have changed very little during the past hundred years.[42]

Whether or not they reflected reality, such qualities seemed to set the state, for good or ill, outside the American mainstream. The 1920s, Lynn Dumenil has said, finally brought the emergence of a modern society in the United States, propelled by the three great transformations that had begun decades earlier: industrialization, immigration, and a sprawling urbanization.[43] Vermont, however, had yet to participate fully in these changes. It remained a rural state, dotted with small towns, and although

Burlington, Winooski, and Rutland were growing, modern industry had done little yet to transform landscape or townscape. Though Vermont had been no stranger to immigration—in 1860 the state's French-Canadians made up by far the largest such group in New England—most of the later arrivals from the north simply crossed the state, riding the new railways down to the mill towns of New Hampshire and southern New England. Other groups of immigrants also arrived in the nineteenth century, including the Irish, joined by pockets of Welsh, Italians, Scotch, and others. But they did not come in large numbers. Even compared with the rest of northern New England, Vermont in the 1920s had the lowest percentage of foreign-born men and women among its population.[44]

To some Vermonters, as well as to many outsiders, it was precisely these qualities of an abiding rurality and apparent ethnic homogeneity that not only set the state apart, but marked its strength (Henry James's Susan Stringham, chaperoning the young Milly Theale around Europe in *The Wings of the Dove,* regards her native Burlington as the "real heart of New England, Boston being 'too far south'"). To others, however, the very lack of change was a cause of anxiety. For decades before the flood, they bemoaned the decline of the hill farms and small towns, the emigration of the best and most ambitious young men and women to other, more promising, parts of the country. Why, asked Millard Newcomb in the *Vermont Review,* did John Deere of Middlebury have to go to Illinois to build the plough that broke the plains? Admiral George Dewey of Montpelier might be a national hero, but his exploits took place on waters far from Lake Champlain; the Northern Pacific Railway, under Frederick Billings of Woodstock, might have become the "Main Street of the Northwest," but it added little to the northeast; and while President Taft's grandparents were Vermonters, he himself was not. Even Calvin Coolidge, that archetypical Vermont character, though born in Plymouth Notch, had been educated in Massachusetts, and made his political career there, before being translated to Washington. Stay in the state, President John Thomas of Middlebury College urged his students in 1913, as he called for educated young men and women to go into the small towns, to share the life of the people, and help to rebuild them (years later, in rather different circumstances, Mao Zedong "sent down" the educated youth of Chinese cities to the impoverished countryside).[45]

For some, of course, as Dorothy Canfield Fisher wrote years later, emigration meant choosing freedom over the monotony of "an unchanging and stable background."[46] Still, none of these anxieties were new, for worries about the state's prospects went back at least to the 1840s. While optimists saw the growth of dairying in the early twentieth century as a bright spot, and cited the shift from sheep raising to milk production as evidence of the Vermont farmer's capacity to change, even they remained concerned about the abandonment of hill farms, where graying houses stood deserted and meadows returned to scrub. No figures better reflected these concerns than those showing the failure of Vermont's population to grow while New England and the rest of the nation advanced. Such findings clearly worried those we might call the "articulate Vermonters," who controlled much of the state's print and publicity, using them to diagnose the illness and propose cures that would lead to a "new Vermont" or a "greater Vermont." Considering themselves progressive, members of this class stood ready to embrace much, if not all of modernity, and were anxious for the state to benefit from the advances being made by the rest of the nation. Their worries gave rise to the "winter thesis," as it's been called, whose proponents, like the historian Harold Wilson in the 1930s, argued that by the late nineteenth century, the quality of rural life was declining along with the quality of the population.[47]

Yet how accurate were such views, and how widely shared were they? As Hal Barron and others have pointed out more recently, Vermont's situation looks rather less bleak in retrospect. Farmers, after all, often saw things differently from those who analyzed their plight, and sometimes, far from being distressed by the growing gap between rural life and the American mainstream, might even welcome it. "This isolation," one of them observed, "keeps out the feverish spirit which troubles most American communities."[48] The view of a darkening winter's onset also ignored the fact that while many left the state, so too, many stayed, and they were often the ones with the most at stake in the futures of their communities.

In a fascinating study of Vermont in the late nineteenth and early twentieth centuries, Paul Searls has drawn attention to a major line of social fracture, dividing "uphill Vermont"—largely the inhabitants of the small towns and the hill farms, with their attachment to old ways—from "downhill Vermont," comprising the entrepreneurs, publicists, and others who, animated by Progressive ideas, sought to move Vermont forward into the modern world. Parochial the uphillers might be in their concerns, and narrow in their view of the world, but they drew

a strength and resiliency from tradition and the endurance of custo-
mary social bonds, and often resisted the prescriptions for improvement that others might try to urge upon them, finding them irrelevant
or even dangerous.[49] Nor were they by any means without a voice, for in
those days, long before the legislature's reapportionment in 1965, rural
and small-town Vermont dominated the House of Representatives in
Montpelier.

Still, whatever future historians might find, at the time of the flood,
the worries and concerns of those who sought to take Vermont's economic and psychic temperature seemed very real. There was no denying
the unchanging population figures, for instance. Hopeful predictions
that such advances as the telephone, rural free delivery, and the increasing use of the automobile, might mitigate the isolation of rural life,
failed to understand the corrosive effect that this last, by drawing people
to the cities, would have on small towns and marginal farms. At the
same time, what others might consider backwardness possibly could be
turned to the state's advantage. Even as articulate Vermonters might despair of any return of prosperity to the hill farms and small towns, they
came to construct an image for the outside world of a state charming in
its solitude, hoping that Vermont, and particularly rural Vermont,
might find some measure of salvation by drawing tourists in from the
outside.[50] Whether or not they shared the anti-modernist and anti-
urban tendencies to which people like Wallace Nutting spoke, they were
quite prepared to capitalize on them.

Therein lay a contradiction. Could the state maintain those qualities—particularly its rural character—that would draw outsiders to it,
and yet at the same time be progressive, as Americans measured the
term in the early twentieth century? How could such a desirable result
best be achieved? Of course this was hardly a question restricted to Vermont. "The central paradox of American history," Lawrence Levine
writes, "has been a belief in progress coupled with a dread of change; an
urge towards the inevitable future combined with a longing for the irre-
trievable past; a deeply ingrained belief in America's unfolding destiny
and a haunting conviction that the nation was in a state of decline."[51]
Levine finds such tensions particularly strong in the twenties, and they
may have been even more so in Vermont. Central to the views of
"downhill Vermont," as Searls describes them, was the need to move the
state forward, while simultaneously preserving its Arcadian rurality in
order to entice visitors from beyond its borders.[52] Yet how could the

state maintain itself as a treasure house of original American virtues, while at the same time standing outside the march of American history, as America itself seemingly stood apart from the history of the rest of the world? For if Americans popularly saw their country as exceptional in its avoidance of the apparently meaningless cycles of violence and tyranny that had so disfigured the old world, little Vermont stood out against even this record of American uniqueness.

History and geography aside, the belief in Vermont's own exceptionalism was based above all upon the real or imagined characteristics of its people. Reflecting on his family's Vermont background, Chief Justice William Howard Taft, in a message to the state's sesquicentennial commission, wrote of his belief "that in that State is maintained, undiluted and undemoralized, that which we like to call the real American character. Its continued maintenance is the strongest security for the future of our country."[53] The local democracy of town meetings, Dorothy Canfield Fisher claimed, kept at bay the bored political cynicism so common in the metropolis. All questions were freely aired, and when they were over,

> and the teams and Fords and lean wiry men stream away from the Town Hall over the rutted roads in the sharp March air, they are all tingling with that wonderfully stimulating experience of having spoken their minds out freely on what concerns them. They step heavily in their great shoes through the mud, which on March–meeting day is horrible beyond belief, but they hold up their heads. They have settled their own affairs.

Norman Rockwell's well-known painting "Freedom of Speech," picturing town meeting in Arlington (where both he and Fisher lived), lay twenty years in the future, but its message was the same. Local democracy was reflected in Vermont's egalitarian lack of social class, or of the extremes of wealth and poverty. The question of what to do with accumulated wealth, Fisher wrote, "bothers us as little as how to fight cobras" (even though Christopher Morley claimed to have discovered a hotel in Manchester reserved for maids and chauffeurs—but of course they, like their masters and mistresses, came from out of state).[54]

Thrift, prudence, self-reliance, independence, integrity, a practical conservatism—these qualities were by no means peculiar to Vermonters, but within the borders of the state they could be found, so it was believed, in greater concentration than elsewhere in the country. "Vermont," wrote the Kansan William Allen White in 1925, quoting the state's constitution, "has preserved perfectly the fundamentals of American life, 'firm adherence to justice, moderation, temperance, industry and frugality,' and thereby has preserved with remarkable fidelity 'the blessings of liberty and a free government.'" "The state's citizens, he continued, "live near the economic margin without want. Good-looking farm and village houses . . . houses built on straight colonial lines, houses built by straight colonial ancestors, adorn the fields."

Was this why, as White believed, in a time of inwardness and conservatism after the crusading zeal of Teddy Roosevelt and Woodrow Wilson, it was Calvin Coolidge, the incarnation of Vermont Yankee virtues, who captured the moment's *Zeitgeist*?[55] His image, hand raised, taking the oath of office from his father in a simple clapboard farm house, illuminated only by a flickering kerosene lamp, was burned into the American imagination. Granted, the image was not always entirely flattering. "The mention of Vermont," R. L. Duffus (who had escaped from Waterbury to California) wrote in the *New York Times Magazine* in August 1927, "doubtless calls up for most persons the thought of a steady-going, hard-working God-fearing, but rather unimaginative and unadventurous race. Mr. Coolidge, the first native-born Vermonter to be elected to the Presidency, has done nothing to shatter this conception."

On the other hand, he continued, "[a] new Vermont, with a growing joy of living, is taking the place of the Vermont of Mr. Coolidge's sober-sided youth."[56] Duffus was only one of many thinking he could make out the shape, however dimly, of an emerging Vermont. Was this entirely a good thing? Was progress to be equated with change? Could there be such a thing as progress without change, at least change in the state's fundamental character? Moderate advance, even the "growing joy of living" was one thing; the reckless hedonism of the jazz age and all that went with it, was something else, however, and few outlanders wanted the state to abandon the qualities they so much valued there. Yet for all his encomium to the character of Coolidge's native state, White darkly reminded his readers that "Vermont has preserved these things in isolation, harking back to a day that has passed in America."

Precisely because the state was largely agricultural and not industrial, precisely because so many of its inhabitants sprang from the old stock, Vermont had held on to the qualities—rural, Protestant, individualistic—that had set America apart at the time of its founding, and now seemed to be in danger of erosion by the transformations changing so much of the nation. "[I]it is an American tide of life which flows through these valleys, with hardly a trace of the alien stocks which have inundated the Atlantic seaboard since the Civil War," Bruce Bliven told the readers of the *New Republic* (for reasons not entirely clear, he wrote in the persona of a Vermonter). A southern New Englander entering Vermont for the first time, wrote H. P. Lovecraft, in the overwrought style familiar to the readers of his horror stories, would find there a sense of "mystic revivification," leaving behind (presumably in places like Massachusetts and Rhode Island) a landscape forgetful of its tradition, where "[s]wart alien forms, heirs of moods and impulses antipodal to those which moulded our heritage, surge in endless streams along smoke-clouded and lamp-dazzled streets, moving to strange measures and inculcating strange customs."[57]

Lovecraft had come to Vermont in 1928 at the invitation of Vrest Orton, who had been associated with H. L. Mencken's *American Mercury,* and behind his views, as behind those of Wallace Nutting and others, lie several related impulses: a distrust of modernity and urbanism, fears of immigration and radical politics, an idealization of folk-life and folklore, and a belief in the virtues of rural life and its rhythms. Views such as these, Lynn Dumenil suggests, reflect a general sense of crisis among old-stock Americans, who saw what they imagined as an earlier homogeneous and harmonious society—native, Protestant, and middle-class—challenged by a modern culture increasingly influenced by immigrants, Catholics, and Jews. Even those lovely white churches adorning the village greens were no longer as much a part of the lives of Vermonters as they once had been. "Papists Have Increased 20% in Ten Years," read a headline in the *Rutland Herald,* and though in the United States as a whole, Protestant church membership was rising at roughly the same rate, that was not true of Vermont.[58] A study of President Coolidge's home county of Windsor revealed a severe drop in Protestant church-going, and in 1931 a committee chaired by John Weeks—himself a man of profound Protestant convictions—discovered that while 51.9 percent of adult Vermonters were church members, without the Papists, the figure would have been far worse, for only 36 percent of the state's non-Catholic population over the age of thirteen belonged to any congregation (the national average was 46.5 percent).[59]

Still, if the rest of the country was in danger of being submerged by Lovecraft's "swart, alien forms," perhaps Vermont, with its high percentage of old native stock, could still be saved, and not just for its own sake, but for the benefit of the nation as a whole. That would only happen, though, if the old stock was able to revivify itself, rather than sliding into degeneracy, watching its most enterprising members emigrate to greener pastures, leaving behind a weakened remnant to breed amongst themselves. Perhaps it was no accident that not only should the American eugenics movement find a substantial foothold in Vermont, but that a Vermont senator—William Dillingham—had been a leader in the battle to restrict immigration that ultimately triumphed in the act of 1924.[60]

The dominant view of the state, then, even as late as 1927, continued to be Yankee, reflecting, as André Sénécal points out, a long history of Vermont's unease with its ethnic past. There was little room for Barre, with its diverse nationalities and history of labor activism, or for the Russians and Poles working in Springfield's machine-tool industry. French-Canadians—the state's largest immigrant group—tended to be seen either as objects of patronizing humor, or as vaguely threatening outsiders, clustering in "plank-built ghettoes," or taking over the farmlands left by emigrating natives. Though Wallace Nutting, at least, found even that preferable to seeing good land go back to wilderness, the prevailing attitude was one of regret. In 1923, William Rossiter of New Hampshire, who had studied the agricultural economy of northern New England, made a familiar diagnosis: the over-reliance on farming, the young and the ambitious leaving the region for other parts of the country, the failure of the old stock to reproduce itself. A new wave of immigration was needed, bearing with it the right sort of people, "people of the sort not afraid of either cold weather or work," coming from elsewhere in the nation, or from the Nordic countries of Europe— England, Scotland, Holland, Scandinavia. "Wake up, northern New England!" he cried. "You need more people of a strong and resourceful type, not of the peasant class."(Did Rossiter know, one wonders, of Redfield Proctor's abortive attempt to settle Swedish and Finnish farmers in and around Rutland county in the late nineteenth century?)[61]

Some of this talk, of course, reflected the influence of the broader American nativism of the twenties (Fisher's paean to Vermont democracy in *The Nation* was one of a series of articles on different states published by that magazine; the one describing Massachusetts was entitled "A Roman Conquest").[62] One prescription for dealing with such threats in the 1920s lay in the revival of the Ku Klux Klan, a phenomenon to which Vermont was by no means immune. In the mid-twenties, there were cross-burnings, a few attacks on Catholic churches, and in 1925, a gathering of the organization drew almost twenty thousand people in

Fig. 8. Four months before the flood, the Klan rallies for its July 4th march through Montpelier. *Courtesy of the Vermont Historical Society.*

Montpelier. Though the press generally opposed the Klan, two governors—Proctor and Billings—intervened to pardon convicted Klansmen, and in 1927, the turnout of an estimated fifteen thousand people for a July Fourth rally in the state capital itself drew no editorial comment other than praise for the police in preventing traffic jams.[63]

If this sort of xenophobia was, as Walter Lippman said at the time, an expression of American village civilization making its last stand against urban modernity, the mirror image of the Klan's prescription, coming from very different circles, lay in the phenomenon brilliantly analyzed by Nancy Gallagher in her study of the state's eugenics movement.[64] Directed by the zoologist Henry F. Perkins of the University of Vermont—a man who himself incarnated the attitudes and privileges of the old stock—this enterprise ultimately sought to define an overarching vision for the state built on the preservation of its old Yankee population, which, depleted by emigration and diluted by newcomers, might no longer produce the sorts of men and women in which the state had taken such pride. Perkins's role will be considered more fully later, but it's worth noting here that, unlike the Klan, he and his colleagues considered themselves to be progressive reformists, priding themselves on their ability to bring a disinterested scientific approach to their work. It's ironic, of course, that while the state's population of French-Canadians

was one of Perkins's particular *bêtes noirs* (as it was for others like him)
we can see now that what he and his colleagues were trying to do by preserving the traditional virtues of the old Protestant stock was almost the
exact mirror of the ideology of *survivance,* developed by the Franco-
American elites, as they sought to maintain their religion, language, culture, and ethnicity in the face of American assimilation (in 1869, it had
been in Rutland that the first Francophone parochial school in New England opened).[65]

Though written for a British audience, the piece by Shane Leslie earlier referred to, was reprinted in at least three Vermont journals in the
months right after the flood.[66] For one of the characteristics, at least of
articulate Vermonters, was an intense curiosity about what the outer
world thought of them and their state. In reading through the daily
press and the journals of the period, it's impossible not to be struck by
how much such Vermonters needed reassurance that, despite the
future's uncertainties, their state still mattered, and more particularly,
that its character, its values, and its traditions, remained relevant to a
changing world. The editorial pages of papers like the *Burlington Free
Press* and the *Rutland Herald* were filled with articles analyzing the
state's reputation beyond its borders, reprinting flattering editorials
from the metropolitan papers, or the statements of leading men and
women praising Vermont and its ways. "So much has been said in the
newspapers of this State about Vermont," began a *Free Press* editorial
some five months before the rains came, "that some readers may be inclined to consider the writers of laudatory articles as prejudiced in favor
of our own commonwealth." Thus it was helpful to examine the views of
outsiders, and the *Free Press* did so by quoting at length from an article
in the *Springfield Republican,* conveniently overlooking the fact that the
Massachusetts paper depended a good deal on a piece originally appearing in the *Vermont Review.*[67]

Particularly after the flood, articles such as Leslie's, editorials from
papers in Boston, New York, Chicago, and elsewhere, even lengthy ex-
cerpts from reviews of A. E. Thomas's gloomy play, *Vermont* (which
opened and closed rapidly on Broadway in early 1929) found their way
into the local press.[68] Added to them was a spate of articles, editorials,
and the like proclaiming, or at least ruminating upon, the state's virtues
(and, less often, on its shortcomings as well). Was there any other state
in the union that engaged in such intense examination of itself, and
cared so much what others thought of it? Did any other state show the

kind of continual need for reassurance that so many of these articulate Vermonters reflected?

Perhaps the same phenomenon could be found in parts of the old Confederacy, still recovering from the wounds of a war fought and lost six decades earlier, insisting that their history, too, must be valued as part of the nation's experience. There are many differences, but also more than a few similarities, between Vermont's editorial soul-searching and *I'll Take My Stand,* the famous 1930 manifesto of the Southern Agrarians such as John Crowe Ransom and Allen Tate. But Vermont's perspective, of course, was very different, for it lacked not only the Southern history of defeat, but also of slavery's shameful past, as it lacked, too, the more obvious manifestations of current racism (whatever the hooded marchers might be doing back home, in 1924, when the Democratic national convention tied itself in knots over the party's attitude toward the Klan, Vermont's tiny delegation voted on the side of the angels).

Still, the kind of regionalism reflected both by southern agrarians and articulate Vermonters (to say nothing of the protagonists of similar movements in the middle west and mountain states), may perhaps be seen as a kind of defensive answer by those feeling themselves left behind, or, as Michael Steiner suggests, "a desire for a sense of place in a perilously dislocated world."[69] They also reflect a concern with authenticity that is characteristic of the twenties and thirties, a need to discover (and to be reassured about) what was genuinely American, genuinely part of the country's history and tradition. Unlike the Rockefellers's "national historic shrine" of Colonial Williamsburg or Henry Ford's Greenfield Village, with its replica of Philadelphia's Independence Hall, both products of these years, Vermont did not need to be rebuilt, or reconstructed, except perhaps in the minds of those observing it. An island of stability in an increasingly uncertain world, Vermont was simply *there,* as it always had been, and must be preserved to remind Americans from whence they had come, and to which they could return, to be reinvigorated and reassured of the continuing validity of their character and traditions.

How Vermonters might preserve their own particular virtues of industry, sobriety, thrift, and prudence, reaffirming their relevance in an age of rapid change, became a continuing theme of editorialists and writers. Shortly after the flood, *The Drift-Wind* (a quirky little literary journal started in 1926 by Walter Coates, a writer and sometime Universalist minister), began to debate this question. In its pages, Vrest Orton feared that modern highways would bring a replication of the land-scapes of New Jersey or Florida, "nothing but Jerry-built roadside shacks, summer camps, hot dog stands . . . cable railways to mountain tops . . . towns of cheap-john houses alike as so many peas, factories belching smoke, crushing the workers and breaking their souls . . . the list could easily go on." Others, however, warned that poverty could be degrading, and that a "lack of forceful development of . . . resources, tended towards physical and mental decadence." Summing up much of the debate, in 1929 Orton came back with a proposal (allegedly drawn up by a Committee of Public Safety) for "A Declaration of Independence for Vermont." One section will give its flavor:

Against the Babbitts in Vermont, WE DECLARE:
1. *That inlanders of the Babbitt classes* are working internal havoc and de-struction by preaching the doctrine that accumulation is the true measure of happiness; a doctrine which presupposes that supremacy of materialism responsible for the fall of *Greece, Rome* and other great powers of antiquity.
2. That these inlanders are inviting into *Vermont* the most undesirable tourists and the most destructive moneyed exploiters.
3. That they are inducing the farmer to leave his farm for the quicker but far less valuable profits of urban commerce and manufacturing in-dustry.
4. That they are forming into strong bands they call *Rotary, Kiwanis, Lions and so forth,* whereby they may wreak an organized and collec-tive destruction and sooner accomplish the ruin of Vermont.

His state's true destiny, Orton concluded, was not to become a mirror of Sinclair Lewis's Zenith, as the boosters of a Greater Vermont seemed to wish, but "to constitute an *ARCADIA* for persons of free thought, ac-tive mind, high standards and aspirations, and cultivated imagina-tion."[70] All very much tongue in cheek, to be sure, but the debate, though in a tiny journal read by very few people, echoes much of the other writing of the time, breathing a real sense of anxiety and uncer-tainty. A visitor like Lovecraft might prefer the "elder and familiar rib-bons of rutted whiteness which curl past alluring valleys and traverse old wooden bridges in the lee of green slopes" to the "tar and concrete roads, and the vulgar world that bred them." But John Southwick of the *Free Press,* and Governor Weeks himself, were passionate advocates both of their state's traditions, and of the modern highways that would lead to Greater Vermont's future.

Behind these contradictions of rurality and modern progress, of the state's imagined exceptionalism and its *Ur*-Americanism, lay the stark contrast between two Vermonts. On the one hand was a hard, socio-economic reality, with its near-stagnant population, its failure to enjoy the material advances of the twenties. On the other was what might be called the subjective "state of Vermont," that psychic and emotional entity whose demarcations appeared in no published atlas, and yet which, mapped by cartographers of the mind, existed fully realized in the imaginations of many beyond the state in those years. In the uncertain decade of the 1920s, this Vermont of the mind served a very particular purpose both within the state and beyond its borders. In part, it reflected an image assiduously constructed by articulate Vermonters such as Dorothy Canfield Fisher and Vrest Orton, by journalists and editors, and, of course, by the State Publicity Bureau, which had been started in 1911, and now was under the direction of the historian and state senator Walter Crockett. But it also came from outsiders, who wanted to believe that somewhere, in a time of unsettling innovation, the old values lived on—"the strongest security for the future of our country," as Taft had called them—and could still be drawn upon as necessary, almost as if they lay in a psychic bank account.

The views of outsiders and the pride of Vermonters in their native tradition reflected more than simply admiration or self-congratulation on having remained true to the faith of the fathers. Yet there was no point in turning Vermont into a vast theme park, whose charm lay simply in its refusal (or inability) to keep abreast of the world, the better to attract summer trippers or to find New York and Boston buyers for its abandoned farm houses. But how to preserve the state's particular qualities while simultaneously advancing toward Greater Vermont? The deep-seated uncertainties that underlay such a question, while mirroring those of the nation as a whole, seemed to be particularly acute in Vermont, taking such disparate forms as the Klan's brief eruption, the eugenics project, editorial concerns with the views of outsiders, or the debate in *The Drift-Wind*. Each of these sought to meet the challenges of those changes that, as they swept over Vermont, might wash away even more than the waters of November had done. The "imagined community" of Vermont, as Paul Searls calls it, "as much an idea as a place," thus spoke not only to Vermont's hopes and fears for the future, but also to larger national anxieties about change and modernism.[71]

Those qualities, real or imagined, that Vermonters liked to find among themselves, and outsiders liked to find in them, would be severely tested, not only by the horrifying experience of the flood itself, but even more by the long and painful process of reconstruction that followed. Yet this testing also made it possible, at least for the moment, to overcome the contradictions between these two Vermonts, the subjective Vermont of the mind and the physical Vermont of socio-economic reality. Vermont's qualities, Vermont's characteristics were now going to be called upon, and the state united in a heroic effort to put itself back together. For it was those qualities that, as a thousand voices repeated at the time, would assure not simply Vermont's survival, but its emergence from reconstruction as a better place with a brighter future. More than that, it had to survive, not just for its own sake, but for the nation's sake. As E. S. Martin, an editor of *Life*, put it at the time, Vermont should be considered less a commonwealth than a school for the nation—"[h]er great product is character and people who have it."[72]

As Paul Searls remarks, Vermont might remain marginal to the national economy, but "its identity as the repository of ancient, simple, republican values made [it] central to the national psyche."[73] That is why the flood of 1927 was not simply a local event, but a truly American one.

3

"Sympathy Flowed in from the Hills"
The Provision of Emergency Relief

Though the downpour finally began to abate by late Friday, 4 November, the wreckage of bridges, houses, and barns, joined by the bodies of dead livestock, still jammed the swollen creeks and rivers. Falling almost as fast as they had risen, the waters left behind a starkly changed landscape, reminiscent of those grainy wartime pictures from France and Belgium a decade earlier. Photographs show towns looking like battle zones, debris piled against surviving bridges, houses collapsed or torn from their foundations, resting crookedly in meadows, or lying on their sides across roads and railroad tracks. In what had once been a meadow near Bolton, dead cattle lie in rows, waiting for burial. Roads show gaping holes or are simply collapsed into stream beds, while the steel tracks of rail lines lie broken and buckled, curving down into the rivers or bending their twisted ends, like November's bare tree limbs, toward the cold sky.

Through November and into December, nights and days of rain alternated with snow and ice, the endless heavy weather a reminder of oncoming winter, fraying nerves still not recovered from the earlier shocks. "It is raining hard to-night and I just hate to hear it . . ." wrote Ethel Colby from Waterbury to her sister in Randolph, on the 17th. "I'm not afraid but it sounds altogether too much like the rain two weeks ago."[1] With highways and railways torn up and bridges gone, those who had to travel found both stamina and ingenuity tested. Five women, caught by the water in Johnson after a day's outing in Burlington, were anxious enough to get home to Morrisville the day after the flood that they picked their way over five miles of muddy roads and fields to a farm in Hyde Park, and from there were rowed across the "inland sea" to a point

Fig. 9. An iron bridge near Waterbury, overturned by the Winooski River. *Courtesy of the Vermont State Archives.*

where a car could carry them the rest of the way. The *Rutland Herald*'s aptly named Roger Flood left the city at 1:30 on the morning of 5 November, carrying photographs for the metropolitan newspapers, was twice stymied in his attempt to find a route west to New York and the railway, eventually managed to reach Burlington, and finally rode a steamer across the lake to Port Kent in time to deliver his pictures to a southbound train. A day or so later, George Thompson, who headed the State Highway Board, had to travel fully two hundred and fifty miles from Montpelier, into New Hampshire and back up through southern Vermont, to reach his home in Proctor, some seventy miles from the capital.[2] Trying to get back to St. Albans from Randolph, Foster Wilson covered 850 miles on a journey that took him to both Montreal and New Rochelle, New York. Still, he arrived a few days after the flood, and thus did better than Carrie Ormsbee, who had been addressing a group in Randolph's Congregational church on the evening of 3 November and watching her audience shrink as the rain poured down outside. Determined, she stayed to finish her lecture, only to find herself stranded "on the island of Randolph," as she put it, unable to get back over the mountains to her home in Brandon. Not for two weeks did she return, and only then by a circuitous route first through Northfield (where she observed the Central Vermont's stranded *Ambassador*), and then through Montpelier, Waterbury, and Burlington.[3]

Even Burlington, though largely undamaged, saw its rail and highway lines cut, and was forced to depend on the *Chateaugay,* which ferried passengers, mails, and telegrams nine miles across Lake Champlain to New York and the main line of the Delaware and Hudson. The old steamer (built in 1888, she had been the first iron-hulled ship on the lake) soon became overburdened, filled to capacity on every trip— "[w]hen she left Burlington this afternoon, you couldn't have put a chicken on her," the company's manager observed.

Within days, the Rutland Railway did manage to restore a skeleton service from Burlington as far south as Middlebury, making possible, among other things, the annual football game between that college and the University of Vermont (Vermont won, and the proceeds went to flood relief). On the 14th, the first train pulled into Rutland from the north, after a slow detour over the tracks of a marble railway, since the main line through Proctor was still impassable.[4] In many places, however, rail bridges remained collapsed and tracks destroyed, and it would be weeks or months before any service was restored.

Meanwhile, the Army shipped up a pontoon bridge from Delaware to restore Burlington's link to industrial Winooski. Brought by an engineering company under Lieutenant Leslie R. Groves, later to become famous as the head of the Manhattan Project in World War II, the bridge was put in place within twenty-four hours, only to sink almost immediately. The pontoons, it turned out, had been in dry storage since the Civil War, and needed to be hauled out and caulked before going back in the water. Though it served its immediate purpose until a permanent replacement could be built, the temporary bridge proved to be a continuing source of trouble during the winter. Both high water and ice made necessary its occasional removal, and in one instance in February, the effort to dynamite an ice block killed a sergeant, and injured Lt. Groves himself.[5]

For those forced to flee who were now returning home, the view from the flooded districts was bleak almost beyond belief. Alice Jennings, a Waterbury teacher, found a nearby bridge simply "a tangled mass full of wreckage," houses lifted off their foundations, and trees "hung with grass so they resemble the Spanish moss in Florida and

Fig. 10. The pontoon bridge put in place by the Army to replace the Burlington-Winooski span destroyed by the flood. In the background is the American Woolen Mill of Winooski. *Courtesy of the Vermont State Archives.*

over everything is the filthy mud." Amid this scene of destruction, people were "chopping up their pianos and furniture for kindling." Making his way along the Winooski Valley, a reporter noted household possessions crowding porches and lining roads, being cleaned off and dried out before being taken back inside, while families did their best to cook what food they had "on parlor drum stoves and impoverished gypsy camp fires in the yards."[6] His ninety-year-old mother, daringly rescued the night of the flood, "never broke down until they brought her home," wrote R. W. Germain of Jonesville. "Her carpet spoiled and lots of keepsakes that she had kept for years, the front yard from a foot up to two feet of mud, the back yard buried up in sand and gravel. She went to pieces for a few days and I did not blame her. I came near going myself."[7]

Those returning to their houses found doors jammed, and often had to smash windows to gain entry. Inside, bureaus and desks were over-turned, chairs and tables tilted at crazy angles. Pianos, the prize posses-sions of many families, lay ruined on parlor floors, keys broken and soundboards warped (Mr. Germain himself lost a parlor organ). And everywhere—in houses, in cellars, in yards, gardens, and streets—lay a thick coat of slimy, foul silt, fine enough to have worked its way into even the tiniest crevices—"*the smell* is a *stench*—the mud is the *slipperyest* stuff & the nastiest of its kind," as Clara Harvey wrote of Montpelier.[8]

"Conditions here are unthinkable," she observed, almost three weeks after the flood. "[T]he papers do not portray the utter ruin and desola-tion on every side. The few venturesome spirits who come to town are appalled—practically every merchant is ruined and business at a stand-still; the banks are standing behind their people nobly, but they will be strained to the limit."[9] "The flood reduced many communities to their essentials of one hundred and fifty years ago," wrote the *Rutland Herald,* describing villages with no power, no telephones or telegraphs, no roads or railroads, and no food or fuel save what was already on hand. Unable to get their milk to market, dairy farmers rummaged in their attics for old churns, to make and store butter against the day when it could once more be sold.[10]

While food was often short, and strict rationing imposed in such places as Waterbury and Montpelier, early alarms of widespread hun-ger proved baseless. "This talk of food famine is mere hysteria," de-clared the manager of a Rutland grocery store, and though the city's gas remained cut off, within two days enough electricity had been re-stored to allow the bakeries to start working again, and the town had ample supplies of coal and food. In Waterbury, milk came from a Cen-tral Vermont train marooned by the waters, while the Montpelier *Times-Argus* reported the presence of a farm woman come to town to sell chickens—but only to customers who were members of the Klan![11] Ordinary yeast suddenly became a precious commodity, for in a day before large commercial bakeries were common, most families either made bread at home or depended on the local bakery. In some flooded towns, it was one of the first emergency supplies to be brought in, while in others, local ingenuity met the problem. A Glover woman who knew how to "start yeast" made enough to share with the small town's other housewives, while a Mrs. Butterfield, working with her son to make yeast from potatoes, was able to keep the Rochester town bakery supplied. Such measures, however, were of little help to Ludlow, where the local bakery—"perhaps the most important building in town," as the *New York Times* remarked—burned down days after the flood.[12]

More immediate was the threat of disease from broken water and sewage systems or from dead cattle decomposing despite the cold. Health officials quickly began campaigns of mandatory inoculation against typhoid, the serum brought in by automobiles and pack animals, or sometimes parachuted from aircraft into isolated villages. Even towns unaffected by the flood took no chances; Stowe, for instance, insisted on inoculating 150 men who returned from helping to clean up Waterbury. In the end, despite some cases of diphtheria in Waterbury, the incidence of disease was surprisingly low.[13]

Cut off from the outside, towns and villages found themselves forced back on their own immediate resources. National Guard units, unable to reach the adjutant-general in beleaguered Montpelier, mobilized on their own to help in rescue work, and to enforce martial law to prevent looting and protect stores of food and fuel.[14] Emergency disaster committees, often working with local Red Cross chapters, set up shelters and messes for the homeless and provided medical care. Armories, schools, churches, church halls, and private houses were pressed into service. Refugees from Barre's North End found food and shelter at a local school, while in Waterbury four hundred people crowded into the Stowe Street school, where Flora Carpenter had found refuge after her rescue by a canvas canoe. There she joined other volunteers in preparing a breakfast on Friday morning, coffee and doughnuts coming from stores that had escaped the flooding. Meanwhile, the town's Congregational church, standing on high ground, was turned into a mess that not only fed the town's refugees, but also sent out boats carrying food to marooned families or floated downriver to Bolton on craft fashioned from coffins lashed together.[15]

Waterbury was one of several badly wounded towns fortunate enough to receive substantial help from its undamaged neighbors. By late Thursday, word of its plight had already reached Stowe, only eleven miles distant, but high enough up in the hills to escape the waters. There, at midnight, Craig Burt, a lumber dealer, received a telephone call from the owner of the Waterbury Inn, a Mrs. Davis, who told him a dam must have broken. "We have several hundred people in the hotel. We have lost some lives. We don't know how many. Water is over the desk in the lobby and rising fast. We must have help. We need boats, food, blankets, and everything." Burt immediately went to work, rounding up others to help and requisitioning boats from the Lake Mansfield Trout Club, then setting out with a friend in his Buick to reach a farmhouse from which he could call Morrisville for more boats. Soon after daybreak, trucks carrying a hundred men from Morrisville and Stowe were on their way to repair the road to Waterbury and throw up temporary bridges.

By late morning, the caravan had covered ten miles, reaching the outskirts of the flooded town, from where Burt was rowed to the Waterbury Inn and deposited on the second-floor fire escape. There he learned of the plight of the nearby State Hospital, where over a thousand patients and staff were without food or drinking water. Burt immediately went back to Stowe for supplies, descending again that evening to the hospital, to find Dr. Eugene Stanley, the superintendent, looking haggard and worn in the light of a kerosene lamp. There, with Burt's help, more volunteers from Stowe were mobilized to help clean up the hospital.[16]

Meanwhile, the women of Stowe and Morrisville stayed up for nights preparing food, so that for several days, as the local paper put it, "Waterbury was practically fed" from those towns. Stowe in fact rationed its own supplies to send bedding, kerosene stoves, and other provisions for their neighbors, while raising over $500 for flood relief, as well as providing asylum for about a hundred Waterbury mothers and children, evacuated because of the threat of typhoid. "The people in Stowe were just wonderful," wrote Minnie Nelson two weeks later. "They opened up their homes and helped in every possible way . . . I stayed a whole week with one family, then last week we were taken to another. You see they wanted to divide the people so each family that wanted to take us could do their share."[17]

In much the same way, the citizens of stricken Johnson benefited from the help given by Hyde Park, six miles away and several hundred feet higher. Two Johnson schoolboys brought the news of their town's predicament on Friday, and immediately three men set out packing food on their backs. Presently, under the direction of Mrs. Harry Noyes, chapter chairman of the Lamoille County Red Cross, men from the American Legion loaded a truck with supplies and set out. Shattered roads and flooded fields forced its abandonment, the men then carrying what they could, wading in some places through waist-deep water, helped by ropes tied to trees, before entering the town, where the flood still reached the second story of Johnson's houses.[18]

Meanwhile, Mrs. Noyes set to work to organize a relief program, asking Red Cross headquarters in Burlington for help. Arriving in Johnson, she joined Mrs. Saleeby, who headed the town's Red Cross organization, setting up an emergency canteen in the Opera House, and arranging for cooked food to be sent in from Morrisville and Hyde Park. She also arranged shelter for refugees and relief workers in the Congregational church, and called for volunteers, both men and women, to help clean the houses and streets, later reporting that many had turned out, including not only workers from Johnson's damaged woolen mill, but also some of "our very best people, unaccustomed to such labor" (among them three of the town's ministers, all seen shoveling mud into the same cart).[19]

One of the helpers was the young Arecca Urban, a student at the Johnson State Normal School, whose first thought when the waters came had been to try to get home to Cabot, some thirty miles distant. The school principal, however, convinced her and her roommate that travel was impossible, and that they should stay to help clean up, sending them into a flooded house, where they discovered a beautiful piano in ruins, while gummy silt covered everything and even had to be scraped off the windows. "Those poor people . . ." she recalled, "they lost everything." Another volunteer described the difficulty of getting into a flood-damaged house, "as we struggled with doors that would not open, and when forcibly opened refused to shut, with cookstoves covered with mud, and furniture that had lost its glue, and didn't know which leg to limp on, and clothes and bedding soaked in filthy water" (the energetic Mrs. Noyes also arranged for dirty linen to be taken to nearby towns for washing by volunteers). By Sunday afternoon, four cars from Burlington managed to reach the town after a difficult detour over mountain roads, bringing yeast, canned food, and insulin. Meanwhile, an emergency board of six men and three women was constituted to oversee relief. Shortly thereafter, Colin Herrle, appointed by the National Red Cross as director of relief work for Lamoille, Chittenden, Franklin, and Orleans counties, arrived in Hyde Park.[20]

Johnson and Waterbury were simply two examples of places benefiting from the aid given by neighboring towns spared the ravages of the flood—"[s]ympathy flowed in from the hills," wrote Ida Morgan Anderson of Cambridge some years later.[21] A reporter from the *Boston Evening Transcript* found himself "impressed, almost astonished to find how adequate local resources have been to meet . . . most of the immediate or 'first-period' needs of the sufferers." Such sharing was a

Fig. 11. Clean-up on State Street, Montpelier. To the right, above, is the capitol with its golden dome, and on the left is the headquarters of National Life. *Courtesy of Special Collections, Bailey/Howe Library, University of Vermont.*

common virtue in the face of privation, reflecting a kind of community sense perhaps still stronger in a rural society than in the more-developed parts of the country. Rallying local help in a time of disaster was part of a long and venerable New England rural tradition of what Karen Hansen characterizes as "mutuality, reciprocity, volunteerism, and localism," and these social values were still alive in rural Vermont well into the twentieth century, changed in form, perhaps, but not in substance.[22] As New England neighbors had come together in the past when a family's house or barn burned down, in 1927 they joined to help not only in their own communities, but those of neighboring towns as well, the sense of commonality heightened by such acts as Stowe's sharing of responsibility in the housing of refugees.

Nor were these examples limited to the smaller towns. Montpelier had something of a reputation for aloofness, even coldness, its inhabitants often transients working for the state government or National Life, whose huge building adjoined the golden-domed capitol on State Street. Yet here, Clara Harvey and her family, only recently moved to town, were still settling in when they began sheltering others, fourteen people crammed together for five days, with no gas, but only an electric grill and a coffee percolator used when the power came back on. "We had four double beds & two cots doing business part of the time . . . It was quite interesting to prepare food for so many under such circumstances in a *strange place,* and not knowing just where to find things, as I really had been here so few days that I felt about as strange as the others."[23]

Perhaps no group responded to the calls for help as enthusiastically as did the college students. Earliest in the field were the Norwich University cadets, who in addition to the help they gave to Northfield, also formed a pack train to carry badly needed supplies of food nine miles over hills already swept by snow and ice to destitute Moretown in the Mad River Valley. Scores of young men from the University of Vermont, Middlebury College, and Dartmouth eagerly volunteered for work in other devastated towns. On Tuesday, 15 November, 150 men from the university left Burlington in a convoy of automobiles provided by the local Rotary and Exchange clubs, making their way slowly over the washed-out roads to Waterbury, carrying picks, shovels, and galvanized steel baskets. To house and feed them, cots were put up in the Stowe Street school, while Fort Ethan Allen sent an army field kitchen. Here, under the command of two professors, the students were divided into squads and assigned houses to clean up. They began by digging out the cellars, which were not only the hardest places to clean, but also potentially dangerous sources of disease, where supplies of food, stored up against the winter, had now become part of the stinking mass of filth and sediment.[24]

Four days later, they returned to classes, replaced by 150 volunteers from Middlebury College, who arrived in cars provided by the town's residents and driven over the all but impassable mountain roads leading to Waterbury. They continued the work begun by their predecessors, and also cleaned out the second floor of the Waterbury town hall for use as Red Cross headquarters. Other volunteers—from the university, from St. Michael's College in Winooski, from Burlington's high schools—went to other Winooski Valley towns such as Richmond, Bolton, and Jonesville or to nearby farms to clean up. Sixty university students made their way to beleaguered Johnson, while cadets from Norwich, who had worked heroically during the Northfield flood, formed pack trains to carry supplies and mail to Barre, Montpelier, and Randolph.[25] Newbury's high school students were dismissed from class for three days to help, the boys shovelling, while the girls collected clothing and provided hot coffee, sandwiches, and doughnuts. Meanwhile, a thousand Dartmouth students (the young Nelson Rockefeller among them) were excused from

Fig. 12. Camp kitchen set up near the Waterbury High School. Those enjoying its amenities are presumably students from the University of Vermont helping in the clean-up. *Courtesy of Special Collections, Bailey/Howe Library, University of Vermont.*

classes on 11 November, boarding flat cars for White River Junction and Hartford across the river, to help those towns dig out.[26]

Women students also did their part, adding (as one observer, predictably enough, put it) "comforts, cheer and sunshine" to the "rugged, elemental things" provided by men.[27] In fact, in Massachusetts, the students of Smith College worked hard with the Red Cross when the flood struck the lower Connecticut Valley, and Middlebury College's women had been among the first in town to respond, holding a bridge party to raise money for sewing materials, and providing clothing for babies and young children. Thus, as a thoroughly patronizing article in the student paper put it, they kept busy enough so they "just barely had time to notice the men's absence, and surely no time to spend in tears."[28] Some also went to the flood zone, like Dorothy Claflin McColl of the university, who spent Thanksgiving weekend volunteering with her mother in Waterbury, sorting out clothing, ridding a damaged house of mud and wet wallpaper, sleeping in the Knights of Columbus hall, and taking her

Fig. 13. Clean-up workers take a break near the Perry Granite Corporation in Waterbury. *Courtesy of Special Collections, Bailey/Howe Library, University of Vermont.*

meals with other workers in the Congregational church mess (she also became violently ill when she ate an improperly cooked chicken pie).[29]

Between them, the students managed to clean up more than three-quarters of the damaged cellars in Waterbury, thus helping to restore normal living conditions before winter set in, a task characterized by the local paper as almost "impossible of accomplishment." More than that, they brought a sense of badly needed hope. "The boys came in with the strength and enthusiasm of young manhood," wrote a Waterbury resident to President Moody of Middlebury, "and, with singing and joy found in service, have helped shoulder the burden and given us courage." "Those who find selfishness the uppermost motive in the much criticized youth of today," the Middlebury student newspaper lectured its readers, "might take note of the present situation and realize that heroism and willing self-sacrifice remain latent in modern young people, ready to rise when the emergencies of peace-time make a worthwhile demand." Only in Northfield, apparently, did some residents think the cadets should have stayed on the job longer, rather than returning to class after a long weekend of clean-up and rescue work.[30]

Such volunteer activities, widely reported in the press, both within the state and beyond, underlined popular views of Vermont self-reliance and community, even if occasionally unorthodox means were used to recruit the able-bodied to serve. A Burlington deputy sheriff, for instance, rounded up twenty denizens of a local pool hall by threatening them with a night in jail if they didn't follow him to Bolton ("give me the college men every time when it comes to doing a real job," he told the *Burlington Free Press*). Within days, local groups were collecting food and clothing, churches were taking up special collections, and groups like the Lions, Elks, Rotarians, Knights of Columbus, and others were raising money or helping to provide supplies. Benefits were organized, such as "The Romantic Young Lady: Three Acts of Spanish Romance," which took the stage of the Strong Theater in Burlington, its proceeds, as well as those of the Armistice Day ball (music by the ten-piece Algonquin Band), going to flood relief. The press even reported that Babe Ruth, fresh from his record-setting sixty home runs that year, also wanted to help the victims, but it's unclear if anything came of his initiative.[31]

It's fruitless to try to distinguish at this point between the work done by local Red Cross chapters and the various emergency committees that quickly came together in the damaged towns. "LOCAL RED CROSS PURELY WOMEN'S ORGANIZATION AND CONSIDERED WEAK," Colin Herrle of the Red Cross's national office wired Washington when he arrived a few days later in St. Johnsbury.[32] But whether he was right in that particular case or not, it's likely that most local chapters depended heavily on volunteer workers, many of whom were the women who organized them, ran them, and made up most of the membership. Clearly there was nothing weak about the enterprising Mrs. Noyes of Hyde Park, or Mrs. Saleeby of Johnson, or Mrs. Field of Rutland, wife of the chairman of that town's emergency committee, and supervisor of food and housing arrangements. Nor is it material whether their work in organizing relief was undertaken because of their ties to the Red Cross or simply because they were community leaders joining their relief efforts with other groups. "Every woman's club in Vermont is now cooperating with the local branch of the Red Cross," noted the *Middlebury Register* on 16 December, "or taking some special part in meeting the needs and conditions in their own localities," and the same was true of church groups and benevolent societies.

Within days of the flood, representatives of the national Red Cross began arriving in Vermont. Some of them, like Charles Carr, who went to Rutland, and vice-chairman James Fieser, came fresh from their work in the Mississippi disaster. William Harris, who for the next two months would head the state's relief effort, reached Montpelier after a difficult automobile trip through a snowstorm over Hunger Mountain, establishing his headquarters in the same school building that temporarily housed Governor Weeks and several state offices. Later on, there would be some questions about the Red Cross's relief work, but for the moment there was only praise. "What is this Red Cross?" an old man asked Marie Dohm, who managed to make her way from Woodstock over Hunger Mountain to stricken Gaysville, walking the last three miles. "I never heard of it before." "The Red Cross certainly has done wonderful work in supplying people with food and clothing," wrote Estelle Slack from Montpelier on 15 November. It was "our 'backbone,'" another woman remembered many years later. "Their help will never be forgotten."[33] On 7 November, Weeks wired John Barton Payne, the national chairman, designating the Red Cross as the official relief agency.[34]

The Response from Montpelier

By then the governor and his officials were beginning the long process of rallying the state's resources for the task ahead of them. It was mere coincidence that Weeks and his wife found themselves in Montpelier that afternoon when the waters rose. It was a fortunate coincidence, however, for it meant that he was at the center of things when disaster struck. Yet had he been back home in unscathed Middlebury, rather than in a capital city with no communications, he would have realized more quickly the full extent of the damage to his state.

In later years, perhaps nothing did more to shape Vermont's public memory of the disaster than the phrase—supposedly uttered by a plucky John Weeks when the first offers of outside aid reached the capital—that "Vermont can take care of its own." Over the years, this proud declaration has been repeated in a variety of forms as a reflection of the state's tradition of self-reliance and its reluctance to accept charity, even at a time when the rest of America was learning to look more and more toward Washington for help in difficulty.

Yet not until later did Weeks's declaration become part of the flood's folklore. A typical version is that found in 1937, when the *Rutland Herald,* commemorating the tenth anniversary, told of a boatload of reporters rowing to the governor's hotel to ask what the state needed, only to be given the "classic reply: 'Vermont will take care of its own.'"[35] A year later, similar stories appeared in Governor George Aiken's *Speaking from Vermont,* and since then can be found in various other accounts, including, most recently, James Jeffords' *An Independent Man* (published in 2003).[36]

"We hope to be able to take care of the situation ourselves," the *Boston Post*'s Herbert Baldwin reported Weeks as saying, and while praising the governor for his hard work, the reporter faulted him for his optimism. "[T]he cheerful predictions of officials that 'Vermont can take care of itself' cannot be fulfilled . . . the job of restoring the state of Vermont is one that the people of the United States must do. And they may as well realize it right now."[37] Yet nowhere else, either in the main Vermont papers or in the other New York and Boston dailies, does Weeks's remark appear, and though the *Burlington Free Press* published a statement from him on Sunday, 6 November, it suggested no reluctance to take outside help.[38]

Perhaps the *Post*'s story had a different source. Eighteen years later, Earle Kinsley, one of the state's Republican leaders, published an account, presumably given him by Weeks, in which the governor recalled telephoning the White House on Sunday night to ask Coolidge to send Secretary of Commerce Herbert Hoover to Vermont.

> As I left the telephone booth a group of pressmen were waiting, of whom one remarked "Vermont has gone to hell! She can never come back!" He kept repeating it. I was mad clear through, and I walked up to him and said, "You shut up. Don't let me hear you say those words again. Vermont will come back, and she can come back on her own, too!"
>
> In my excitement I forgot myself for the moment, but I have never regretted saying it.
>
> The newspapers made a good deal of my statement that we could come back on our own, and they attempted to fix the idea that Vermont's governor didn't want any help, and he was going to do it all himself. Naturally that was not my feeling about it. People were very kind and generous with money, gifts of clothing, drugs and medicines—but we really did the job ourselves.[39]

Was it perhaps the *Post*'s reporter who earned the governor's ire with his irreverent predictions? There's no way of knowing, of course, but in any case, the impression was soon abroad that Montpelier was rejecting offers of outside aid. Was the capital so thoroughly cut off that Weeks still had no idea of the extent of the devastation elsewhere? That view seemed to be confirmed by the later account of Charles Ferrin, at the time a captain at Fort Ethan Allen, who recalled traveling on horseback over Smuggler's Notch and down through Waterbury, finally reaching Montpelier to offer the Army's help. "Captain," Weeks responded, looking at him, "Vermont can take care of its own," not knowing, as Ferrin put it, "that the streets of Waterbury were littered with dead cattle and the railroad station was being used as a morgue." Herbert T. Johnson, the adjutant-general, had a more realistic view, however. "Charles," he told Ferrin, "send the troops."[40]

Yet Ferrin's retrospective account raises at least as many questions as it answers. The Army was indeed trying to reach Montpelier, urged on by Senator Frank Greene in St. Albans who, unable to telephone the governor, wired the War Department on Saturday for help in reestablishing communication with the capital.[41] From Boston, Major-General Preston Brown, commander of the Army's First Corps area, who had already organized the first relief flights to Vermont, managed himself to reach Burlington by air on Sunday. There he called Greene, telling him not only of the terrible devastation he'd seen, but also of his sense that the Army's help was not wanted. Greene thereupon managed to get a message through to Montpelier, imploring the governor to accept military aid, though a few days later he was almost apologetic about his initiative, telling Weeks he hoped he had not embarrassed him.[42]

But was it from Ferrin that the army concluded that its help was unwelcome? Oddly enough, his name never appears in an official report by the adjutant-general later in the month, and indeed the press reported—inaccurately, no doubt—that he had never reached the capital.[43] At 8:30 on Saturday evening, Captain William Mayer, accompanied by a small radio detachment, did arrive from the Fort, after walking all the way from Waterbury Center. There, once he had conferred with state officials, it was decided not to bring cavalry into the capital, where the police and National Guard were in control, but to send them instead to places where they could be more useful. Weeks considered the situation under control, Mayer told his superiors, and Montpelier needed no further help from the Fort.

"At that time, however," Adjutant-General Johnson's report dryly commented, "very little was known of the real situation." His account is carefully worded, and its judicious use of the passive voice leaves a good deal of uncertainty about which actors actually made which decisions, or how much coordination, if any, there was between Captain Mayer and Captain Ferrin. Mayer left Montpelier early on Sunday, assured that help from federal troops in the Winooski Valley would be welcome.[44] "The situation [in the capital] is serious," Weeks told the *Burlington Free Press* that day, "but we do not need more help just at present," and he cited instead Bolton, Waterbury, and Bethel as examples of places that needed aid more desperately. Finally, early on Monday morning, Johnson received a call from one of General Brown's officers suggesting that Brown himself believed the governor wanted no assistance from Federal troops. He quickly explained that was not the case, that Weeks was grateful for the offers, and that the troops were indeed needed in the Winooski and Lamoille valleys, but not in the capital region.[45]

Why the misunderstanding, then? Even if Weeks thought that Montpelier could do without the army, other sorts of help were certainly welcome, and even before Mayer's arrival, the first call made over a jury-rigged telephone system on Saturday afternoon was an urgent message by the local Red Cross asking for food, medical supplies, and money. Presumably this was made with the governor's blessing; whatever else he was, Weeks was certainly unlike Austin Peay of Tennessee, who, during the spring floods in his state, had rejected even the aid of the Red Cross, on the grounds that people should learn to provide for themselves.[46] Still, it's possible that the governor might well have thought at first that if things elsewhere in the state were no worse than in Montpelier, Vermont could indeed handle the emergency alone. But Captain Mayer's report, and perhaps Captain Ferrin's unrecorded appearance, changed his mind. A few weeks later, in a letter to Senator Greene, Adjutant-General Johnson denied that Weeks had ever rejected the Army's help. What actually happened, he suggested, was that on Sunday morning General Brown had spoken not to the governor, but to H. J. M. Jones, just appointed Montpelier's emergency food and fuel commissioner. When Jones told him no help was needed, he was speaking only of the capital, but the general took it to mean the state at large. "Never for a moment," concluded Johnson, had Weeks refused any help for the state as a whole.[47]

"Vermont can take care of its own." Whether or not Weeks ever actually made the statement is almost beside the point. For the historian, its importance lies in the way the story entered into Vermont's consciousness and became part of its folklore, so that what actually happened seemed less important than what people wanted to think had happened. "VERMONT FOLK TOO PROUD TO ADMIT NEED TO WORLD," ran a headline in the *Boston Globe,* and one report, quickly denied, even had Weeks rejecting an offer of three million dollars.[48] Real or imagined, the governor's words reflected, in the eyes of both Vermonters and sympathetic outsiders, something about Vermont virtues and the Vermont character, all the more so because they came at a time when the Mississippi Valley states were actively importuning Washington for massive federal intervention to prevent a recurrence of the disasters they had seen that spring. Vermont was different, Vermont was proud, Vermont would keep its hands off the public purse, relying on its own resources. As Mr. Germain had said of his ninety-year-old mother, rescued from her house in Jonesville the night of the flood, "she has the grit."

Whatever may lie behind the early reports, offers of outside help began to pour in almost immediately. The New England Council volunteered its assistance, and from Albany, which had seen some flooding itself, Governor Al Smith immediately wired offers of help to the New England states. When three New York National Guard aircraft arrived in Montpelier on Monday, Weeks asked them to stay on.[49] Two days later, praising the army's work, he added that "[r]umors have gone out that Federal aid was unnecessary which is entirely wrong." "Our loss has been so great," he wired Coolidge the same day, "that we shall need all the assistance the government and the Red Cross can give," and in a broadcast on the 9th, he spoke of the "appalling toll of human life and loss of property," thanked all those who had offered help, and appealed for contributions to a relief fund. "The plea now comes through with exceptional strength," wrote the *Boston Evening Transcript.* Not the sort of man ever to cry Wolf! and look around immediately for outside help, Governor Weeks had now concluded that some aid was necessary, and the paper promised that Boston, at least, would be generous.[50]

On 8 November, Weeks established a set of committees to direct the work of relief and rehabilitation, and to act as a structure for the state's emergency administration. Among the most important of the steps taken was the appointment of Fred Howland, one of the state's leading businessmen. A Dartmouth graduate, Howland had read law in the office of former Governor William Dillingham in Waterbury. After practicing

Fig. 14. Fred Howland, who headed the National Life Insurance Company, became Vermont's emergency finance commissioner after the flood. *Arthur F. Stone,* The Vermont of Today: With Its Historical Backgrounds, Attractions, and People, *4 (New York: Lewis Historical Publishing Co., 1929).*

briefly in Minneapolis, he had returned to Montpelier, becoming coun-
sel to National Life in 1903, and rising to its presidency in 1916. That put
him at the helm of one of the two nationally most important and influential Vermont corporations (the other, of course, was Vermont
Marble, run by the Proctor family and its protégés). Howland had earlier served in several state posts, becoming a member of the Public
Safety Committee during the war, and had played an active role in Republican affairs, chairing the state's delegation to the national convention in 1924. Long a friend of Weeks, he was now named financial commissioner, whose duties the governor had earlier assumed himself, to
save the state the expense of an extra salary (Howland also turned down
the salary offered him). For the next two years, he would be the
governor's right-hand man in the work of reconstruction, and to call
him "the director of Vermont's emergency government," said the *Boston
Evening Transcript*, "by no means overstates either the authority or the
responsibility committed into his hands."[51]

That paper's reporter, W. H. MacDonald, left his readers a vivid picture of Howland at work (the "Hoover of Vermont," he called him). Arriving a few days later in wet, cold, and musty-smelling Montpelier, he
found the new commissioner in the large, marble National Life building
flanking the State House, dressed in gray golf clothes and heavy boots,
"a big, mild-mannered man, with snow-white hair and a white mous-
tache. His face was ruddy with out of doors." Though napping at his
desk when MacDonald entered ("like everybody else in Vermont he had
been working hard"), he awoke at once, and went on as if he'd never
taken his mind off his work. At pains to assure MacDonald that his state
had never rejected outside help, Howland spoke of his gratitude for the
assistance now pouring in, and of the importance of restoring rail and
road lines, estimating that highway and bridge repairs alone would run
some five to six million dollars. Thoroughly optimistic about the state's
future, he suggested that conservative Vermont might in the end actually profit from the shock of the flood, and showed MacDonald a letter
from Senator Greene, predicting a newly unified Vermont rising from
the catastrophe—"[w]hile we are reading a somber page in her history
the next one will be brighter than ever." As the two men parted, wrote
MacDonald, "[h]is cigar was going, and his blue eyes gleamed mildly in
his ruddy face. He was cheerful and busy. He was like others one might
talk to in Montpelier and Barre. One felt," concluded the reporter, "that
confidence like this was to be the making of a new Vermont."[52]

Herbert Hoover Comes to Vermont

By the time MacDonald visited the "Hoover of Vermont" at work, the real secretary of commerce had already come and gone. On 6 November, when he had called Coolidge, Weeks had asked the president to send Hoover, and a day later, after some initial doubts, Coolidge agreed.[53] As Weeks and those around him knew, such a visit would have considerable political and symbolic value. The "Great Humanitarian," as he was known, had built up a reputation as an able and energetic relief administrator in Europe during and after the war, and that spring Coolidge had put him in charge of the Special Mississippi Flood Committee, a body that included five cabinet secretaries, to oversee relief measures in regions devastated by the big river. A man with an almost apocalyptic faith in the power of engineering to provide rational solutions to natural and social questions, he threw himself into his work, drawing praise from all circles, and the energy and activity that radiated from his Memphis headquarters contrasted with the president's seemingly do-nothing approach, and made him a national hero.[54]

Even though a whole week passed before the White House publicly announced his trip (the delay inevitably leading to speculation about Coolidge's lack of sympathy for his secretary's presidential aspirations), his coming would hearten those facing the task of rebuilding as winter drew on.[55] "Hoover, Sargent [Attorney-General John Sargent, a native of Ludlow], Howland, and Fieser—the sight of these four men conferring together in Vermont gives all New England a real sense of encouragement," wrote the *Evening Transcript,* before their meeting actually took place.[56] On the 13th, Sargent reached Burlington, though the next day Reuben Slaight, Hoover's personal assistant, perished when his aircraft crashed trying to land in Montpelier.

The secretary himself arrived in Vermont on the 16th, his special train cheered by over a hundred schoolchildren turned out to greet him at Essex Junction. From Burlington, a convoy of nine automobiles edged its way slowly through the ravaged landscape and over the broken roads to Montpelier. In Waterbury, where they stopped to mount chains on the tires, a Boston paper saw "[t]he spirit of the whole valley . . . manifested when one Vermonter smiled his welcome and declared: 'Well, sir, we have nothing left, but plenty of courage.'" Fifty years later, the Waterbury journalist Lloyd Squier remembered, rather less reverently, that when

Hoover's car stalled in trying to scrabble over a temporary corduroy road at Middlesex Notch, one of the workers, seeing him waiting in the back seat, called to him to get out and help push.[57]

That evening, meeting in Montpelier with state and Red Cross officials, Hoover listened to reports of what was being done, promising whatever help he could give, and praising the spirit he had seen. Next morning, he gave Weeks his recommendations: the Red Cross to assume full responsibility for emergency relief; a way found to provide emergency credits to damaged businesses; and finally, an estimate to be made by the Federal Highway Bureau of the cost of restoring federal aid roads, while the state and federal agencies worked out the responsibilities for reconstruction.[58]

In later years, the story grew that Weeks had proudly refused Hoover's offer of aid from Washington. "Thank you, Mr. Hoover," went one version of the tale. "Tell the president, not one red cent, Vermont will take care of her own."[59] Nothing of the sort actually took place, of course. On the contrary, Hoover's suggestion that money might come from Washington must have been heartening, particularly to the state's congressional delegation, which was already exploring the possibility. On the occasion of the flood's fifth anniversary, John Weeks—by now a congressman—praised Hoover's "keen analysis" of the state's needs, and his "comprehensive program for restoring the state to its normal condition." But that was in 1932, of course, just days before the national election that was to pit President Hoover against Governor Franklin D. Roosevelt of New York.[60]

Though undoubtedly grateful for the secretary's visit, Vermonters might have been surprised by the notion that their reconstruction was the brainchild of the Great Humanitarian. "I have seen Vermont at its worst and Vermonters at their best," Hoover said, but the fact is that he saw neither the state nor its inhabitants for very long, and after delivering his advice to the governor, left to address the gathering of the New England Council in Springfield, Massachusetts. "Herbert Hoover came—and saw—and suggested—and left," Clara Harvey complained from Montpelier. "We do not consider that he made any very wonderful or constructive suggestions or [said?] anything new. I understand that some of the men who really expected something from his visitation were utterly discouraged after his coming."[61]

How common her view was, it's hard to say (her mother was rather a pessimist, Clara Harvey's daughter admitted), but for all the acclaim in the press, the fact was that he had been in the state no more that twenty-four hours.[62] Harvey's strictures missed an important point, however, for, as F. Lauriston Bullard pointed out (he wrote frequently on New England affairs for the *New York Times*), the story of reconstruction was less newsworthy than the flood itself, and Hoover's arrival would put Vermont's difficulties back on the front page where they belonged. Still, whatever might be the symbolic value of the visit, the secretary's recommendations owed more to common sense (and to his Mississippi experience) than to any careful study of the particularities of Vermont's situation. In one respect, however, Bullard—reflecting the belief in the state's proud independence—was quite wrong. "[R]umor, garbed in robes of plausibility and even of probability," he wrote, "has it that Vermont did not at first look forward with undiluted pleasure to the visit of the national almoner," fearing that the secretary was simply coming to see how much help they needed, but "Vermonters are not used to charity."[63]

Yet, of course Hoover came because Weeks asked for him. It was fortuitous too that the New England Council was just then meeting in Springfield, where the flood's ravages, if not so bad as those farther north, were still visible. There too, the secretary repeated his warm praise for Vermont, calling on outsiders to help, not out of charity but because it was in the national interest to see Vermont put back on its feet. Again, he recommended finding a way to provide emergency credits to damaged businesses, suggesting that their very availability, because of their stabilizing effect, would be worth millions "without actual supply of money" (out of a fund of $11 million in the south, he said, less than $1 million had actually been used).[64]

The Finances of Reconstruction

"[D]o not let any one or any department tell you that you do not need Federal aid," H. J. Page of the Canadian National Railroad told a Vermont audience a week after the flood. "Rather seek the government's assistance at once in rebuilding your bridges, re-opening your farm counties and re-stocking your valleys, so that like the people of the stricken village of Waterbury you can say, we are back on the map, bigger and better than ever."[65] Easy to say, perhaps even easier for one who was an official of a huge, state-run corporation. But where would the money come from? "Five thousand or more cattle drowned! The horror of it to the struggling owners crushes the bravest spirit," wrote John Southwick in the *Free Press*, dismissing the idea that Vermont could take care of its own. "What avail is Vermont pride in the tradition? Funds far in excess of Vermont's ability to furnish must be provided."[66] In times past, however, ever since a great fire in Portsmouth, New Hampshire, in 1803, Washington had responded to disaster both at home and abroad (the giant Kanto earthquake that leveled much of Tokyo and Yokohama in 1923 was a recent example), and Representative Elbert Brigham presently would be showing his House colleagues a long list of these occasions for their reflection. But who would help private enterprises ravaged by the flood? Not the Red Cross, whose interest lay primarily in family rehabilitation. Who would restore the rail lines, vital as they were in getting Vermont's goods to market? Above all, who would rebuild the thousands of miles of washed-out roads, and the more than twelve hundred downed bridges? Even if Washington were to help those highways on the federal aid system, as Hoover suggested, the rest were the responsibility of the state and its individual towns, and they would have to provide.

By state law, Montpelier could give the towns no more than $5,000 for each bridge that needed repair or replacement. The amount was obviously woefully inadequate, and as early as 8 November, Walter H. Crockett of the State Publicity Department suggested to the governor the need of a bond issue to avoid bankrupting towns (he also saw the disaster as a splendid chance for the state to move in and take over responsibility for roads and bridges, thus avoiding the troublesome dealings in recent years with individual towns that, jealous of their prerogatives, sometimes refused repairs to the trunk roads passing through them).[67] When the attorney-general ruled that the State Emergency Board had no authority to borrow the estimated $10 million needed for rebuilding, its members promptly urged Weeks to call the legislature into emergency session. By then, in fact, Fred Howland was already anticipating their action, talking to Boston banking circles about a $5 million bond issue, undismayed by their predictions that the interest rate of 3¾ percent that he proposed was too low.[68]

Even in a day when the lawmakers met for only three months every two years, extraordinary sessions were extremely rare. The last had been in 1916, when the General Assembly gathered to vote the pay of the Vermont National Guard, called up to serve on the Mexican border. On 17 November 1927, as soon as Hoover had left, Weeks summoned a special

Fig. 15. Temporary footbridge over the White River near Bethel. *Courtesy of Special Collections, Bailey/Howe Library, University of Vermont.*

session to meet on the last day of the month to deal with repairs to highways and state buildings. Nothing was said about other losses, such as those suffered by farmers, by businesses, or by the railways. Though the *Burlington Free Press* earlier had grumbled that such a meeting would be premature, it now backed the call, though still wondering if there would be a quorum, given the hazards of travel and the need for legislators to cover the expenses of the trip out of their own pockets.[69]

On 29 November, the New Hampshire General Court held its own emergency session, raising the state's gasoline tax and appropriating $3 million for highway repairs.[70] While some of the members descending on Concord may have found difficulties getting there, they faced few of the problems of their colleagues trying to make their way to Montpelier. Though a temporary bridge had been thrown across the Winooski River at Waterbury and a foot bridge joined Moretown and Middlesex, making some traffic possible in those directions, many members still faced the prospect of a long detour. The Montpelier and Wells River Railway was now sufficiently restored to run a "Legislative Special" for those who could find their way up the Connecticut Valley to Wells River, but some had to go as far south as Massachusetts to do so. Even then, the Special, supposed to leave Wells River at five in the afternoon, was held up for hours by reports of a weakened bridge on the line, and not until nearly midnight on the 29th did it finally steam into the capital (one of its pas-sengers reported that he felt the bridge sag under the train's weight).[71]

Despite such difficulties, very few members were absent when on the morning of the 30th, under a cold rain, the General Assembly gathered under the golden dome of the state house to take up its work. Entering the chamber to address them, Governor Weeks looked tired and preoc-cupied, noted Edward Rockwood of the *Vermont Review,* "yet with a firmness of carriage and a simplicity of manner which is arresting." As he had at his inauguration eleven months earlier, he opened by turning to the Bible.

> He is introduced [Rockwood continued; the ellipses are his]. He re-sponds by quoting scripture: The Lord is my . . . He quotes it passion-ately—like the lines of a favorite poet made sacred by past associations. He is praying. O, Lord upon whom . . . and he prays eloquently—like a gifted divine, gaining momentum and volume with each sentence.

Actually, the governor's psalm was not the Twenty-third, as Rock-wood reported, but the more apt Forty-sixth (suggested to him, inci-dentally, by John Thomas, the former president of Middlebury Col-lege and now heading Rutgers). "God is our refuge and strength," Weeks began,

> a very present help in trouble. Therefore will we not fear, though the earth be removed, and though the mountains be carried into the midst of the sea; though the waters thereof roar and be troubled, though the mountains shake with the swelling thereof. There is a river, the streams whereof shall make glad the city of God, the holy place of the tabernacles of the Most High . . .

There followed a prosaic, sobering report of the destruction and damage. To make repairs, Vermont had no alternative but to raise the extraordinarily large sum of $8,500,000. Furthermore, because the ad-vent of the automobile meant that highways no longer simply served in-dividual towns, but the entire state, and because of the limits on state aid to towns for bridge construction, Weeks proposed the rebuilding should be centrally undertaken, carried out under the supervision of the Highway Department.

So, at any rate, went the dry-as-dust talk as it was officially re-corded. "This does not go over so big—psychologically speaking," Rockwood noted.

It lacks literary value, is short, business-like, and statistical. It falls rather prosaic on a gathering unconsciously responsive to dramatic values. The Governor senses the situation. Laying aside the mss., he talks extemp. Now the full forces of his sincerity and earnestness is felt. He rededicates himself to his task; he pledges all his strength and ability; he reaffirms his confidence in the good judgment of the Senators and Representatives; and he pleads for an abandonment of all selfish desires in the interest of a rehabilitated state. The effect is highly dramatic. A climax is reached. He sits down. The applause is instantaneous. It continues. It grows in volume—louder, louder, and still louder. The Governor rises to leave. The joint assembly rises, and continues to applaud. The Governor makes his exit. Once again he has scored.[72]

"Vermont has a future before her that she has not realized," Weeks concluded, and he promised "to reconsecrate every ounce of my strength to the work of making Vermont a stronger power in the outside world and a happier place to live in." Rockwood was not the only one moved, for Weeks's remarks, said the *Rutland Herald,* brought tears to the eyes of his audience. After such a beginning, his program passed easily. The main item was the $8,500,000 bond issue, an amount Weeks had sought, though others had argued for $10 million. In addition, there was an enabling act for the kind of credit mechanism that Hoover had recommended, and a provision allowing the governor to seek expert advice on questions of flood control. Somewhat more controversially, the Assembly also authorized a loan to the St. Johnsbury and Lake Champlain Railway, which the previous evening had busily lobbied a group of legislators for help.

"The greatest work ever done in a single day by the Vermont Legislature," House Speaker Loren Pierce called it, when the tired lawmakers finally rose after more than thirteen hours of work. Certainly it was a personal triumph for John Weeks. If his success with a fractious legislature earlier that year demonstrated his political astuteness, his actions now showed his qualities as leader of an afflicted state, in his refusal to be cowed by hardship, and as an incarnation of optimism and hope, exemplifying the sort of hard work and self-reliance that Vermonters valued in themselves, and the outside world valued in them.

And, while the ramifications would not be clear for some time, the rebuilding now made possible would prove a godsend to the governor's larger program. Though hardly a man to advocate a blind acceptance of the new, he already had proved himself a passionate champion of a modern highway system. Until now, he had followed a prudent, pay-as-you-go policy, rather than choosing to borrow to speed up the work. It would soon become clear, though, that reconstruction did not mean simply bringing the roads back to where they had been before November. This sudden rush of new money would provide both the excuse and the means to modernize the highway system far more rapidly than any could have predicted. "[T]he next time your out-of-state friends laud Coolidge for the cleverness of his political tactics," the *Vermont Review* advised its readers, "just tell them we have a Governor in Vermont that is a veritable Socrates when it comes to political sagacity. He belongs to the pragmatic school; and he always gets what he goes after, be it eight millions of dollars or forty miles of cement."

Meanwhile, as the year drew to its close, at least some of the flood's victims were cheered by the support that came flowing in from their neighbors. A deeply religious man, Governor Weeks used his Thanksgiving proclamation of 12 November not only to recall the blessings bestowed by the "Author of all mercies," but to express the state's profound gratitude to those who had come to its aid, and the hope that November's tribulations would lead Vermonters to restore loss and become a better people. His wish, suggested the *Boston Evening Transcript*, was based on sound enough Puritan theology, but under the circumstances, "slightly supererogatory. The Vermonters are already a very good people . . . honest, virtuous and rather more than to the average extent godly." Surely this "greatest calamity in their history" was due to natural causes, and must not to be seen (as a letter to the paper had suggested), as divine judgment on the state's alleged laxness toward rum-runners bringing their illicit wares down from Canada.[73]

Be that as it may, the spirit of cooperation continued in the weeks after the flood. Johnson put on a communal Thanksgiving dinner, as did the First Congregational Church of St. Johnsbury, which had become a haven for refugees. From Burlington came a Thanksgiving feast for the entire town of Waterbury in the Congregational church, which was still serving as a general mess (though organized by men, the *Waterbury Record* pointed out, they thoughtfully brought "their own waitresses").[74] Other towns participated as well (Middlebury, for example, furnished ice cream). The event was such a success that an even larger dinner was planned for Christmas, and so much money poured in that similar gatherings were prepared for other hard-hit towns.

Meanwhile, as Christmas approached, from all over the northeast trucks pulled into Waterbury, filled with clothes and children's toys to be distributed by churches and benevolent societies (the children of Waterbury town, noted the *Record,* were attracted by bright red hats and fashionable sweaters, while those from the farms sensibly chose warm stockings and mufflers).[75] On Christmas day, more than fifteen hundred people, arriving in different shifts, crowded into the Congregational church for the feast (this time, rather than waitresses, seventy prominent business and professional men, adorned with white caps, green and red garlands around their necks, and "cute little gingham aprons" did the serving). "I can't describe the feeling that existed, but it was certainly more than food and chocolates we carried away from the church." "What a Christmas! What a Christmas!" wrote the local paper. "Don't ever say to anyone living in Waterbury and vicinity . . . that there is no such thing as the brotherhood of man."

The celebration was, the *New York Times* reported, the biggest event of its kind ever to have taken place in the state. And, as one observer noted, for Burlington itself, it "proved to be national advertising and worth all that it cost."[76]

4

〜〜〜〜

"New Experiences in Disaster Relief"

Reconstruction Begins

In all the tangled wreckage of bridges, houses, and barns borne away on the swollen waters of the Winooski River that harrowing November night, was the debris of one particular building that was soon to become famous beyond the borders of Vermont. The little schoolhouse that stood on Pinneo Flats, just above the river near Bolton, had been abandoned for more than a decade when, through a community effort, it had been repaired and put back into use, reopening in the autumn of 1926. A year later, it counted seventeen pupils, with the twenty-year-old Clara Thompson as their teacher. That night, watching with horror from a nearby house, she had seen the river overwhelm the building and bear it off downstream.

Edward Clark, the school superintendent, was determined to rebuild it, but was also realist enough to know that the money would not be found in his shattered town. Writing to John Southwick of the *Burlington Free Press,* he promised that if he could raise $1,000, he would renovate an empty barn, so that the school might reopen again in early January. Overly optimistic, perhaps, but his tactics worked. Southwick ran an editorial on 18 November to rally public support, and a second piece four days later, calling the story of the school's destruction "one of the most heart-wrenching of the flood," urged all, school children as well as adults, to help.[1]

That did it. Not only did children contribute their pennies (one Waterbury youngster told the press that he was depriving himself of chewing gum to help), but mother's clubs, parent-teacher associations, and other such groups raised money. Donations came not only from within the state, but from as far away as Florida, Illinois, and Alabama, both in cash and in kind: building materials, books, desks, and other furnishings (some from J. L. Hammett of Boston), to say nothing of an organ (from Mrs. P. E. Kingsley of Middlebury), a stained-glass window, and a school bell. By 30 November, when Clarence H. Dempsey, the state commissioner of education, appealed for support, the decision had been made to build a brand-new school on higher ground, and the goal was raised to $3,000. All the world responded, the Associated Press asserted (on the strength of one or two contributions from Europe), no gift more touching than the $500 that came from schoolchildren in the Mississippi Valley.[2] On 25 January 1928, the new Bolton Memorial School, named to commemorate the town's twenty-six victims, opened, not only safer than before, but larger and considerably better equipped than it earlier had been. Clara Thompson returned to her position as teacher, although, as the *Rutland Herald* noted sadly, several of her former students had been lost in the flood.[3]

"An educational epic," Southwick called the story. "We are glad this Memorial School was not created by one beneficent (sic) giver. That would have robbed a host of boys and girls of the abiding joy that will ever be there as they visit or drive past the structure and realize they had a part in this fine memorial." Perhaps because it might detract from the vision of a school, "erected," as the *St. Albans Messenger* later put it, "by the pennies and dimes of the little school folks and the dollars of the older ones," no mention was made of the leading gift, a contribution of $1,000 by the seventy-eight-year-old Ellen Pinneo Smilie of Montpelier, who, years earlier, had been a student in the old school.[4]

Pinneo Flats was precisely the story the times demanded, wonderfully suiting the upbeat coverage of reconstruction given by the press. A small victory in a tiny town, perhaps, but as a "splendid memorial to the great-heartedness of the people of Vermont and other states who contributed," to quote the *Free Press,* its symbolic value was far reaching.[5] The rebuilding of this little schoolhouse in a wasted landscape provided something immediately tangible: a small, local, and successful undertaking that combined care for children and future generations with community effort, outside support, and dollars well, but thriftily, spent, all coming together in a happy ending.

The Bolton school story thus served not only to raise spirits during the hardships of a long, dark winter, but also served as a popular illustration of the larger story of Vermont's character and its response to disaster. It also helped to counteract the gloomy predictions made by some right after the flood about the state's capacity for recovery. "When the millions for Mississippi were too few," wrote Louis Lyons in the *Boston Globe* ten days after the Vermont cataclysm, "Will Rogers said if it was New England the money would have come in unasked in a flood." But Rogers was wrong, concluded Lyons. The money "has not flowed in like water, nor even like wine. It has not begun to flow at all," and the "pitiable" amount appropriated thus far by the Red Cross was less than Boston had raised in a single week for the relief of the southern states.[6]

Lyons was wrong, though. In fact, almost as soon as the waters went down, money began arriving in Governor Weeks's office, and in a ceremony at the state house on 16 November, he presented James Fieser of the Red Cross with a check for $75,000, representing contributions thus far received. More came later, much of it from within the state. It came from individuals, from town canvasses, from church collection plates, from service organizations like the Elks and the Freemasons, and from corporations (the Vermont Marble Company contributed $1,000). But it also arrived from outside the state: from the *Knickerbocker Press* of Albany, which sent some $16,000 raised in that city, from theater owners in Boston and other cities that held benefit performances, from places such as the Boston women's store that turned over proceeds from a special sale to the local Daughters of Vermont, and from many, many small groups, like the Hanscom Ladies Nest of Owls in Nashua, New Hampshire, which contributed $25.[7]

Eventually, of the somewhat more than $1 million spent by the Red Cross in the state, Vermonters themselves contributed roughly $300,000.[8] That figure probably includes funds from expatriate Vermonters—men and women who, though born in the state or owning property there, lived elsewhere. Vermont Societies in Boston, New York, and Washington were particularly active; as early as 12 November, this last group had already called on President Coolidge to solicit his support for their plan to raise money. The New York society canceled its annual tea dance, holding a benefit at the Hotel Roosevelt instead, with Col. Theodore Roosevelt in the chair. From Park Avenue, Anna Louise Orvis, Republican national comitteewoman, owner of the Equinox Hotel in Manchester, and former president of the Village of Manchester, raised some $4,000 by appealing to New York's Vermonters to share their Thanksgiving plenty with the flood sufferers.[9]

Though Weeks had promised to turn over to the Red Cross all the funds coming into his office when he designated it as the official relief

Fig. 16. Governor Weeks hands a check for $75,000 to James L. Fieser, vice-chairman of the National Red Cross, 18 November 1927. Herbert Hoover stands at his right. *Courtesy of the Vermont State Archives.*

agency for the state, some would have preferred that the governor handle the money himself. A letter from Connecticut enclosing $10 expressed no confidence in either the Red Cross or the Y.M.C.A. because of their "gouging and profiteering" during the war. A Mrs. A. P. Cross gave $5 to a vice-president of the Shawmut Bank in Boston, asking that it to go directly to someone in need, rather than being passed through the Red Cross (given her age and condition, the banker inferred, her gift was the equivalent of $5,000 from someone more fortunate). Fred Howland wrote her later to say that the money had been given to a Mrs. Pape, with four children, left homeless by the flood. And C. F. Harrington, of Salem, Massachusetts, asked, his tongue presumably firmly in his cheek, that his contribution go to "DEMOCRATIC sufferers . . . all Democrats in New England are in need of relief, and most particularly those who are residents of Vermont." But perhaps most important was the sort of view expressed by John Barrett, a former diplomat then living in Grafton, who wrote Weeks about the funds raised by members of his church. "The . . . point I want to emphasize is that they were all keen on sending the money to you because to them you are the embodiment of the state's soul and body, so to speak, in this great catastrophe. They all feel deep confidence in you personally and believe you will spend the money 'however and wherever best.'"[10]

Nor was money all that arrived, as the flood of toys and clothes sent to towns like Waterbury at Christmastime showed. Some three or four public libraries were badly damaged, including those in Johnson and Waterbury and, most seriously of all, the Kellogg-Hubbard Library of Montpelier, which lost some sixteen thousand volumes kept in the basement, as well as pictures and files. Thanks to an appeal by the American Library Association and a grant from the Carnegie Foundation, help for these institutions came from other libraries and occasionally from publishers. The state Free Public Library Department received $8,200, the Kellogg-Hubbard $6,000, and Waterbury $3,000 (interestingly enough, the largest grant made in the south was $2,000 to the Mississippi Department of Education, while none of the other grants in that region amounted to more than several hundred dollars).[11]

As is true after any great disaster, Vermont's broader reconstruction had two different aspects. The first was physical: the repair and replacement of buildings and property, such as the Bolton school, the damaged State Hospital in Waterbury, the ruined stores of merchants in towns such as Montpelier and Johnson, the farmhouses and barns lost to the waters, and the herds and flocks that they had once sheltered, and the highways and rail lines linking Vermont to the greater world. The second was human: the need to help the injured back to their feet, keeping up their spirits in the face of a winter promising little but privation. Vermonters had to believe in their own recuperative powers, had to believe that their state could come back, as Governor Weeks and others were fond of putting it, stronger and better than ever before.

Yet they would scarcely have been human had not some of them been crushed by despair. The Nichols family of Middlesex, having barely managed to get out of their house in time, returned to find it gone, the store that was their livelihood ruined, its stock destroyed. "Oh how much better it would have been if we had all stayed in the house and gone together," wrote their despondent daughter, "better than to live in poverty in father & mother's old age." "We simply exist, we don't live," added her mother. "What the future has in store for us remains to be seen. How we dread the long cold winter with no income." The shattered town of Gaysville had "completely lost its spirit," R. E. Savage wrote to Governor Weeks from nearby Bethel, and its people "are doing absolutely nothing for themselves." A Red Cross worker echoed his conclusions, finding those who lived there little interested in rebuilding, asking only for funds to tide them through the winter.[12]

There was also some carping as well, at least in private, about the legislature's foolhardy readiness to saddle the state with a huge debt, as well as at the favoritism shown the St. Johnsbury and Lake Champlain Railway ("a piece of bad business and vicious precedent," the *Rutland Herald* called it, blaming "the celebrated Lamoille Valley lobby" for the move).[13] But such voices were few, drowned out by the tide of public and private admiration for Vermont's actions, both within the state and beyond. "You have shown the Mississippi Valley fellows that you are ready to help yourselves instead of spending all your time for months asking other folks to come to your aid," wrote the Boston publisher Lewis Parkhurst to Fred Howland. "People in general like to help those who are ready to help themselves, and Vermont will not suffer in the end from this action."[14]

Fair or not, the perceived contrast here between southern passivity and Yankee roll-up-your-sleeves activism (pictured in a *Boston Globe* cartoon of 9 November), once again suggested that the governor's boast of his state's ability to care for its own did nothing to hurt Vermont's cause. Certainly no one did more to keep spirits up than John Weeks himself. With an energy belying his years, he used every pulpit available to him to hold out the promise of a brighter future for the state, after it met and overcame its trial by water. It was there in his Thanksgiving proclamation, days after the flood, it was there in his statements to the legislature and the press, and it was there in his ringing declaration of 22 January that Vermont had already come back, its farms and businesses once more flourishing (on that occasion his words drew an alarmed response from Elbert Brigham: Don't make the recovery sound too successful, he warned, lest Congress decide that the state could do without Washington's help).[15]

Meanwhile, despite cautions from the Boston bankers, Fred Howland persisted in his efforts to market the newly authorized bonds at as low an interest rate as possible. It's not clear precisely whether he first approached J. P. Morgan & Company in New York or whether Morgan approached him, but by early December an agreement was close whereby the banking house would not only take $5 million worth of the bonds at

3¾ percent but also would cover the normal cost of issue while charging no commission. In mid-January, the arrangement was made public (to the considerable upset of other bond dealers, of course), but, as Howland told John Grissingham of the *Wall Street Journal,* Morgan considered the arrangement their contribution to Vermont's relief. "This price was so favorable and so much lower than any dealer had suggested it would be possible to secure, as well as so much better than the price at which state bonds generally were selling, that we had no hesitation in accepting the proposal." Whatever the unhappiness of the other dealers, the arrangement, seen as a coup for the state, was welcomed at home. "The great international firm of J. P. Morgan," wrote the *Randolph Herald and News,* "has disproved the conception that all concerns of that type are Shylocks, ready to take the pound of flesh from hapless victims . . . A handsome thing, we say, and one that Vermont should not and will not forget."[16]

National Assistance and Local Enterprise:
The Red Cross and the Vermont Flood Credit Corporation

Much was made in the press of the day about the reluctance of many Vermonters to take what they considered to be charity. "They are not built right to pass the hat for themselves," as the *Boston Globe* put it, and town histories have many accounts bearing out this reluctance. A Red Cross worker, however, noted that while farmers spurned offers of aid with a brusqueness that verged on discourtesy, in the towns and larger villages, people were apt to take whatever they could get and even ask for more.[17] "They are really a pretty good bunch," wrote Colin Herrle of the national office in early December about the Lamoille County Red Cross committee in Johnson, "except for one bird who is out to stick us to the limit & one other, who wants to see everyone get as much replacement of losses as possible." But he also noted that rumors were reaching Johnson about large awards made in Waterbury and Montpelier, leading the local committee to suspect it was asking for and perhaps getting too little.[18]

Such fears were not restricted to Lamoille County, and they reflect, if not the quality of the Red Cross's work, then the often uneasy relationship between the agency and the state. Despite its role in the Great War, the Red Cross remained unfamiliar to many Vermonters, who were unused to the idea of a national organization, technically independent of the federal government, yet working closely with it and identified with it (the president of the Red Cross was also president of the United States). Indeed, after the war the organization had come under attack, particularly from the Hearst press, for self-aggrandizement and extravagance, while at the same time facing a struggle within its own ranks between those wanting to restrict it to relief in times of emergency and those arguing for a broader mission embracing more general welfare.[19] Meanwhile, by the mid-twenties, its work on the national level had been increasingly professionalized, reflecting the impetus towards new forms of professional association and cooperation between government and private organizations that, as Ellis Hawley has argued, were such a marked aspect of the period. General public support fell off after the war, but that began to change after the great Miami hurricane of 1926. Although efforts by Florida authorities to play down the disaster may have been responsible for the Red Cross's failure to find the $5 million it sought for relief, when President Coolidge appealed for funds in 1927 for Mississippi flood sufferers, the agency was able to raise $17 million.[20]

On the local level, however, the Red Cross depended on individual chapters (there were roughly nineteen in Vermont) staffed by volunteers. Not surprisingly, tensions could arise between these national and local, professional and amateur, sides of the organization, and Vermont was by no means immune to them. Questions of how funds were to be raised and distributed were particularly troublesome. The Red Cross, while ready to cooperate with local groups, insisted that once it assumed responsibility for disaster relief, all assistance should be administered under its aegis, following policies worked out on the basis of its own experience. The point, of course, was to ensure equity of treatment among its beneficiaries, rather than allowing regions or even individuals to dictate differences. Too often, national officials believed, local chapters were apt to be overly generous in making awards, failing to understand the real needs of the applicants and wasting scarce resources. Yet the volunteers who ran them, not surprisingly, thought themselves far better informed about local conditions than were outside professionals, and perceived the outsiders as too fettered by bureaucratic procedures and red tape of their own making.[21]

The stage was thus set in Vermont for a probably unavoidable clash of cultures. Earlier that year, a Red Cross worker on the Mississippi had complained about the "native indolence" that kept communities from taking any steps to help themselves, while "expecting substantial help in leadership and in wealth from the outside."[22] Native indolence and passivity, however, were hardly problems in New England. Experienced professionals found themselves up against independently minded, not to say stiff-necked Yankees, long in the habit of forming local groups to meet local needs, reluctant to accept policies in whose making they had no voice, and indisposed to take orders from the outside. The situation was exacerbated because, in Vermont at least, some chapters were better organized than others, and because when communities set up disaster relief committees right after the flood, they sometimes worked with the Red Cross and at other times went their own way.

Unfortunately, not a single scrap of paper remains from Vermont's Red Cross chapters, and the story has to be put together from the records kept by national headquarters in Washington. These suggest that while some of the local emergency committees worked well with the Red Cross, in other cases there was friction. Rutland's disaster relief committee, for example, appears to have distrusted the Red Cross and taken over the granting of damage awards by itself, while in nearby Proctor, headquarters of the huge Vermont Marble Company, a local committee made generous awards with no oversight ("some very influential state people live there," wrote a Red Cross official to Washington, presumably including those whose surnames happened to be Proctor).[23] On the other hand, William Harris, then in charge of New England relief for the Red Cross, advised that although Addison County had suffered relatively little, it should receive generous awards, because that was where Governor Weeks lived, and it was important to please him.[24]

Generally, on the question of financial control over all aid awards, the Red Cross got its way—at least in theory. Though rejecting a special appeal for funds, as there had been in the South, it promised sufficient resources from private donations and from its own treasury.[25] Learning of Montpelier's plans to raise funds separately to "supplement" the agency's work, the Red Cross officials objected and won their case, persuading the Vermonters that, as Fred Howland said, they would "receive such generous and liberal treatment from that organization that it is the best way to handle it."[26] Although Governor Weeks initially had promised to turn over to the Red Cross all the relief funds coming into his office, as time went on, it became evident that not only was he holding back money, but several chapters were doing the same, presumably planning to make their own disbursals after seeing what the National Red Cross would do.[27]

Thus there were tensions from the very start. The Red Cross, as it kept reminding people, was not an insurance agency, there to make good on all losses; its purpose was family rehabilitation, and families with sufficient resources to continue could expect little help, while those left destitute would be treated generously.[28] Governor Weeks himself appealed to the Red Cross to help Montpelier's merchants, but the Red Cross's Henry Baker suspected that local banks were being overly cautious in granting credit, waiting to see, like rivals in a poker game, what cards the Red Cross would play before putting down their own (he did point out, in any case, that awards for stock and equipment had been made to fifty-eight families in the city).[29] Barre, too, saw a good deal of friction between the authorities—particularly the mayor, Frank Small—and the Red Cross, though this eventually seems to have been smoothed over.[30]

There were other complaints, sometimes about inequities among awards and sometimes about their size. A particularly awkward problem threatened to arise in Cavendish. There, Red Cross officials suspected that Leon Gay, chairman of the local chapter, was using financial awards to placate those hurt by the failure of a dam belonging to the Vermont Hydro-Electric Corporation, with which Gay was associated, so they would be less likely to sue. An investigation by a Red Cross legal adviser concluded, however, that litigation by the agency was likely to fail, partly because of the flood's unprecedented nature, and partly because behind the Hydro-Electric Corporation stood the huge Insull utilities empire, with all its batteries of corporate lawyers.[31]

Although Fred Howland generally was satisfied with the Red Cross's work, and thought most of the complaints unfounded, he—as well as Weeks—was less pleased with some of the officials from Washington. "There has been one worker here who should never have been connected with work of this kind," wrote Weeks. "He has assumed the responsibility of slashing awards made by the Committee with the threat that if his award is [illegible: disturbed?] the Red Cross will withdraw. You will realize that such a procedure would be very unhappy in any instance."[32] Although Howland considered William Harris, in charge of the relief effort, to be a man of ability, he found him also undiplomatic, and some of his subordinates simply incompetent.

If the state's leaders complained that the Red Cross officials could sometimes be tactless, these latter also had their problems. Rumors, and the appearance of the occasional charlatan, were no help. Right after the flood, the enterprising "Doctor" Matthew Spiero showed up in Montpelier, carrying a gold-headed cane (a good-luck charm from his work in Mississippi, he told the press). Passing himself off as a water pollution expert from the Rockefeller Foundation, he apparently managed to extract $500 in Red Cross funds to pursue his work before he decamped (ultimately his wealthy father appears to have paid his bills).[33] Meanwhile, from Johnson came stories that the Red Cross was charging the Elmore Hotel for restocking its food supplies after it had fed and housed a hundred refugees for several days, and shortly thereafter Harris had to deny reports that the agency was selling clothes to the needy.[34]

Did the Red Cross underestimate both the cost and the amount of time it would need to handle New England's flood relief? It's impossible to say. In any case, matters came to a head in January, when either Harris himself or his colleague Colin Herrle announced that their work was almost done and most of the awards now made.[35] Shortly thereafter, Harris left, to be replaced by Henry M. Baker, the Red Cross's national director of disaster relief. Australian-born and now forty-four years old, Baker had assumed his present position in 1922, and his handbook on the subject had become the standard treatment, distributed to local committees to help them prepare for emergencies. Very much a representative of the new professionalism, it was Baker who had been sent to Miami after the destructive hurricane of 1926. In early 1927, he had become what the press called the "Flood Relief Dictator," working with Hoover in the Mississippi Valley.[36]

The Red Cross records are silent about the change of command in January, and on the whole, the press was uncommonly discreet in its coverage (the *Burlington Free Press*, for example, chose not to publicize complaints about the agency's work, but sent them privately to the Red Cross).[37] The *Burlington Daily News*, however, suggested that Harris had either spoken out of turn when he said the Red Cross's work would soon wind up, or else was being made the "goat" by a national headquarters intent on covering its own mistakes. A few days later, the paper professed itself satisfied with the new director's summary of progress, and there's no doubt that Baker's arrival in Montpelier helped clear the air (Howland gave credit for the change to the intervention behind the scenes of both Herbert Hoover and A. C. Ratshesky, a Boston banker who headed the Red Cross in that city to whom Howland often turned for advice).[38] For the moment, the troubles were stilled. That would change, however, when the winter snows began to melt.

If the Red Cross insisted that it was not an insurance agency, neither was it an agency to extend credit to shattered businesses so that they could rebuild. Yet such help was necessary for Vermont's human reconstruction, and there was inevitably some overlap between the Red Cross and the new Vermont Flood Credit Corporation (VTFCC), which emerged in December. This latter organization grew out of the work of a committee set up by the New England Council at its Springfield meeting three weeks after the flood, in response to suggestions from Herbert Hoover, who had actively promoted such schemes in the Mississippi states. Its particular form, though, which Boston bankers praised as superior to its southern analogue, seems to have been the brainchild of Frank Partridge, a former diplomat and long-standing ally of the Proctor interests, now president of the Vermont Marble Company.[39] Neither a relief nor a charitable organization, the VTFCC was charged with helping farmers and small businessmen gain access to credit that otherwise might be denied them. To this end, the VTFCC worked with local banks, assessing the worthiness of applicants, and then guaranteeing 75 percent of the loans made by the banks, so that in case of a default a bank would lose only a quarter of its outlay.

The VTFCC was incorporated on 1 December 1927, a day after its authorization by the legislature as a $1 million entity, the capital coming not only from Vermont but from New York and the rest of New England as well.[40] Frank Partridge was elected president, and Herbert Comings, a former commissioner of finance and Democratic gubernatorial candidate in 1926, who had also chaired the Vermont delegation to the New England Council, was chosen as vice-president. By late January 1928, the executive committee was meeting weekly at the National Life building in Montpelier to consider the cases brought to it. As Partridge put it, the enterprise represented something new, and its officers had to make up many of the rules as they went along. That meant on the one hand sticking "as closely to business principles as the circumstances will warrant," seeing little point in helping those who already had been in financial trouble before the flood or who could not succeed even with help. On the other hand, the corporation had to be ready to run some risks, in order to meet its "altruistic purposes."[41]

By the time it held its first annual meeting in March 1928, the VTFCC had already approved guarantees for twenty-five loans, for a total of $261,700. While it was still too early to judge the corporation's effect, Partridge considered that its very existence was helping to restore business confidence. His judgment was echoed in a flattering review of Vermont's recovery efforts appearing in the *New York Times* two months later, which praised the work of Partridge and his colleagues as "the big item in the account." However, it's worth pointing out that the author, F. Lauriston Bullard, was one of the state's consistent champions in the press, and his article was based largely on materials obligingly furnished him by Fred Howland's office in Montpelier.[42]

Yet by the time of the March meeting, no farmers had yet come forth seeking loans, though the VTFCC had a particular interest in their well-being, and E. H. Jones, the commissioner of agriculture, was vice-chairman of its executive committee. Partridge, however, was sure that once the snows melted, and the damage to agriculture became more visible, they would do so. It was precisely over this question that friction arose with the Red Cross. In February, the corporation wrote to all farmers who had applied to the Red Cross, offering its help, and Jones and B. R. Demeritt, chairman of the executive committee, were named to work with the agency on such matters. Although Henry Baker professed himself optimistic about their cooperation, Demeritt and Jones were less happy, claiming that the Red Cross had settled most of the farm cases without consulting the VTFCC. They thereupon carried out their own set of farm inspections in the spring, looking particularly at questions of land damage—that is, those fields that either had been washed away or ruined by heavy deposits of mud, gravel, or silt—on which Baker apparently had agreed earlier to defer action until the snow melted and accurate assessments could be made. Then, however, when Jones told Baker that he was ready to proceed with the work, Baker replied that the Red Cross had changed its policy, believing that awards made for the replacement of buildings and livestock had been sufficiently generous that land damage should no longer be an issue.

Wishful thinking, of course, and it is impossible to know what lay behind Baker's apparent change of front. By way of example, in Richmond, M. D. Dimick lost not only sixty cows but also his farm tools, while his buildings were badly damaged and much of his land left covered with silt. All in all, he put his losses at $15,000. He asked the Red Cross for a grant of $3,500, but was told to wait until the spring when his damaged land could be considered with his other losses, only to be told later that his application was denied. "Before the flood, the farm was one of the best, with a beautiful herd of jersey cows," he wrote Senator Frank Greene, appealing for help. "I have done everything that I can do and as I said before have come to the end of my resources. There is only one thing left for me to do if I do not get help, and that is to dispose of what personal property I have there and abandon the farm."

Perhaps the Red Cross decided that Dimick had sufficient resources of his own to continue. While he tried to borrow against his house in the village, he did not turn to the Flood Credit Corporation, although his plight would have seemed to fall precisely within their purview. Henry Bashaw, a Richford farmer, whose flood losses amounted to over $18,000, received not only $5,000 from the Red Cross (apparently the largest grant made in the state), but also $1,500 from the Flood Credit Corporation, to which he had applied at Comings's urging.[43] No doubt there were other cases of this sort as well, but without the local Red Cross records, it's impossible to know how they were judged.

Such questions were among the reasons that Baker and his colleagues ran into troubles of their own as they tried to finish up the Red Cross's local work (Vermont, after all, was hardly the only place in the country struck by disaster). But there were other reasons as well. Kathryn Monroe, the Red Cross's highly experienced supervisor of family rehabilitation, described an encounter with the Waterbury group as "[o]n the whole . . . one of the most unpleasant committee meetings I ever sat in." Several members, including C. B. Adams, its chairman (who tried to "domineer" the meeting), objected to any questioning of his committee's decisions, accusing the Red Cross of seeking to use it as a rubber stamp. "Frankly," Monroe concluded, "I think it will be necessary to watch this situation very closely as I believe that we will be paying for services other than disaster relief if we are not exceedingly careful." Elsewhere, the Red Cross had to deal with William Tracy, an attorney who, according to Colin Herrle, "aspires to be the political boss of Johnson," and who was "exceedingly put out because he was not placed in charge of Red Cross work." (Tracy, in fact, appears to have had a rather bumptious local reputation).[44] Above all, perhaps, Baker found himself frustrated by the continual discovery that emergency committees were holding back relief money, using it as a way of "supplementing our awards . . . according to their own desires." This was not just a problem on the local level; Baker suspected that John Weeks himself was still sitting on some $55,000 that had been contributed to the Governor's Fund.[45]

Thus Baker's announcement in late April that awards would be completed by the first of June proved too optimistic.[46] After a long meeting on 4 May, during which Baker thought that he had reached agreement with Jones and Demeritt on the question of land damage, he was summoned to the governor's office, where he found the two others apparently complaining of his attitude. Believing it was time for some "plain talk," Baker told Weeks that, unless he was ready to charge the Red Cross with misuse of funds, he had no rights in the matter. "I am afraid," he wrote Fieser, "that I do not have very much influence or weight with the Governor and his associates as he seems to think that I am just one more person trying to camouflage the work in such a way that I can slip out of the state as quickly as possible." However, he did agree to meet with an advisory committee that had been set up right after the flood to coordinate the state's work with that of the Red Cross, but had never yet met. At a further meeting on 21 May, Baker promised to review the land cases himself, thus blocking the formation of a special committee to do it. "I am hopeful," he wired Fieser, "that above plan . . . will hold situation in line."[47]

Meanwhile, Weeks, presumably without Baker's knowledge, asked the local Red Cross chapters and emergency committees to report in confidence on the quality of the agency's work in their regions. The reports were mixed; some praised the agency, others faulted it over the land damage question, and one, from the redoubtable C. B. Adams of Waterbury, was a five-page, single-spaced litany of complaints.[48] Then, when the meeting with the advisory committee was to take place on 1 June in the State House, Baker appeared, joined by Fieser and several other representatives from Washington, only to find themselves cooling their heels in an outer office for an hour or more, while Weeks met the committee in executive session. Invited in at last, they were then (in Fieser's ironic words) "informed that their [the advisory committee's] review pointed first to the unsatisfactory conduct of relief in Vermont and, secondly to their desire that Mr. Baker should continue until September first."

To Fieser, at least, it seemed that there were no complaints about the Red Cross's work in the towns and villages, and the only problems had to do with a small group of farmers whose claims were still debatable. In vain did Baker point out that Vermont farmers had received almost twice as much in awards as was usual in such rural relief operations and that the Red Cross had dug deeper into its own treasury than in most other disasters. "None of these statements," Fieser continued, "were at all impressive, nor was there any expression of appreciation for any of the work of the Red Cross." By the end of the afternoon, he agreed to keep

Baker in Vermont until Jones finished his farm survey, and while Baker would then review the remaining land damage cases, his decision was final. In Fieser's view, Weeks had to pose as "the friend of the farmer," as he prepared to run for re-election, while Baker thought privately that various interests, including the banks holding farm mortgages, were keeping the pot stirred, urging farmers to press their claims. No wonder then that, as an addendum to the notes of the meeting put it,

> All three representatives of the National Organization expressed the opinion that their contact with Vermont Yankees had given them some new experiences in disaster relief. The committee's taking the meeting out of their hands was indicative of a less hearty cooperative attitude than they had usually experienced in other sections of the country. All three saw the humor of this particular action by the committee and were not especially worried about it.

Humor indeed. Clipped to the Red Cross's copy of the minutes is a handwritten note from Judge Payne, the national chairman, to Fieser: "Tell Baker to sit tight—use his judgment in the Vermont manner. Cold [?]—do not permit himself to be influenced by demands."[49]

By late July, Baker and Jones had cut down the number of land damage claims from over two hundred to sixty-three. Another meeting with state leaders in mid-month threatened to end in a deadlock until James McClintock of the national office proposed a plan: Governor Weeks would turn over to the Red Cross the balance held in his relief fund, and Baker would then allot it to the disputed cases. By 2 August, after a series of all-day meetings, Baker and Jones reached agreement, awarding almost $29,000 in the final sixty-three cases. Weeks, for his part, turned over the $28,000 that he was still holding.[50]

Baker, however, insisted that the Red Cross must not leave Vermont without a public expression of gratitude from the state's leaders. State Auditor Benjamin Gates, who chaired the advisory committee, agreed to a resolution of appreciation, and he and Commissioner Jones also issued public statements of their own, praising the agency's work. Weeks said that he would write his own personal thanks to John Barton Payne, the Red Cross chairman, which he did a few days later, though in a singularly brief and tepid letter.[51]

Thus on 4 August 1928, the Red Cross officially ended its work in Vermont. The last problems, Fred Howland wrote Judge Payne two days later, had been settled "as satisfactorily as could be expected," leaving a

Fig. 17. Governor Weeks and Henry M. Baker of the National Red Cross on 2 August 1928, at the conclusion of the Red Cross's work in Vermont. *Courtesy of the Vermont State Archives.*

"fine and unblemished record" for the Red Cross in the state. "I feel that the Red Cross has been very generous in its handling of the Vermont situation, which has undoubtedly presented new and troublesome problems somewhat different than the organization has had to cope with in other parts of the country." He was also effusive in his praise for the "wise and diplomatic" conduct of Henry Baker. "All in all," he concluded in a separate letter to Ratshesky in Boston, "I believe the Red Cross has done a wonderfully fine piece of work in the state, and I attribute the ironing out of some of the difficulties very largely to your interest and intercession."[52]

The figures published at the time leave no doubt of the Red Cross's role in rebuilding the state. Compared to the Mississippi Valley, Vermont's disaster might be small, but the final report—issued in late 1928—concluded that it nonetheless "precipitated the most extensive reconstruction program the Red Cross has ever had to carry through in the northeastern section of the country." Of the 5,800 New England families registering for aid, 4,718 came from Vermont, and of the 3,504 families awarded aid, 2,721 were Vermonters. Though the report does not break down the dollar amounts given to each state, other sources show that of the almost $1.3 million spent on relief and rehabilitation in all New England, well over $1 million went to Vermont. Not all of this was outside money, of course, for well over $300,000 came from donations made by Vermonters themselves.[53]

Such figures also provide a context within which to understand the friction between the Red Cross and Vermonters. The difficulties should not be overemphasized, and against them we need to place the many, many tributes paid to the Red Cross by individuals, by towns, by newspaper editorials, all seeing its work as absolutely vital to the state's well-being. Still, the episode is instructive. "Professional expertise," Nancy Gallagher has suggested in another context, "was not necessarily appreciated in Vermont unless it had local roots and was supported by reputable Vermonters."[54] Governor Weeks, after all, was a man of great courtesy, not the sort of person generally to keep distinguished visitors like Fieser and his colleagues waiting outside his office before admitting them. Yet he was an old Vermont farmer himself, with an old Vermont outlook, not to say prejudices, and while deeply concerned with issues of social welfare, he was no doubt suspicious of any suggestion that Washington experts could handle his state's problems better than could he and his colleagues. Fred Howland, on the other hand, was a good deal more cosmopolitan in experience and outlook than Weeks, and there's no reason to believe that he and others were anything but sincere in their praise for the agency. Still, the tensions provide an interesting preview of what would happen in the next decade, when Vermont found itself faced with the depression: support, even gratitude, for help given, but a deep distrust of the New Deal bureaucracy through which it was mediated.

Little more than a month after closing the New England office, Henry Baker, along with several others who had been active in Vermont, were in southern Florida. There, the huge Caribbean hurricane that had already torn through Puerto Rico, pounded ashore at Palm Beach on 16 September 1928, swept inland over Lake Okeechobee, and probably killed more than twenty-five hundred people. In Vermont, the local chapters of the Red Cross once again began raising money for aid. Later that month, at a celebration in Woodstock, Governor Weeks, presumably with no sense of irony, accepted on behalf of Vermont the Red Cross Honor Flag, given each year to the state with the highest percentage of its population enrolled in the Red Cross. Vermont's figure stood at 11.6 percent. It was not only a rise of 7.8 percent over the previous year, but also a national record.[55]

If the Red Cross's contribution to Vermont's rebuilding is clear, the work of the Flood Credit Corporation is rather less so, even though in this case, its records have survived. What is clear is that the rush of applications from farmers in the spring of 1928 never materialized. In the end, only six came forward asking for loan guarantees, all of which were approved. Were others discouraged from applying? Or did they simply depend upon their own resources and the help given by the Red Cross? In all likelihood, many of them were already too deeply in debt to take on further obligations. Even before the flood, half of all Vermont farms were already mortgaged, Thomas Bradlee of the Agricultural Extension Service had pointed out back in November, and those hit by the flood were simply unable to raise the money they needed to rebuild. A year and a half later, at the VTFCC's annual meeting in March 1929, Frank Partridge gloomily agreed. "As one such farmer expressed it," he concluded, "'I already have all the debt I can carry and do not care to assume any further obligations.' It is to be borne in mind that our farmers are for the most part small operators. Their cases apparently were for the Red Cross and not for us."[56]

Several of the cases do show a cooperation between the Red Cross and the VTFCC. H. N. Bashaw, who received both a large Red Cross grant and a guarantee for a bank loan, enabling him to buy a new farm and a new herd, was one example. Another was Arthur Burnor of Cambridge, who lost his farm and had to buy a new one. The Red Cross advanced him $1,500 for the first payment, and through the corporation he received a loan of $1,925, secured on sixteen cows and a Ford truck.[57]

Not only did all the farmers who applied for loan guarantees get them, but so did most of the businesses. Ultimately, guarantees were approved to thirty-eight individuals and enterprises, for loans totalling $268,270, the amounts ranging from $25,000 to the Nantanna Worsted Company of Northfield, which suffered heavy losses of buildings and stock, to the $500 granted Frank Orne, an Irasburg farmer. In the end, only two applications, together worth $3,000, were declined.

The guarantees were usually valid for ten years, though the officers hoped that most of the work would be finished by 1932. Although most loans were issued for five years, the corporation seems to have been liberal in granting extensions, no doubt because of the difficulties settling over the land by the early thirties. By the time the VTFCC voted itself out of existence, ten years after the flood, ten of the loans had gone into complete or partial default, including two of the largest, one to the Nantanna Mills, the other to an automobile company in Waterbury, as well as a smaller loan to A. J. Saleeby in Johnson, leading to $26,709.30 in losses to the corporation. All others were repaid.

In retrospect, the *Times*'s optimistic estimate of the corporation's work as the "big item in the account" may well be overdrawn. Given the ravages of the flood, a total of thirty-eight enterprises does not sound very high. It seems odd also that almost all the applicants came from the northern part of the state, including thirteen in Montpelier and six in Waterbury. A loan in Bethel was the single example in the ravaged White River Valley, and none appear to have been either sought or given in such places as Rutland, Bennington, or Windsor, all of which were badly hurt. "Our operations have not perhaps been so extensive as was originally expected," Partridge admitted to the annual meeting of 1929, "but the number of loans guaranteed is not the measure of the helpfulness of the corporation. By the spirit of confidence which it inspired, the corporation has contributed much to the revival of industry and business in our flood stricken state."[58]

Herbert Hoover had made the same argument, when he told the New England Council that the very availability of credit might well be worth more than its actual provision. Perhaps so, but the limited use made of these resources may also reflect the fragile nature of sectors of Vermont's economy even before the flood. John Barry, examining similar efforts in the Mississippi Valley, points out that although Hoover was able to raise $13 million in credit for state reconstruction corporations in Arkansas, Mississippi, and Louisiana (despite the reluctance of many bankers to contribute), most of that sum went unused. The provision of credit, after all, demands either the promise of reasonable return or sufficient collateral that can be pledged to mitigate the risks. As one Mississippi banker put it, although there was a superabundance of funds, there was a shortage of collateral. Raising money was easy; lending it was not.[59]

Was Vermont's problem also not so much a shortage of credit as a shortage of collateral? Perhaps so, particularly given farm indebtedness before the flood. In any case, by guaranteeing loans to a total of almost 27 percent of the corporation's capital, the Vermont Flood Credit Corporation did considerably better than the roughly 5 percent reached by Hoover's credit corporations in the three southern states. And credits, of course, were better than nothing, in an age when direct aid, apart from that given by the Red Cross, was unlikely to be in the cards. Perhaps the very availability of credit did something to restore confidence, even though the confidence may well have been felt more by Vermont's businessmen than by its farms. Still, the corporation seems to have had a mixed record, through no fault of its own, and given the widespread destruction of November 1927, the number of loan guarantees sought was surprisingly low.

Rebuilding the Railways

> Transportation by rail is an absolute necessity in Vermont. The flood has taught us that lesson. Why, a year ago some people didn't care whether we had any railroads or not. They thought the trucks and busses were all that were needed, but now many thank God when the railroads get running.[60]

So the state highway commissioner Stoddard Bates told a gathering in Montpelier in January 1928. It was an apt reminder, since even under the best conditions, the trucks of the day were hardly capable of bringing in the food and fuel the state needed or of carrying quantities of Vermont's milk, granite, and marble to market over dirt and gravel roads. Yet more graphically than any facts and figures, photographs of the time tell the story of what happened to New England's rail network. Bridges vanished or fallen into rivers, tracks washed away or buried by landslides, locomotives and rolling stock lying on their sides, all give a dramatic sense of the disaster.

The amount of track torn up in New England was the equal of a line running from Boston to Chicago, said a Boston and Maine spokesman, and a Canadian National official thought the damage inflicted on Vermont's railways to be "in excess of that suffered by any railroad at any time."[61] Along the 413 miles of the Rutland Railroad, there were some 356 separate washouts, and eleven bridges destroyed, including the great iron span linking Burlington to Winooski. All in all, some $750,000 was needed for repairs, and the disruption cost the line another $285,000 in lost revenues. The St. Johnsbury and Lake Champlain (Slow, Jerky, and Late Coming, as many called it even when it was running) was fortunate in losing none of its locomotives, but damage to its line and bridges was estimated at $454,000. By early 1928, the Canadian Pacific had already spent over $1 million restoring its lines in Vermont, New Hampshire, and Quebec, while almost every foot of track of the little White River line from Bethel to Rochester was destroyed, and fifteen major washouts cut the brief fourteen miles of the Woodstock Railway. Other short lines, like the Montpelier and Barre and the Montpelier and Wells River, suffered as well, while larger lines such as the Boston and Maine, Maine Central, and Boston and Albany were all badly damaged.[62]

Unlike the Central Vermont, which formed part of the huge Canadian National empire, the Rutland had no rich parent to look after it, though the New York Central's work trains and crews came to its aid. As early as 5 November, a passenger train from Burlington reached Middlebury, but water blocked any passage farther south until 12 November, when the first train steamed into Rutland from the north. Later in the month, the services between Montreal, New York, and Boston were resumed, albeit on a diminished schedule. Still, the losses wiped out not only all the line's net earnings for that year, but also its surplus.[63] Meanwhile, other lines slowly came back to life. On 16 November, the first train ran between Barre and Montpelier, and the day after Christmas, in a scene typical of the time, all Morrisville turned out to welcome the bunting-hung locomotive drawing the first train into town, while whistles sounded from the mills and granite sheds, and the local military band struck up. Still, it was not until 15 January 1928 that the first train ran the whole distance from St. Johnsbury to Swanton, and not for another month yet was the whole of the St.J.&L.C. back in operation.[64]

The stories of two lines, one big and one small, best capture the sense of the slow climb back up from the dark days of November. The big one was the Central Vermont, the most seriously hurt of all. Winding through the Winooski Valley as it cuts through the main range of the Green Mountains, the C.V. saw bridge after bridge destroyed and whole sections of track uprooted, while the destruction it suffered in the White River Valley, particularly near Bethel, was almost as bad. "Words fail me in attempting to describe the damage . . . between Middlesex and Montpelier," Agriculture Commissioner Jones wrote to his son in Boston. "Ties and track hang in the air and long stretches of the track are completely torn up, ties standing on end or washed to one side and tangled like telephone wires," and he predicted no trains would run there until well into the following summer.[65] A month after the flood, the cost of repairs and replacement was put at over $2 million, but that figure climbed steadily as work progressed, rising to some $4,500,000 later.[66]

The C.V. was, however, a line "fortunate in its friends," as a study of the time put it, for it was the Canadian National, owner of two-thirds of its stock, that came to the rescue.[67] Although some of its own officials doubted whether reconstruction was even feasible, that was emphatically not true of Sir Henry Thornton, the C.N.'s American-born president. "Go ahead. Rebuild. Don't spare the horses," he wired from England, promising the full resources of the parent line for the work. Within days came a report that the Canadian National was pledging $3 million to the task, and one of the line's officials predicted that the speed of the reconstruction would be a "revelation" to the people of Vermont.[68]

In a desperate time, such optimism was heartening, and to many, Thornton's readiness to help Vermont back to its feet made him one of the recovery's heroes. A native of Indiana, he was a big man in every sense, who had played football at the University of Pennsylvania before going to work for the Pennsylvania Railroad, where he became general superintendent of the Long Island after its merger with the Pennsylvania in 1911. In 1914, he moved to London to reorganize the Great Eastern, and during the war became Inspector-General of Transportation for the British Expeditionary Forces, where his abilities to coordinate British and French rail services helped to stem the German advance. Returning to North America a British subject with a knighthood, in 1922 he became chief of the new Canadian National, which had been formed by a

Fig. 18. Central Vermont repair crew at work in winter weather near Duxbury. *Collection of Harriet and Heath Riggs.*

union of several smaller lines, including the Grand Trunk, of which the Central Vermont had been a part. There he quickly built a reputation as an able and efficient administrator, inspiring the loyalty of his employees, working with rather than against the unions, rapidly raising the net earnings of his line. Although a few years later, Canadian politics would bring about his downfall, in the late twenties he stood at the zenith of his career, becoming, in the words of a Canadian journalist, "more than a national figure; he was in a sense a Canadian ambassador without official credentials."[69]

Though the C.V. soon resumed limited service between Essex Junction and St. Albans, in the Winooski and White River valleys traffic remained at a standstill. The sixty-six miles of track from Sharon to Williston were completely useless, while at the aptly named Slip Hill near Waterbury, a hundred-foot-high embankment had collapsed, spilling two thousand feet of track into the Winooski, where it lay "like the skeleton of a great amphibian," as one observer put it.[70] By the end of November, some eighteen hundred men were at work, living in camps along the line, many of them Canadians, whose passage had been eased by immigration officials. By early December, the night expresses between Montreal and Washington ran again, although detouring over the tracks of other lines, while the Boston to Montreal

Fig. 19. Slip Hill, two miles from Middlesex in the Winooski Valley, presented Central Vermont with one of its most difficult problems. *Courtesy of the Vermont State Archives.*

connection followed a roundabout route through Portland, Maine. Before Christmas, trains once again reached Northfield, and a month later passengers could travel to Montpelier Junction from the south. Beyond that, however, the difficulties at Slip Hill continued to frustrate the best efforts of the tracklayers.

Meanwhile, on 12 December, the Canadian National went to court to petition the Central Vermont into the hands of receivers. Although Elbert Brigham fretted over the possibility that the railroad's headquarters might move from St. Albans to Montreal, the action was in fact a friendly one, taken to protect the C.V. against legal disruptions during its recovery.[71] By early January, the receivers were negotiating a $5 million loan in New York, and in a move that took Wall Street by surprise, the Canadian National not only promised that it would look after the C.V.'s pensioners during the reorganization, but also offered to redeem the line's outstanding bonds at par. Very few bondholders took advantage of the offer, a sign of their continuing confidence in the line's future.[72]

Late in January, the repair of a 440-foot bridge north of Waterbury closed the last link, and on the morning of the 29th, Waterbury, as the local paper put it, "once more heard the long gone but not forgotten sound of whistles, bells, and cars being shunted around the railway yards." That afternoon, the first train pulled in from Montpelier, taking aboard several passengers who rode it as far as Middlesex, and then walked back six miles in the cold, all for the sake of being on the first train out of town in eighty-seven days.[73]

Then, at eight in the morning of 4 February, a large crowd gathered at the St. Albans station to see off the first train that would travel the whole breadth of the state, a hundred and twenty miles to White River Junction. Church bells rang, fire whistles sounded, a row of Boy Scouts saluted as it pulled away, its seven private cars and Pullmans carrying Governor Weeks, Sir Henry Thornton, former Governor E. C. Smith (president of the line before the receivership), Fred Howland, and a number of other prominent Vermonters. At Essex Junction, the welcoming crowd included a high school band, and at Waterbury two thousand cheered as Roy Demeritt, the village president, presented four members of the party with the key to the city, and the Stowe Military Band, come down from the hills, played "God Save the King" in

Fig. 20. On 4 February 1928, Waterbury welcomed the passage of the first Central Vermont train across the state since the flood. *Jim Murphy Collection.*

Thornton's honor. "BELIEVE ME!!!" Catherine Adams Church wrote years later, "WHEN THAT TRAIN CAME THROUGH IN FEBRUARY, EVERYONE IN TOWN WAS AT THE STATION TO GREET IT!!! There was nothing or no where else to be that day. What a celebration!!!"[74]

At Montpelier, the official party left the train, walking through lines of flag-bearing schoolchildren standing at salute. In the audience at the State House was Dexter Taylor—who as a boy of six had watched the first train come through in 1849—listening to Mayor Edward Deavitt, Governor Weeks, and others pay tribute to all those who had helped the railroad to run again. "Vermont has come back," the governor assured his listeners, while Thornton called the cooperation between Canada and Vermont a "magnificent example" to other nations of "[w]hat great results would be accomplished if the hand of friendship should be stretched out from every boundary line." Then, as the journey resumed, more flags flew, sirens sounded, and welcome parties made their speeches at every stop the train made. The local Rotary turned out in Randolph under a frigid drenching rain to sing "I've been Working on De Railroad," while the approach to White River Junction, at the end of its run, was "announced by aerial bombs."[75]

The day was a triumph. "A new epoch in rail construction," the *Burlington Free Press* called it, in an understandable burst of hyperbole. "Never before in the recollection of Vermonters was the distant shriek of a locomotive so welcome," wrote the *New York Times*'s reporter, describing people flocking to country railway stations in fur caps and heavy mufflers, flags waving, musicians puffing at their instruments, their fingers blue with cold. "Vermont villages," said Louis Lyons in the *Boston Globe,* "that have been reduced to frontier communications this Winter are knit again into the fabric of this modern age whose threads are steel." "The successful accomplishment of a feat of engineering that has never been equalled on the American continent," he called it, but he was also ironist enough to marvel both at the reception given Thornton, earlier seen as an ogre anxious to gobble up Vermont's small railways, and at the way staunch Yankee Republicans turned out to "proclaim the strength and virtue of what is probably the most far-reaching Government-owned utility in the world."[76]

Perhaps more than any other single event of the time, the journey made that February day symbolized the state's recovery, although it would take almost another year for the Central Vermont to return to the level it had known before the flood. Not until late May did the Washingtonian

Fig. 21. The White River Railway, running from Rochester to Bethel (shown above) was almost totally destroyed by the waters. *Wes Herwig Collection, reprinted from Wes Herwig, Miriam Herwig, and Robert C. Jones,* A Whistle Up the Valley, The Story of the Peavine, Vermont's White River Railroad *(Burlington, Vt.: Evergreen Press, 2005).*

and Montrealer run once more over their former routes, not until 24 June did the crack Ambassador renew its old itinerary from Montreal to Boston, and it was another two months before service was resumed between Essex Junction and Burlington. Finally, in mid-December 1928, more than thirteen months after the flood, the receivers could declare the railroad fully restored, ready in the coming years to resume business and to start earning back some of the great expenses incurred in its rebuilding.[77]

Vital as was the rebuilding of the Central Vermont, in some ways the story of the little White River Railway seemed most emblematic of Vermont's rejoinder to disaster.[78] Built at the turn of the century, the Peavine, as it was known locally, twisted its way nineteen miles along the river from Rochester to Bethel, and its almost total destruction appeared to bring to an end a quarter century of operations that had been somewhat uncertain even at the best of times. The White River Valley, noted the *Rutland Herald* in February 1928, was a scene of desolation as great as anywhere in the state, the railway on which its industries depended "physically and financially ruined."[79] Although the line's owner,

Chauncey Parker of Boston, was convinced that it had no future, the Valley was not ready to give up. Working with local businessmen, E. S. French, the railway's vice-president (who later headed the Boston and Maine), helped to form a Rochester Citizens' Railroad Committee, and in the meantime secured Parker's agreement to sell the line's remaining assets. By that time, the estimated cost of reconstruction had been pared to $160,000.[80] Rochester's town meeting voted a $30,000 bond issue, while local industries pitched in: $35,000 from Vermont Marble, $25,000 from the Blair Veneer Mill, and lesser contributions from International Paper and the Eastern Magnesia Talc Company. Middlebury College, by no means a rich institution at the time, contributed $10,000 because of its ownership of large tracts of forest and park land, "the product of which have their natural outlet through the White River Valley."[81] In addition, there were many smaller pledges, some of cash, others contributions in kind: labor, trucking, railroad ties, even legal services from Artemus Townsend, of Ropes, Gray, Boyden & Perkins, in Boston, whose mother lived in Rochester. When the sum still fell short, Governor Weeks put out an appeal that brought in more contributions, including almost $6,000 from Standard Oil.[82]

By July, reconstruction had begun. "Rochester and the valley have tried to work out their own salvation," proclaimed J. B. Henry of the Railroad Committee, adding his firm belief that the rebuilt line would once again pay dividends to its investors. From the ruins of twisted iron and steel and broken, derelict bridges, wrote the *Free Press*, "will arise the new, gleaming and modern railroad."[83] In early September, the first train reached Stockbridge, and then finally, on 1 January 1929, the entire line reopened, as two locomotives puffed their way from Bethel to Rochester, entering that town to the sound of bells pealing from all the churches and schools.

Thrifty Vermonters liked to note that the railroads recovered without recourse to public money. Almost, at any rate, for there were exceptions. The legislature's special treatment of the St. Johnsbury and Lake Champlain has already been noted (although the line's unofficial historian pointed out that the company never received more than $195,000 of the $300,000 voted).[84] A public bond issue helped the Peavine, the voters of Woodstock agreed to a loan of $10,000 to reconstruct the fourteen-mile line up to White River Junction, while in 1929, the legislature approved a $200,000 loan to the West River Railway, formerly a branch of the Central Vermont.[85]

Fig. 22. Bridge repair near Stockbridge, in the White River Valley. *Marcus Blair Collection.*

But the Rutland, the Central Vermont, the Canadian Pacific, and the Boston and Maine lines received no such favors. In retrospect, of course, it's easy enough to see that such reconstruction did little more than simply postpone the inevitable decline of the railways, which now faced forces in the depression and in the automobile far harder to keep dammed up than the flood's waters (within a few years of its rebuilding, the White River Railway was once again closed, this time permanently). Still, the stories of celebrations that greeted the first trains along these lines reflect more than relief at the restoration of links to the outside world. The enthusiastic crowds standing in the cold, the pealing church bells, factory whistles, and fire sirens, the brass bands, Rotarians singing, and Boy Scouts saluting, all responded to a perceived victory over the elements, a triumph of human spirit, celebrating tangible aspects of those Vermont values whose reaffirmation was such an essential part of the recovery. It was not the economic aspect of the Peavine's rebuilding that was important, the editorialists wrote, but rather the "evidence of courage," of a belief in Vermont and its local communities, and the "faith and vision" of those who were determined to save those towns and villages.[86]

The repair of these lines thus gave heart to those who saw the state once more being knit together, both figuratively and physically, by determination and common action. Overblown as his prose may have been, Charles Walter of the St. Johnsbury *Republican* no doubt spoke for many when, after he disembarked from the Central Vermont's special train in February, he looked ahead to the coming summer.

> When thousands of visitors again throng our hills and valleys and inquire where are the signs of the flood about which the whole country has heard, many of the number will view from observation platforms of the trains on this line the worst of the flood-wrecked areas, places where last November all was chaos, devastation and almost despair, [where] now are found smiling valleys responding to the cheerful hearts and faces of contented and joyous people. Then, we shall be glad of the "come back" of the railroads . . . and Nature, which "covers even battlefields with verdure and bloom," and which through the winter months has shrouded with its white mantle these scenes of desolation, will in springtime deck the ravaged fields with living green and cause the woods to blossom again, just as God heals the wounds and covers the scars on human hearts with blessings after the tremendous trials and sacrifices of life.[87]

5

"Squeezed Through After Many Hairbreadth Escapes"

Flood Politics in Washington and Montpelier

While the relatively open winter of 1928 helped the tracklayers and others rebuilding the railways, in many places little more than temporary patching could be done to the roads until the frost was out of the ground. Still, by late January, the Highway Department had spent almost a million dollars in repairs, and before the coming of spring, the state was already awarding contracts for new bridges. With more than twelve hundred spans needing replacement, for a brief period Vermont became a national laboratory for the development of new methods and new designs. The bridge department, which heretofore consisted of a single engineer and a dozen part-time draftsmen, now grew to over thirty-five people, including several engineers and technicians on loan from the federal government, as well as one from the American Bridge Company, a subsidiary of U.S. Steel, and by far the largest concern of its kind in the country.[1]

Cold weather was not the only reason to postpone road reconstruction, however. Although with two small exceptions, the rebuilding of rail lines made no direct demands on the state's pocketbook, Montpelier was going to have to foot the bill for highways. Or most of it, at least. Revenues from the bond would cover the lion's share of the work, but well before its issue, Vermont's leaders were looking for ways to supplement the state's own monies with those from the federal treasury. Such funds, however, were unlikely to arrive before the start of the new fiscal year. Prudent men all, Vermont's authorities did not want to learn in

July that federal largesse was not retroactive and could not be used to pay for repairs already made.

Whatever might be said about Vermont relying only on its own resources, at the time few raised any questions about either the propriety or practicability of seeking Washington's help. Within days of the flood, the congressional delegation was active, with the full backing of Montpelier and the major newspapers. Vermont's misfortunes struck at a time when the nation was deeply embroiled in a debate about the federal government's proper role in dealing with the huge floods that had devastated the Mississippi Valley the prior spring. President Coolidge resolutely resisted calls for a special session of Congress to deal with the emergency, and resisted also the idea that Washington should assume complete responsibility, financial and otherwise, for flood control in the river basin, threatening to veto any measure that did not insist on the states sharing some of the burden. Quite properly so, agreed Vermont's editorial writers in the spring and summer of 1927, coupling their sympathy for the river's victims with warnings that their plight would, as the *Burlington Free Press* predicted, "be seized by interested parties as an excuse . . . to get their hands into Uncle Sam's strong box for the benefit of their own pockets."[2]

Eighty years after these events, it is hard to imagine a time when the federal government would not have been required to respond to such disasters. But in 1927, the Federal Emergency Management Agency (FEMA) lay fifty years in the future, and not for almost another decade would the social programs of the New Deal begin to take shape, including the National Housing Act, which authorized disaster loans. Without the great Mississippi flood six months earlier, would Vermont even have thought of asking for Washington's help? If it had asked, would that help have been forthcoming? When Morgan Brainard of Aetna Life Insurance expressed the hope that Vermont would set an example to the nation by its bond issue, resisting "the temptation to seek help from the common pocketbook," Fred Howland replied that, despite his own dislike of federal intervention, he thought an appeal for highway aid justified. "In any event, the consideration of the Mississippi flood relief measures at this time offers so tempting an opportunity to Vermont to share in the relief to be afforded that I understand our Congressmen are inclined to take advantage of it."[3]

Not that those congressmen were simply falling into line with their southern colleagues. Even though the Mississippi states might seize on the chance to try to recruit New England to their cause against Coolidge's obduracy, Congressman Elbert Brigham, for one, drew a clear line between flood *control* and flood *relief*. The pressing issue for the southerners was control; for New England, however, it was relief. The term, as Brigham used it, meant not the sort of emergency succor that was the purview of the Red Cross, but financial relief from the appalling costs that were the legacy of the flood, and above all the costs of highway repair. His reluctance to see Washington assume responsibility for flood control came no doubt from his Republican suspicion of federal paternalism. But it also came from fiscal prudence. If (as he wrote Warren Austin, then a lawyer and businessman), the federal government were to get into the business of controlling floods "on every little river in the United States . . . the cost of the war would be as nothing compared to it." On the other hand, Brigham was quite pragmatic enough at least to imagine a quid pro quo: New England's support for Mississippi flood control in return for southern support for relief in highway reconstruction.[4]

Brigham prepared his campaign by producing a list of disasters, both foreign and domestic, in which Congress had provided funds for relief (the first such instance came after a fire in Portsmouth, New Hampshire, in 1803). Unfortunately, nowhere was there any precedent for rebuilding highways, and while the Federal Aid Roads Act of 1916 provided funds for construction and upkeep, it was silent about further responsibilities; not until 1934 would the Bureau of Public Roads be authorized to provide funding for highways and bridges damaged by natural disasters. On the other hand, nowhere in Brigham's long list did Vermont's name appear as beneficiary of help, and now perhaps its turn had come. That, at least, was the view of the *Free Press,* inveighing against "pork barrel schemes" along the Mississippi, while implying that Vermont, with its traditions of grit, thrift, and self-reliance, deserved Washington's helping hand at least as much as the states along the big river.[5]

Thus, though a few doubted the wisdom of taking Washington's dollar, for most the question was not whether to seek federal aid, but how to get as much as possible on the best terms. During his November visit, Herbert Hoover himself suggested that Washington would help and Governor Weeks echoed his confidence. Prospects for quick action seemed good; Army and federal engineers were already surveying the damage, and even as the legislature met in Montpelier, Representatives Brigham and Gibson were making the first of several calls at the White

House to talk to Coolidge, although the story that they sought his backing for an $8 million appropriation was almost certainly wrong.[6] They came away much encouraged, heartened by the president's reference in his message to Congress in early December to the "considerable sum of money" that would be available for highway reconstruction through the Department of Agriculture.[7]

Still, hopes for early action were dashed, thanks largely to Congress's fear of setting a precedent, a fear shared even by other New England delegations.[8] In the end, not for another five months, and then only after some extraordinarily complex parliamentary wranglings and maneuverings, was Vermont able to get its money. For the historian, more important than the political details are the ways in which Vermont set out its arguments for help, both in Washington and back home. Three aspects were most prominent. First was the claim that, massive as was the Mississippi disaster, because of Vermont's tiny size, its losses were proportionately far greater. Second, never in the state's long history had it ever approached the national treasury with hands outstretched. Finally, whatever Washington might or might not do, Vermonters had already rolled up their sleeves and gone to work without waiting, willingly shouldering their burden of debt before seeking the help of others.

So, for example, when he appeared before the House Committee on Flood Control on 11 January 1928, Ernest Gibson argued that Vermont's $30-odd million in losses amounted to about half the assessed real property valuation for the whole state. Put another way, it represented a charge of $90 for every Vermonter, man, woman, and child; put yet another way, it was comparable to a loss in the District of Columbia of $60 million, of $150 million in North Carolina, $480 million in Massachusetts, or $570 million in California. None of the Mississippi Valley states, for all their misfortunes, came remotely close to such figures.[9] Although the numbers became more refined as time passed, the arguments remained the same (they were repeated in March by Governor Weeks who told his audience in a broadcast from New York that relatively speaking, Vermont's property damage was ten times that of the Mississippi Valley's losses, and the death toll twelve times as heavy.[10]

On 20 January, Senator Frank Greene and Representative Gibson introduced bills into their respective chambers seeking an appropriation of $2,654,000, a sum earlier reached in consultation with the Federal Bureau of Public Roads, which was to be matched by the state. Both publicly and privately, Brigham tried to argue that the appropriation would set no precedent for future claims, but not everyone saw that point as clearly as he did. Further testimony in the House followed, Brigham and Gibson now joined by Frank Partridge as Governor Weeks's representative.[11] "Vermonters find themselves in a novel situation," Gibson told the full House in March, after the Roads Committee had sent the bill to them. They were "believers in state independence," and if other states were prepared to bear their own losses from disaster, so too would Vermont. Vermont, in short, prided itself on its traditions of independence and self-reliance, but if others, with no such admirable habits, were being helped, common justice demanded that this little state, "suffering from one of the greatest calamities that ever befell the people of a State in the history of the Nation," should be given a share as well.[12]

If the issue of precedent posed one problem, so did the great battle between Congress and the president over who would pay to control the Mississippi's unruly waters. Brigham saw a "mighty serious fight" shaping up over Vermont's appropriation, and his pessimism was justified. A new problem arose in February, when John Robsion of Kentucky brought in his own bill, seeking $1,889,884 for repairs to highways damaged by flash flooding the previous spring. Somewhat ungraciously, perhaps, Brigham thought Kentucky's case weak, fearing that Congress would see through it, refuse to pay, and bring down Vermont's claim as well. Unfortunately, Robsion by now had become acting chair of the House Roads Committee, and in private he let both Brigham and Gibson know that if his state lost its appropriation, they could forget about their own.[13]

Eventually, through a series of complicated maneuvers, on 29 March—a day after the Senate had unanimously passed the huge Jones-Reid Mississippi flood control bill, which put the entire financial burden onto the federal government—the amendment to the agriculture bill "squeaked through" the Senate, carrying funds for Vermont, New Hampshire, and Kentucky. Although Brigham continued to fret that if Kentucky's claims were thrown out by the conference committee, Vermont would suffer, Congress managed to resolve its differences.[14] On 10 May, the House passed the measure, after adding an amendment to make it clear that no precedents were being set (the relief was to be "a contribution in aid . . .without acknowledgment of any liability on the part of the United States").[15] Final action by the Senate followed swiftly, and on 16 May, to the vast relief of the Vermont delegation, Coolidge signed the bill. "The appropriation squeezed through after many hairbreadth escapes," Brigham wrote Frank Partridge, "and we are glad it is over." "I do not believe," he later confessed to Frank Howe of the *Bennington Banner,* "many people who are not familiar with procedure in Congress know the difficulty of securing an appropriation of this kind particularly when there has been no precedent therefore."[16]

With rather less grace, Coolidge also signed the huge Mississippi Valley flood bill the same day—a "pillaging of the public funds," John Southwick of the *Free Press* had called it, darkly hinting at links to Tammany Hall, and contrasting it to Vermont's "splendid example . . . by going ahead with its own measures of relief without waiting for Uncle Sam." The stated cost was $325 million—"the greatest expenditure the government has undertaken except in the World War," the *New York Times* called it, and many predicted the actual price tag might be several times that amount.[17] Of this sum, the New England states received not a penny. But then, after an initial flurry of interest the previous fall, they had not asked for much either, seeing the matter of flood control as one primarily for states to handle. The question, however, did not go away, and Vermont's response to flood control in New England would continue as an issue for years to come.[18]

Finally, for all Brigham's fears that Kentucky might be the spoiler, in the end that state's role actually proved helpful. First, because the final bill made the funds immediately available, so that there was no need to wait for the new fiscal year before claiming the prize. And second, because for all Vermont's earlier promises that Washington's money would be spent only on federal aid roads and their extensions, the final bill removed any such restrictions.[19]

Thus, for the first time in its history, Vermont asked for and received direct federal assistance for disaster relief. It might be argued that, ironically enough, in seeking Washington's aid, the state was doing precisely what many poorer Vermont towns had done for years, as they looked to Montpelier for help in meeting rising local expenses. Those towns, however, paid a price in diminished local authority and autonomy, but now, needless to say, no one drew that parallel or suggested that taking Washington's money would compromise the old traditions of independence.[20] So, at least, argued the *Free Press* and others that spring, losing few chances to contrast Vermont's principled posture with that of other states interested in log rolling, pork barrels, and pillage. Others, the *New*

York Sun commented, might take their troubles "to the wailing wall at Washington," but not "brave, sturdy, self-reliant Vermont," which was working out its own destiny, rather than "filling the woods with lamentations or piercing cries for help." "God helps those who help themselves," observed the *Free Press*. "Inasmuch as man was made in the divine image it is not strange we should admire people who help themselves instead of asking Uncle Sam to support them."[21]

Even the dullest reader would get the point: While the self-seeking arguments from the Mississippi Valley raised red flags against the perils of federal interference and paternalism, Vermont received no more than it deserved. "The amount of publicity gained by Vermont in connection with the rehabilitation of our flooded districts is almost beyond comprehension," wrote the *Free Press*. "Its value is inestimable . . . The feature that appeals to the metropolitan newspapers as well as the public is that we are showing a gratifying degree of self-reliance."[22] In short, whatever Congress might be doing, on the pages of the *Free Press* and even some papers beyond the state, Vermont was still taking care of its own.

Highways, Bridges, and Tourists

As Congress wrangled over the details of the highway bill, April swept into the north country with an unusual burst of warm weather, the mountain snows melting rapidly under the spring sun. Once again, Montpelier's flood warnings sounded, as the ice-swollen Winooski surged over its banks, forcing merchants to haul their stock up out of threatened basements, and in Jonesville a man drowned when the cable of his ferryboat gave way. Highways and railway lines were cut, the Red Wing, bound from Montreal to Boston, was stranded for fifteen hours at Lyndonville, while at Gilman, the dam across the Connecticut failed.[23]

The thaw took its usual toll on the roads. Rutland was almost cut off for a while, automobile traffic in and out of Burlington came to a standstill, buses found themselves mired and unable to move, and Northfield's citizenry turned out for an "indignation meeting," demanding action to improve the road to Montpelier. Complaints filled the papers, though it's hard to disentangle the damage left by the flood from the usual problems of mud season.

This road is not passable,
Not even jackassable,
And he who would travel
Must bring his own gravel.[24]

Yet to the normal annual burden of repairing winter-damaged roads were added the already heavy expenses piled up in the flood's aftermath. By June, the state had already put almost $1.1 million into rebuilding, some of it permanent, some of it simple patch-up to tide travelers over until the warm weather returned. That was just a start, for over the course of the next fiscal year, another $7,765,000 would be spent, and by the end of November 1930, the total would reach $11,836,220.56.[25] Despite earlier hopes that if help arrived from Washington, the final $3.5 million worth of bonds authorized by the legislature would not need to be sold, they were issued in January 1929 at 4 percent, adding to the total available for road construction.[26]

As Samuel Hand has observed, it's pointless to try to separate reconstruction pure and simple from the ways in which the champions of hard roads, from Governor Weeks on down, used this sudden huge influx of funds to further their vision of a modern highway system. After all, there was no point in simply restoring roads that would once again be vulnerable to catastrophe, that even before the flood had already been inadequate, and whose maintenance costs would be greater than if they were rebuilt in a more durable form.[27]

Although spring's coming was welcome enough after what Lloyd Squier called a winter of "unparalleled hardship," the snow at least had the virtue of covering up many of the signs of November's destruction. Now, as it vanished, there was no escaping the reminders throughout the barren land of the enormous tasks remaining, as well as grim reports of the recoveries of more bodies. The Winooski Valley would be turned into a "riot of color" that summer, promised Waterbury, with flowers planted everywhere to cover the damage, and the town declared 3 May a holiday for a general clean-up. Schools, factories, and offices closed down, hundreds of men turned out to work on the roads, helped by trucks and teams of horses, the Central Vermont pitched in, high school girls and their teachers made coffee, sandwiches, and doughnuts, and the Woman's Club served a communal dinner in the Congregational church. Meanwhile, a retired professor from Lehigh University, driving through Quechee, spotted the skull of what he pronounced to be a mammoth or mastodon, sitting on the verandah of a house in town, placed there by a local millworker who had found it during November's clean-up.[28]

Ventures like those in Waterbury and elsewhere were designed not only to keep spirits up, but also to help swell the influx of summer tourists. Or so it was hoped, although the fears of travelers were hardly likely to be allayed by some of the reports of road conditions—the *Rutland Herald*, for example, noted the coming of a carload of early visitors in mid-May who arrived at a hotel "with both vehicle and nerves badly shaken." Although rumors of a sign in New York's Grand Central Station warning travelers away from Vermont turned out to be untrue, there were other alarming reports of cautions being given to tourists in such cities as New York and Montreal. Even in far-off Moose Jaw, Saskatchewan, noted one irate correspondent, a ticket agent had been told to avoid routing travelers through Vermont, since the railways were known to be dangerous and the roads impassable (perhaps that city's location on the Canadian Pacific, rival to the Canadian National, had something to do with the warning).[29]

"[T]he stories of the almost miraculous recovery of Vermont never seems [*sic*] to have caught up with the original tales of ruin and desolation," observed the *Rutland Herald*.[30] The state Chamber of Commerce, the Highway Board, and Governor Weeks himself all did their best to assure nervous visitors that while there might be slight holdups, the highways would be in good condition for the touring season. Vermont was ready for summer visitors, F. Lauriston Bullard told the readers of the *New York Times*, using the material obligingly furnished him by Fred Howland's office, its main highways and rail lines safe and comfortable. The *Boston Evening Transcript* dismissed the fears of those who still envisaged a ravaged landscape, suggesting that the scare stories had been encouraged by "rival resort keepers." Others, including Walter Husband, a native of St. Johnsbury and Coolidge's assistant secretary of labor, as well as Representative Sol Bloom of New York, praised the state's condition after visits there.[31]

It's impossible to know how good or bad the tourist season actually was in 1928. One local paper claimed that the figures showed a vast improvement over 1927 while publishing in the same issue a mournful editorial from the *Albany Evening News* reporting the opposite. Another stated that while June and July did well, there had been a fall-off in late summer, due to adverse propaganda in other states and Canada. Sometimes the problem was too many rather than too few visitors. Thousands turned out to look at Gaysville in the White River Valley, with its huge gully carved out by the river, its power plant in ruins, and the concrete blocks of a shattered dam still lying about. Every Sunday and holiday brought massive traffic jams to Cavendish, as sightseers piled into town to view the spectacular gorge where the main street once had run.[32] An enterprising *Free Press* reporter, after making his own tour of inspection in August, concluded that Vermont's recovery had been so rapid that people looking for "barren lands and wrecked highways" would be disappointed. He did admit, though, that in the White River Valley he'd had to make a detour when the main road came to an end, driving through pastures and hayfields, but left no record of what the property owners thought of such trespassing.[33]

Whatever the disappointments of hotel keepers and others, the summer of 1928 still had room for public celebrations. Thousands turned out in mid-June to mark the opening of the "Gateway Road," seventeen and a half miles of hard surface from Rutland to the New York border near Whitehall ("The Dawn of a New Era of Progress and Prosperity," the *Rutland Herald* called it). On a Saturday in early August, seven or eight thousand listened to band music, watched Miss Grace Cashman (daughter of the contractor) cut the ribbon opening the new bridge once more linking Burlington to Winooski, and heard Governor Weeks invoke the spirits of Thomas Chittenden and Ira Allen, praising the new span as "a lasting monument to the courage and faith and enterprise of the citizens of this state." Meanwhile, several towns in Addison County, hitherto laggards in the good roads movement, competed for the route that would lead to the new bridge, scheduled to open in 1929, crossing Lake Champlain to New York at Crown Point.[34]

Like the festivities that had marked the opening of new roads even before the flood, these gatherings reflected a faith in a new and progressive Vermont, ready to match the achievements of its sister states as it advanced into the modern world. But, like the celebrations that had attended the return of the trains to isolated towns the prior winter, they were also expressions of community pride in the enormous distance that the state had traveled since the dark days of November.

The greatest celebration was yet to come, however. President Coolidge was planning to tour his native state in September, and by that time, Vermont's political landscape would have changed.

Politics and the Mountain Rule

Vacationing in the Black Hills of South Dakota in the summer of 1927 (where, among other things, he was adopted into the Sioux tribe by Henry Standing Bear), President Coolidge managed both to startle and confuse the country when he suddenly announced to the press, "I do not choose to run for president in 1928." Apparently he consulted no one in advance, not even Grace Coolidge, and for months newspapers would spill a considerable amount of ink trying to parse the sentence, and to decide precisely what Silent Cal had meant. Among the more baffled, of course, was Herbert Hoover, his eye firmly set on the White House, but in no mood to challenge his chief.[35] To many of the president's supporters, particularly in Vermont, the cryptic utterance might mean that while the president would not throw his hat actively into the ring, he nevertheless would be amenable to a draft. As the months passed, however, their hopes began to fade, leaving them faced with the reality that Mr. Coolidge not only did not choose to run again, but simply would not do so, in any way, shape, or form.

That left Secretary of Commerce Hoover, buoyed by his work in Mississippi relief, or perhaps Vice-President Charles Dawes, to bear the standard of the Republican Party. Though Senator Porter Dale seems to have favored him, Dawes had little support in Vermont, being closely wedded to the McNary-Haugen agricultural plan, which smacked too much of big government, while offering little to Vermont's farmers. Meanwhile, on his swing through Vermont the prior November, Hoover had found time to round up supporters (Fred Howland among them). Presently, a discreet, but influential, pro-Hoover organization began to take shape in the state.[36]

More important locally was the question of John Weeks's own political future. "I am not a candidate to succeed myself," he told the press in July 1927, during the Governors' Conference at Mackinac Island in Michigan, "because of the unwritten law of my State that a government official be satisfied with one term." His statement caused a minor flurry at the time, not because America was concerned with Weeks's future or with Vermont's political traditions, but because some thought it might bear on the question of the political future of that other Vermonter, Calvin Coolidge, who had not yet revealed his own plans.[37]

The "unwritten law" to which the governor referred was that which Vermonters called the Mountain Rule, or at least was a subsection of that rule. Virtually since the time of the state's founding, the rule's intent had been to balance the different interests of a state geographically and economically bisected by the Green Mountains (as the *New York Times* pointed out, there were still those born in the Connecticut Valley who had never seen Lake Champlain, and never cared to). Vermont's two congressional districts reflected the geographical split and the choice of its two senators customarily respected the divide. Although the men sent to Washington had no term limits, by 1870 the Mountain Rule also came to mean not only that easterners and westerners should alternate in the governorship, but that the incumbent should be limited to a single two-year term.[38]

As Vermont in the latter half of the nineteenth century became for all practical purposes a one-party state, the Mountain Rule gradually evolved from a simple mechanism to balance sectional interests into a way for Republican leaders to control the selection of candidates, minimize factional feuding, and thus to bring a degree of stability to party affairs. To its defenders, the rule explained "the glorious record of this state in the affairs of this nation," as former Governor E. C. Smith put it in 1916. To its detractors, however, it was inefficient and got in the way of the kind of scientific management admired by Progressives. Did it really make sense, they asked, to turn the governor into a lame duck the instant he took office? James Hartness, the Springfield engineer elected in 1920 as an advocate of modern efficiency in government, left office frustrated, recommending that the state appoint a chief executive administrator to serve a term of at least six years, but no such step was taken.[39]

It would be wrong to say that there was a popular groundswell calling for the Mountain Rule's abolition before the flood, but the question was certainly in the air and had been raised during the governorships of Redfield Proctor and Franklin Billings.[40] In the late summer of 1927, the *Free Press* suggested that the time might have come to break the tradition, while admitting that it was unlikely to happen. At a public celebration of the opening of a new highway near Middlebury in late October that year, the Rev. J. J. Fowler, introducing the governor, drew cheers when he called for the overthrow of "the antiquated mountain rule," and the *Free Press* spoke of growing numbers of people who wanted to do just that. Not surprisingly, Weeks's hometown paper also favored his re-election, but thought it unlikely. "Something out of the ordinary must take place before any new system will be devised," the *Middlebury Register* wrote in mid-October. "The mountain division politically, is as firmly established today as at any period in the history of Vermont."[41]

By the late summer of 1927, Lieutenant-Governor S. Hollister Jackson, an easterner from Barre, had apparently already drafted Watson Webb, a westerner from Shelburne, as his running mate in the 1928 campaign.[42] Jackson's high position was no guarantee of victory, however, and he was likely to face a serious rival in Stanley Wilson of Chelsea, another easterner. Might he also have had to face an unexpected rival in Weeks himself? Given the governor's statement in Michigan, it seemed unlikely, yet back home, Weeks appears to have done little to quash any speculation over his future. Then, of course, came that "something out of the ordinary" of which the *Middlebury Register* had spoken, and with Jackson's drowning, the idea of Weeks's re-election began to develop a broader currency.

Samuel Hand, in a retrospective reading of the governor's remarks made to the General Assembly on 30 November 1927, and to the press in the days thereafter, suggests that he must already have been thinking of running again. "Apparently Stanley Wilson has a clear field for the governorship," Walter Crockett wrote Senator Frank Greene in early December, "but it would not take a great deal of effort to start a strong movement for the re-election of Governor Weeks. He is the most popular Governor we have had for a considerable period, and if an organized effort was made to renominate him, which I do not anticipate, it would stand a good chance of success."[43]

Wilson, a forty-nine-year-old lawyer who had served as speaker of the Vermont house in 1917, certainly would have been a logical choice, and after the death of Jackson, was most frequently mentioned as Weeks's successor. By early 1928, however, there began to be heard the argument that the work of reconstruction was too important to be diverted by a divisive political campaign. "The *Herald* attaches no particular importance to the 'mountain rule,'" that Rutland paper stated in March, while admitting that such a tradition would not be broken easily. Like several other papers in the state, it ran a straw ballot for its readers that spring, giving them three choices: the renomination of Weeks, the nomination of Wilson, or the nomination of another easterner (presumably the nomination of another westerner, or even a Democrat, was unthinkable). Meanwhile, Howard Rice of the *Brattleboro Reformer*

wrote the governor, offering his paper's support, but appealed to Weeks
to make his own intentions clear.[44]

Such polls, when the results were in, reflected solid support for a second term. In any other state, the *New York Times* commented, a
governor with Weeks's record would be re-elected without question, but
the paper feared that in Vermont tradition would die hard. What
farmer, asked the *Free Press*, would discharge a faithful and satisfactory
hired man just for the sake of change? And surely, the same paper sensibly commented a few months later, there was no logical connection
between alternating easterners and westerners in the governor's office
and the tradition of the single term.[45]

By then, the Burlington paper was just one of many journals clearly
backing Weeks, although dissenting voices occasionally emerged. In
March, Fred Howland privately assured Weeks that he could be re-
elected, but suggested it might be wiser to retire "without running the
hazard of an anti-climax to his fine record," and Frank Partridge
sounded cool to the project.[46] Why break a tradition that had so long
served the state well, asked Edward Rockwood in the *Vermont Review*.
"The Mountain rule is not a gift from the Gods. It is only a political
scheme, but it is a scheme which is pregnant with virtue." Look at what
was happening in some of America's great cities, he warned, with their
political machines, like the one in Chicago, where office-holders
(Democrats, of course) stayed in forever. Luther Johnson's *Randolph
Herald* also opposed a second term, and Max Powell, who had opposed
Weeks in the Republican primary of 1926, warned darkly of building up
"a Mussolini oligarchy that finds no place in Vermont's politics." It's unlikely, though, that he envisioned John Weeks in a black shirt, his right
arm outstretched as he returned the salute of the admiring masses
below the balcony of the Pavilion Hotel. Fortunately, Powell probably
never knew that, two months after the election, the "Vermont Fascisti"
would wire their congratulations from White River Junction, while several years later, Sinclair Lewis would set his chilling *It Can't Happen Here*
within the state.[47]

Despite a report from Boston in March that Stanley Wilson had
thrown his hat in the ring, apparently he made no such announcement
himself. Meanwhile, after an address to the Bennington Chamber of
Commerce on 27 March, Weeks responded to a question about a second
term with a simple, two-sentence declaration. "If I can be of service, I

am willing. It is for the people to say." He then added that he would like to see through the state's reconstruction, estimating that it would last another three years. Less opaque than Coolidge's statement eight months earlier, the remark drew surprisingly little comment at the time. But what exactly did it mean? How were "the people" to say whether they wished Weeks to continue, unless his name appeared on the ballot? Or was the governor suggesting that he would take the results of the various straw polls (which by now were running heavily in his favor), or the amount of editorial support for his putative candidacy, as evidence that he should or should not run again?

Given the paucity of sources, there's no way of knowing what was in Weeks's mind. Some claimed to know that he really wanted to retire, and only the public demand for his services changed his mind. Others held that such a view "hardly stands the wash," as the *Randolph Herald* put it, suggesting that Weeks had kept his ear to the ground for months, conducting a "very canny canvass" to promote himself for the position. Edward Rockwood speculated in the *New York Times* that Stanley Wilson's political opponents were anxious to derail that candidate's campaign (he had in mind the former supporters of Hollister Jackson and the present supporters of Senator Porter Dale, who, in his coming campaign in 1932, might have to face a former Governor Wilson as his opponent). These "Jacksonians" and "Dalists" thus banded together, flattering Weeks to see himself as a Moses called to lead his people into the Promised Land of a rebuilt Vermont, thus blocking Wilson's own claim to the office.[48] Perhaps so, though surely more important was that Weeks wanted the job and his supporters were making good arguments for his keeping it.

Not until 17 May—a day after Coolidge signed the highway bill, giving Vermont its federal funds—did Weeks put himself forward unambiguously as a candidate. He would have preferred not to have done so yet, he told John Spargo, but was being importuned by friends to make the announcement. He also may have feared that, as Vermont's Republicans planned to meet the next day to choose delegates to the national convention, a resolution supporting the Mountain Rule might be introduced, upsetting his plans.[49] In fact, the resolution was brought up, but only at the end of the meeting and only to be rejected overwhelmingly. Then, a few days later came Stanley Wilson's announcement that he would run for the lieutenant-governorship, not wishing, as he said, to divert the state from the business of reconstruction by a challenge to Weeks. The move also made him Weeks's logical successor, thus (as Guy Bailey, president of the University of Vermont pointed out) frustrating the plans of Senator Dale's supporters to keep him from the office.[50]

Despite the obvious and broad support for the governor, not everyone was happy with the results. The arrangement had been sealed in a Burlington hotel lobby, grumbled Rockwood, conjuring up visions of deals in smoke-filled rooms. All the political excitement was drained from what might have been an energizing campaign (Weeks's re-election, he had suggested earlier, "would be about as exciting as breakfasting with one's grandfather"), and the press was left without a job. "Everything has been arranged. . . . Hindley [of the *Rutland Herald*] can now take up tatting or embroidery and Southwick [of the *Free Press*] can blaze his double-barreled shotgun at such harmless phenomena as economic conditions in Afghanistan or the population problem of Siberia." Meanwhile, only the future would reveal the damage caused to Vermont by Weeks's "tragic political blunder—a blunder which President Coolidge, in a like situation, was wise enough to avoid."[51]

The common rumor at the time, although Rockwood didn't repeat it, was that former Governor Redfield Proctor had brokered the arrangement. Although Southwick strongly denied the story, some others appear to have considered the arrangement as "bolshevik," a term that, like Max Powell's "fascist," was not one commonly slung around in Vermont politics of the day. Whatever the background, Weeks would get his second term, with Wilson as heir-apparent succeeding to the governorship in 1931 and setting a new pattern for the Mountain Rule's application.[52]

Not that Weeks went entirely unopposed, for toward the end of July, Edward Deavitt, the mayor of Montpelier, announced his candidacy. Fifty-seven years old, a graduate of Harvard Law School, former state treasurer and former finance commissioner, his platform consisted of little more than upholding the tradition of the Mountain Rule (he noted that Governor John Stewart—like Weeks a Middlebury native— had tried for a second term in 1872 and had been defeated). Privately, Guy Bailey (with the backing of former Governor Franklin S. Billings) suggested that Weeks, who had persuaded him not to enter the 1926 campaign, should now step down himself, but Weeks, though disappointed by Deavitt's action, stayed in the race.[53] In the end, Deavitt's platform was irrelevant, and he was defeated handily in the Republican primary on 11 September, by a vote of 37,500 to 19,500, carrying only Orange and Washington counties.

So the Mountain Rule, if not dead, was at least transformed by the flood and its aftermath. But not only by the flood, for Weeks's ambitions played a part as well, meshing nicely with a broader desire for modern efficiency and professionalism in state government. Once again, the governor showed himself to be a consummate politician, not by acting as a rural version of the kind of modern urban boss feared by Rockwood or Powell, but in the way of a native Vermont farmer, who watched carefully, allowing support to build, but never actively campaigning for it until he made his statement. "We believe Vermont is to see the greatest two years in its history," wrote a jubilant *Free Press* after the primary, convinced that Weeks and the forthcoming legislature would work together to meet the state's "great expectations."[54] Against him that November, the Democrats tried to rally support for Harry Shurtleff, a Montpelier lawyer. But Vermonters had not elected a Democratic governor since 1852, and would not do so again until 1962.

The Coolidge Tour, September 1928

Before the November election, the last and most important of the celebrations commemorating recovery took place when Calvin Coolidge returned to the state in late September. In March 1926, he had made a hurried journey through the winter snows as his father lay dying in Plymouth, and the following August, while vacationing in the Adirondacks, he visited Burlington and spent several days in Plymouth. Despite the wistful hope of the *Vermont Review* that he might vacation there rather than in the Black Hills, and the appeals of John Spargo and others to have him come to the Bennington Sesquicentennial, the year of 1927 brought no presidential visit. By the spring of 1928, several papers hoped that he would summer in Vermont, noting how badly the state needed tourists, and the *Waterbury Record* called on Coolidge to do his duty to his native state with at least a brief visit.[55] Governor Weeks and others invited him to tour the flood districts early in the summer, but having signed the highway bill, Coolidge immediately headed west, presumably preferring angling for fish in the cool waters of Wisconsin's Brule River to angling for votes in an election year. Particularly angling for the votes of the expected Republican candidate, for according to his biographer Robert Ferrell, one of the reasons that he chose Wisconsin was to absent himself from the Kansas City convention in mid-June, where, to no one's great surprise, Hoover was chosen as candidate on the first ballot (Warren Austin was among those seconding the nomination). A few days later, the successful nominee traveled to Wisconsin, where, in an awkward meeting, he received a cool presidential endorsement.[56]

The Vermont trip was not abandoned, however, but simply postponed. In early September, the White House announced that the president, his summer vacation now concluded, would visit his natal state. On the 19th, accompanied by his wife, Attorney-General Sargent, and a few others, Coolidge left Washington, just after issuing an appeal for $5 million for the Red Cross, which was already at work aiding victims of the terrible hurricane that had swept through Puerto Rico and southern Florida a few days earlier. On the morning of the next day, the presidential train reached Brattleboro, receiving an enthusiastic, if damp welcome in the warm rain spread north by the storm. There were brief stops elsewhere, including one at Montpelier Junction, where Governor Weeks and his party came aboard, although the presidential special swept through Waterbury at forty miles an hour, giving the waiting crowd only the briefest glimpse of the Coolidges on the platform of the observation car.

At Burlington, the couple disembarked to drive through flag-waving crowds to the Green Mount Cemetery, where Grace Coolidge laid a wreath on her father's grave. Four thousand turned out at Middlebury, including all the students and faculty of the college, Mrs. Coolidge received bouquets, while the Legion's drum corps provided music. Another such gathering met him in Rutland late that afternoon, three thousand people cheering, factory whistles blaring, while a drum and bugle corps strove to make itself heard above the din. Finally, the train reached Ludlow, where the president and his wife disembarked, to be driven twelve miles through the autumn dusk to the old Coolidge farmhouse at Plymouth Notch for the night.

The next day, the president inspected his farm, "275 acres in the defiant soil of Vermont," as the New York Times put it, and the herd that earned him $1.46 a day through the sale of milk to the local cheese factory. He also called on relatives, including both his aunt Sarah Pollard (the one who had denied seeing a "great gray monster" rush down from the hills), as well as his firmly Democratic cousin, Clark Pollard, who

Fig. 23. Governor and Mrs. Weeks with President and Mrs. Coolidge, aboard the special train surveying recovery work, 22 September 1928. *Courtesy of the Vermont Historical Society.*

had seconded Al Smith's nomination at the Democratic convention in Houston that summer. At Ludlow, the president recalled his student days at Black River Academy, and then proceeded to Cavendish, where, guided by Leon Gay, the Coolidges spent a half hour examining the chasm left by the flood, before boarding the train to go back to Rutland, and to continue the journey south.[57]

"No returning Vermonter could fail to feel an emotion of pride in traversing her lately ravaged valleys," wrote the *Boston Evening Transcript.* "President Coolidge, deeply loving her every field and stream and forest must be inspired, on his present return, with inexpressible thoughts."[58] At last, however, the inexpressible thoughts found expression. Having earlier resisted all the calls for him to speak, insisting that he was come only to see the state's recovery, he now made up for his silence. In the late afternoon, as the train pulled in to its last stop at Bennington just before crossing back into Massachusetts, some five

Fig. 24. President Coolidge receives a flag from a child at White River Junction, 21 September 1928. *Courtesy of the Vermont Historical Society.*

thousand people surrounded it, and as bands played, the Coolidges stepped out on the observation car's platform, bowed, and smiled. Deeply moved, the president thanked the Vermonters for their kindness and hospitality, expressing his admiration for their splendid work in rebuilding the state.

Then, putting aside whatever notes he may have had, he began to talk from the heart, in words that, as Craig Burt of Stowe later put it, "every school child should be taught."[59]

> Vermont is a state I love. I could not look upon the peaks of Ascutney, Killington, Mansfield, and Equinox, without being moved in a way that no other scene could move me. It was here that I first saw the light of day; here I received my bride, here my dead lie pillowed on the loving breast of our eternal hills.
>
> I love Vermont because of her hills and valleys, her scenery and invigorating climate, but most of all because of her indomitable people. They are a race of pioneers who have almost beggared themselves to serve others. If the spirit of liberty should vanish in other parts of the Union, and support of our institutions should languish, it could all be replenished from the generous store held by the people of this brave little state of Vermont.[60]

"PRESIDENT MOVES AUDIENCE TO TEARS: Profession of Love for Vermont Touches Emotions of Crowd at Bennington," ran the headline the next day in the *Boston Globe*. Whether or not he should have come to Vermont earlier, in that final speech, Calvin Coolidge paid whatever dues he owed the state of his birth. The words spoken that afternoon retain a firm place in Vermont's historical memory; seventy-five years later, in September 2002, they were heard again in a re-enactment in Bennington, and a very physical reminder of them remains on a plaque in the State House in Montpelier.

Like the image that had begun Coolidge's presidency—that midnight oath of office administered by his father in the light shed by a single kerosene lamp in the ancestral farm house—the vision of the president traveling through his state to admire the work done by its inhabitants seemed to validate not only their deeds, but the spirit of Vermont that had inspired them. No one caught the symbolic meaning of the trip better than did Louis Lyons, the *Boston Globe* reporter who had been one of the first to reach Montpelier after the flood, and who years later would become curator of the Nieman Fellowships at Harvard. The Vermont through which the president's train steamed for those two early autumn days emerges from Lyons' writing as an Arcadian landscape, unchanged by the years, a countryside where children stand outside a district school to cheer the passing train, where people at a country store look up and wave, where farmers haul the summer's sileage corn along dusty country roads, where red maples already flame in the forests, and crimson sumac grows under sunlit gray stone walls. "President Coolidge finds his home country at its loveliest," Lyons observed. "This countryside has scarcely changed since the President was a boy. Hardly another man of his generation could return to find his home country as much the same."[61]

Whatever may have been Coolidge's private views of his successor, seven weeks later Hoover swept into office. Vermont stood by him, of course, despite a plaintive reminder by Montpelier's Democrats that the first public official from outside the state to respond to the disaster a year earlier had been their party's own "Great Humanitarian," Governor Al Smith of New York. Vermont leaders remained grateful for Hoover's visit after the flood, brief as it was, and presumably agreed with Elbert Brigham's views that only if Hoover were elected could Vermont meet the heavy economic burdens imposed by the recovery. A victory for Smith, on the other hand, would bring high taxes, a removal of the protective tariff, and a lowering of the barriers against alien immigrants, none of which Vermont could afford.[62] Herbert Hoover, wrote the *Rutland Herald,* had proved his "fidelity and ability in big things," while Smith was a man "whose principles are repugnant to almost every Vermont tradition" (though the paper also reprinted, with no sense of irony, an editorial from the *New York Times* referring to Governor Weeks as "the Al Smith of Vermont").[63]

To the *Free Press,* Hoover's election was "a victory for American ideas and ideals as opposed to European theories and fads"—or, as a Middle Western paper put it, "Main Street is still the principal thoroughfare of the nation."[64] More recently, historians have used their privilege of retrospection to suggest that despite the magnitude of Hoover's sweep, the signs of Franklin Roosevelt's future victory and the formation of the New Deal coalition were already visible. At the time, indeed, the *Rutland Herald,* while applauding Hoover's success, wrung its hands over the figures showing that while the Republicans had picked up ten thousand votes since 1924, the Democrats gained twenty-eight thousand. They came within an ace, moreover, of taking Franklin County and actually carried Chittenden County as well as several of the larger towns, such as Winooski, Burlington, Shelburne, Rutland, and Randolph. Barre, however, despite its strong working-class traditions, stayed in the Republican column.

On the other hand, John Weeks's popular vote of ninety-five thousand set a record that would remain unbroken until 1976.[65]

The 1929 Legislature

The governor had little time to bask in the glow of his easy victory, for two months after the election, on 10 January 1929, he stood once more before the lawmakers gathered in the State House for their biennial session. After taking the oath of office, the first governor since John B. Page in 1869 to do so for a second term, he opened the proceedings with a prayer and then spoke to the two houses of the main issues facing them. Two were perhaps the most important: First, how to pay for the continuation of the hard-roads program launched two years earlier? And second, how to pay off the bond issue authorized at the special session, the last $3.5 million of which had just been sold?

Though some, like Senator W. A. Simpson of the Highway Board, pushed for further borrowing to speed the pace of construction, hoping to add perhaps as many as five hundred miles of hard roads over the next two years, Weeks remained cautious. The state should continue its earlier pay-as-you-go policies, he advised, avoiding further bond issues, while raising the gasoline tax by a penny, to permit both the building of a hundred miles of road over the next two years and meeting payments on the bond issue. He did, however, hedge his bets, pledging not to stand in the way of more ambitious proposals, as long as they accorded with "sound business principles, sane judgment, and wise economy."[66]

Generally speaking, once more he got his way. Two months later, the session came to an end after eighty-six days, the shortest gathering since 1900, and one, as the *Rutland Herald* commented, as notable for what it did not do as what it did do.[67] What it did was to authorize the building of 125 miles of hard road over the next two years, and to raise the gasoline tax by a penny. Following the recommendations of a committee reviewing the tax structure, chaired by former governor Redfield Proctor, it continued a $.075 state tax, first passed in 1927, and authorized a $2.50 poll tax to help pay off the bonds. New laws encouraged the development of aviation, which had proved its importance at the time of the flood. Another authorized a $200,000 loan to rebuild the West River Railway (an unprofitable branch line, legally abandoned within hours of the flood by the Central Vermont) and yet another enabled the Canadian National, a foreign corporation, to maintain its earlier relationship with the Central Vermont, now emerging from bankruptcy as a new company. This last brought a thoroughly appreciative letter from Sir Henry Thornton to the governor, citing the legislation as a splendid example of international cooperation, as well as a promise that the C.N. would never abandon its "perpetual responsibility" to the Vermont line.[68]

What the General Assembly did not do that winter was to authorize an income tax, a measure pushed by farm interests for some years, as a way of mitigating the property tax that fell so heavily on their sector. Weeks opposed it, Senate President Levi Smith denounced it as an inducement to class warfare, and though the House passed it in a highly amended form, the Senate killed it, twenty-five to four (two years later, under different circumstances, it would go through). Another bill, championed by Senator Walter Crockett and passed by the Senate, would have given the state control over federal aid roads. Although the *Rutland Herald* backed it as a progressive step forward to a modern highway system, it also predicted—rightly—its defeat. "This is the biggest curse put on us so far," Representative Sawyer of Sharon told his colleagues in the House, "and if you want 'Stod' Bates [Stoddard Bates, the highway commissioner] to run your whole state, for God's sake, vote for this bill."[69] The memories of the flood and the efficiencies of a reconstruction directed by Montpelier were not enough to save it, and, dominated by small town interests fearful of anything that might smell of the loss of local control, the House sent the bill down to defeat.

Finally, before it went home, the legislature considered the preliminary report of a committee, set up by the Public Service Commission and chaired by J. W. Votey, dean of the University of Vermont's engineering school, to study questions of flood control. Its final work will be considered later, and in 1929 the legislature did no more than vote funds, to be matched by the power companies, to bring the study to its conclusion.

Brief as it was, the meeting of the lawmakers was yet another success for Governor Weeks, and the measures taken did nothing to affect his continuing popularity. Only on the last day did he veto a single bill, one that would have lowered the fines for liquor violations. Apart from that, he once again had succeeded, as the *Free Press* pointed out, in working without coming into conflict with the two houses, while keeping Vermont on a "safe and thrifty and at the same time progressive basis," just as Coolidge had in the nation as a whole.[70] By now, reconstruction was well on its way, and the bigger, better, and more progressive Vermont that Weeks had promised had seemingly suffered no more than a temporary check from the water's ravages. No one could have foretold how drastically the picture would have changed by the time the next legislature met in the early months of 1931.

6

"Any Great Catastrophe Brings a Good Many Changes in Its Wake"

The Flood and Vermont's Future

The Unfinished Business of Flood Control

Even before Vermont's rivers had subsided that gray November, Representative Frank Reid of Illinois, chairman of the House Flood Control Committee, was calling for an act of national scope, to cover not only the Mississippi, but other river systems as well. Although Coolidge thought the state's peculiar topography made flood control in Vermont a hopeless task, others disagreed, like Lt.-Col. Robert Ralston of the Corps of Engineers, who suggested that precisely because of the mountains, the problems were simpler than those found in the flat lands of the delta. Right after the flood, John Southwick of the *Burlington Free Press* called for federal intervention in New England, as in the Mississippi valley, for no single state could deal with flood problems by itself. "Failure to take precautions in one state may visit its sins on other states. This is a case where Federal action is essential. Indeed, one State alone may be absolutely helpless."[1]

Still, by the time Reid's committee heard their testimony, Vermont's congressmen had few ideas to offer, reflecting Elbert Brigham's earlier view that flood relief, not flood control, was the issue. So too, the *Free Press*'s Southwick, with whom Brigham had corresponded privately, drew the same distinction between control and relief, and while he, like Brigham, was concerned by the enormous costs of flood control, he continued to argue that New England deserved as much of Congress's attention as did the Mississippi states.[2]

At the time, many blamed the loss of Vermont's woodlands over the years for leaving the state particularly vulnerable, although State Forester Robert Ross, among others, thought that no amount of cover would have sufficed to deal with November's rains. A more practical approach appeared to be the building of storage reservoirs. The new Molly's Falls dam near Marshfield had kept the Winooski's flooding from being even worse than it was, and the New England Power Association dams on the Deerfield River substantially limited the damage in southern Vermont and western Massachusetts. Bad flooding was seen primarily as an autumn phenomenon, and the reservoirs, normally low by summer's end, would have ample room to trap the waters. Not only that, of course, but they could be adapted relatively easily and cheaply to help generate hydroelectricity, thus providing additional resources of "white coal" for the region's benefit.[3]

Although in early March Governor Weeks still promised that something would be done, by the spring of 1928, Vermont's interest in flood control seemed to be waning in the face of the enormous costs projected by Representative Reid's bill. That proposal now called for the federal government to pick up all the expenses of harnessing the Mississippi, despite Coolidge's protestations that the river states should contribute as well. Unlike the southern states, which looked to the federal government and the national treasury, Vermont, the *Free Press* said, after the proper surveys, would work out its own methods of flood prevention through a system of dams and reservoirs.[4]

The Votey Committee and the Barrows Plan

In March 1928, the Vermont Public Service Commission, which for the last three months had been studying flood control, appointed an Advisory Committee of Engineers to take charge of the investigation. Chaired by J. W. Votey, dean of the University of Vermont's engineering school, it included also Harry Barker, a New York engineer, as its secretary, and H. W. Barrows of the Massachusetts Institute of Technology, as consulting engineer. They were charged with carrying out a survey of the state's main river valleys, the study's costs to be met by $5,000 from the federal government (whose Geological Survey would also install gaging stations and pay half the cost of their maintenance), and by grants of $16,000 each from the state's emergency funds and from

Vermont's private power companies. By December, the committee gave Governor Weeks a preliminary study, which he passed on to the legislature a month later, as it opened its 1929 biennial session. Largely the work of Barrows, it included an initial survey of five of the state's principle river systems: the Missisquoi, the Lamoille, the Winooski, the White, and the Passumpsic.[5]

"It is likely," Barrows and his colleagues wrote, "that such a storm as 1927 may be expected in Vermont *on the average* perhaps once in 50 to 75 years, but of course *it may occur at any time*" (41). Citing the effectiveness of the Deerfield river dams in southern Vermont, the report concluded that the only feasible solution lay in the construction of a system of reservoirs to hold back the waters when the rains came. By themselves, they would cost roughly $40 million. An additional $34 million, however, would make them suitable for power generation, producing nearly a billion kilowatt hours per year, far more than was necessary at the time, but power that would be needed presently.

To allow this, the General Assembly first would have to pass legislation enabling the state to take land, property, and water rights for such projects, modeled (Barrows suggested) on the New York Storage Act of 1915, which established river regulating districts. The most important initial undertakings would include a single large dam and power station on the White River, probably near Gaysville; and two dams each on the Winooski, Passumpsic, Lamoille, and Missisquoi rivers. Somewhat optimistically, the Barrows report suggested that the costs to the state would be minimal, and that rather than making any direct appropriations for construction, Montpelier need simply "encourage in every way possible the development of such projects by the power companies, under proper state control and supervision" (49). The state would do its part by helping the power companies secure low interest on bonds, and by making whatever changes to the highway routing might be necessitated by these new bodies of water.

Although most legislators seem to have favored a system of reservoirs for flood control, as long as the power companies helped foot the bill, the General Assembly did little with Barrows's initial recommendations, other than to go along with the governor's request to vote further funds (matched by the power companies) to allow the engineers to complete their study.[6] Two years later, on 15 December 1930, Votey and his colleagues presented their final recommendations to Governor Weeks, a month before he was to turn his office over to Stanley Wilson. By now, the survey had been broadened to cover seventeen river basins—including such streams as the Otter, the Black, and others—which, fully developed, would produce 1,862 million kilowatt hours per year. Again, Barrows pointed out that while this was far more than the present market called for, electrical usage was growing rapidly, and indeed within ten years the power system earlier proposed for the Winooski would be needed.[7]

This time the committee appended a series of detailed tables spelling out the steps necessary, estimating that the entire project would cost some $149 million (15), not including some channel improvements on various rivers (17–19), and setting forth its benefits. An accompanying map also gave a sense of the dramatic changes that would take place in the state's topography if the project, which called for the building of some eighty-five new reservoirs of varying sizes, were adopted in full. Thus, for example, in the Champlain Valley, a big lake, fed by the New Haven River, would flood much of the land between Middlebury and Bristol, while nearby another would reach almost from Cornwall to Shoreham. A large new lake would appear between Gaysville and Rochester in the White River Valley, and others would be found near such places as Newfane, Johnson, and between Burlington and Essex Junction. Fully carried through, such a scheme no doubt would insure the state against massive damage in the future. It would also drastically change the face of Vermont, and, among other things, submerge large amounts of good farm land.

Again, the committee urged the establishment of river regulating districts on New York's model, and now suggested the initial financing and construction of seventeen of the eighty-five reservoirs on their master plan. Here, however, the Barrows proposals ran into opposition. The sheer expense of the project, as the national depression deepened, must have seemed overwhelming. But another problem lay in the very concept of combining flood control with the generation of power. Votey and his colleagues were engineers, not politicians or economists, and while their proposals no doubt made perfect sense from the point of view of strict engineering, they left unaddressed several important political questions.

Large amounts of privately held land—much of it good farm land—would have to be condemned and taken over by the state. That was bad enough, of course, in a state that took private property very seriously, and continued to look to a future dependent upon agriculture. What was even worse, in some eyes, was an unnatural arranged marriage between public water resources and private power companies, and this at a time when many in the nation at large saw the power trust, as its enemies disparagingly called it, virtually unchecked and seeking to extend its control by every means possible. Admittedly, Barrows recommended that the power companies pursue their projects "under proper state control and supervision." But ideas about what was proper control might well differ, and the Public Service Commission, since its establishment in 1909, had proved itself a somewhat toothless watchdog. Although much of Vermont's earlier power generation had come from small companies locally owned, by the the end of the twenties this had changed. Now the generation and transmission of electricity in Vermont was largely in the hands of two companies, Green Mountain Power, controlled by the Forshay and Ohrstrom interests in Minneapolis, and Central Vermont Public Service, controlled by the Insull interests of Chicago. In addition to them, the Boston-based New England Power Company was responsible for several huge dams on the Connecticut and the Deerfield rivers, whose primary purpose was the provision of electricity to eastern Massachusetts. Vermont had become the largest exporter of power in New England, and it was by no means clear that Vermonters, particularly the farmers, were benefiting.[8]

Back in 1926, Governor Billings had wanted to tax hydropower exported from the state, only to see his measure defeated by the legislature. Then, during Governor Weeks's two administrations, the issue took a back seat to highway improvement. Now, in his outgoing message to the legislature on 8 January 1931, the governor stated that the Votey commission's work had "shown clearly enough that flood protection for Vermont must rely upon storage-power reservoir systems," and called on the legislature to take the appropriate action. A few hours later, however, after he had been sworn in, his successor Stanley Wilson sounded a far more cautious note, warning in his own inaugural address against

> giving to public service corporations, under the guise of flood control, rights in our beautiful and fertile valleys without adequate compensation both to the individuals concerned and the State.
>
> Storage reservoirs and power developments are not things of beauty and themselves uncontrolled may have as devastating effect on a valley as an occasional flood. We should not sacrifice the cream of our farm land to the development of additional electric energy unless satisfied that it will be beneficial to the State.

> The State of Vermont should have first claim on the electric current developed in the State. These developments should be for the growth and betterment of Vermont and not be the sacrifice of Vermont for the benefit of other states and communities.[9]

The contrast between the views of the two governors is surprising. Perhaps Weeks's overriding concerns with reconstruction and the extension of modern highways led him to turn a blind eye to the power interests that by now had become so dominant. Perhaps he assumed that in the long run, Vermonters, including the many farmers who still had no electricity, would profit from the development of its hydropower resources. Still, it seems inexplicable that he should have overlooked the flooding of so much good farm land. In any case, nothing was done until two months later, when Speaker Edward Deavitt of Montpelier introduced a bill on 17 March to "regulate the flow of rivers by storage reservoirs." Following Barrows's suggestion, it called for river regulation districts on the New York model, each to be administered by a board of three people, appointed by the governor, to prepare plans for the control of water flows, and empowered to condemn any land needed for reservoir use.

Although Deavitt himself expected no action on a bill brought in so late in the session, he hoped that it would at least be recommended for further study.[10] Even that minor victory was denied him, however. The bill was sent to the House Committee on Conservation and Development, and there it met the opposition of a freshman representative from Putney named George Aiken. "Certain people," Aiken recalled later,

> interested in harnessing the rivers worked out a plan for development that had some elements of public financing and yet did not require the use of State credit or taxation as such. This plan was presented to the Legislature as a flood control measure.
>
> Careful examination of the bill made it evident that, in effect, it would give the power companies control of the destiny of the State. For this reason it was defeated in the legislative committee of which I was a member.[11]

True enough, no doubt, but perhaps not the full story. Aiken, whose seat on the committee was due to his profession as nurseryman and his authorship of a book on Vermont wildflowers, was able to get his way only by waiting until six of the committee's fifteen members were absent, and then calling for a vote. His opposition to the Barrows plan, it was later suggested, came not only from his support for local control and his fears for the future of rural living, but also because one of the dams would have flooded his ancestral farm in Putney.[12] Be that as it may, the vote effectively ended consideration of the bill, and on 1 April Deavitt withdrew it.

Surely it is an overstatement, though, to call the Barrows proposal, as one observer does, "an ambitious new plan by the private utilities to build more power dams in Vermont," as if the engineers were somehow doing the work of the power trust.[13] Although their charge had been flood prevention and not power generation, in a time of tight budgets, it would have seemed perfectly sensible to engage the electric companies in a scheme that would save the state from another great flood and to reward them for their investment. Perfectly sensible, of course, within the context of a Hooverian alliance between engineers and private enterprise, but less than perfectly sensible within the context of local politics, particularly in a state with Vermont's traditions.

In 1937, George Aiken, the freshman legislator from Putney, would rise to the governorship. His coup of 1931, as it turned out, was the first skirmish in a long battle that he would fight over the forthcoming years, capitalizing on a widespread distrust of both the private power companies and the federal government under Franklin Roosevelt, each of which, in his eyes, was determined to chip away at the principles of states' rights and local control. In the spring of 1935, the worst floods in living memory devastated parts of western Massachusetts and Connecticut, and brought a renewed interest in flood control in southern New England. Yet if the Connecticut River were to be tamed, the dams would have to be built in Vermont and New Hampshire. Those two states, however, escaped the worst of the flood's ravages, and were relatively indifferent to the plight of their southern neighbors. Under Governor Aiken, the Green Mountain State, standing high on its principles, managed to block much of the proposed project to contain the Connecticut, and remained firmly opposed to intervention by either Washington or private power companies.[14]

In 1931, neither the press nor the public apparently paid much attention to Deavitt's proposal or to its defeat. More surprising is how little was said of the larger Barrows plan at the time. Although it would have drastically changed the face of Vermont, and would have had a considerable effect on the state's agriculture, it received not a single mention, for instance, in *Rural Vermont,* the report issued after three years of study by the Vermont Commission on Country Life in 1931. A few years later, the Winooski watershed would see the construction of three dams, built largely by members of the Civilian Conservation Corps under the direction of the Army Corps of Engineers. That work, though valuable to Vermont, was undertaken largely as part of the public works projects of the New Deal (and fully backed by Vermont's senators).[15] More dams would come later, but Barrows's grand plan of eighty-five reservoirs—Vermont's equivalent of China's Three Gorges project, perhaps—never came to fruition (New Hampshire, on the other hand, which also took Barrows on as a consultant, did establish a state Water Resources Board in 1935 and planned two dams in the Merrimac Valley).[16] In 1931, though, when Deavitt introduced his bill to start implementing the recommendations of the Barrows report, funds were short. It is hard to avoid the conclusion that by now, as the Depression deepened over the nation and the world, flood control, which had been such a burning issue a few years earlier, no longer seemed of great interest to Vermont.

Looking Beyond the Flood: The Commission on Country Life, 1928–1931

"Vermont will take longer strides forward on the path to progress . . . than ever before," a speaker promised the Vermont Bankers' Association in early 1928. On the other hand, he warned them not to allow themselves to be blinded by Vermont's traditions of individualism and self-reliance, so that they would miss the big picture and find it hard to devise any common plan of action for the benefit of the state as a whole and the rest of New England.[17]

Grand planning had never played an important role in the minds of Vermont's leaders. James Hartness, the Springfield factory executive who had been elected governor in 1920 over the opposition of the Republican establishment, tried to bring an engineer's rational efficiency to public affairs. Yet his "Blueprint for Progress," looking to the orderly development of industry and the creation of jobs in the state, failed, thanks to his political inexperience and the limitations of a single two-year term.[18] Individual agencies, such as those concerned with education or tourism or agriculture, also looked ahead from time to time, seeking ways to help with production or with marketing. But for all the talk in the newspapers about the emergence of a "Greater Vermont," or "the re-creation of Rural Vermont," there was little broad vision for the future. Addressing the state Chamber of Commerce in July 1930, John Nolen, a city planner and landscape architect from Massachusetts, berated Vermont for its backwardness in this regard: "there is no state plan and no modern comprehensive plan for any city, any village, or any town in the whole state of Vermont."[19] Vrest Orton and his fellow writers in *Driftwind* might argue that Vermont must not become another Florida or New Jersey, and Governor Weeks might argue that the state's future would inevitably be tightly bound to agriculture. Beyond such generalizations, however, it would have been difficult, on the eve of the flood, to draw a picture of what shape Vermont might assume in the years to come.

That is one reason why the creation of the Vermont Commission on Country Life, in May 1928, is important. Although the Commission's origins go back before the flood, it was the events of November 1927 that gave its formation a new urgency. In one sense, its appearance also marks Vermont's belated response to the national Country Life movement, which, though it had flourished briefly in the decades before the first world war, had now become a much less potent force, its largely urban and academic membership failing to establish real connections to rural populations. Reflecting the persistence of an American agrarian and yeoman myth, its hope that rural communities might be revitalized in the face of a growing industrialization and urbanism would have seemed particularly attractive in a state like Vermont.[20]

On a yet broader level, the Commission's formation also reflected the growing influence of the regionalist movement in the years between the wars. Partly a response to modernism, to the growth of cities, and to the spread of a homogenized mass culture, regionalism was most prominent in the South and the West, but New England was also a participant.[21] There were differences, of course. For many writers and artists, such as the Southern Agrarians around Allan Tate and John Crowe Ransom, or those who gathered in Santa Fe and Taos, regionalism and agrarianism were aesthetic and cultural choices, part of a search to redefine an authentic America in terms that broke with the old Eurocentric values of the northeast, or the new post-war urban modernism. Vermont, however, had its own clear views of what were authentic American values. Yet it lacked the luxury of choice: For solid economic and geographical reasons, many (like Governor Weeks) believed that the state had either an agricultural future or no future.

Finally, Vermont's country life movement also owed something to the kinds of phenomena that historians like Ellis Hawley have found in the period: the belief, for example, in the powers of bureaucratic and managerial rationalism, animated by the prescriptions of experts in the natural and social sciences, and a faith that the amassing of data would allow sensible planning to meet future change.[22] One example of this could be found in the Eugenics Survey, launched in 1925 by Henry F. Perkins, a University of Vermont zoologist, and several like-minded colleagues. Upset by the apparently high rate of defectiveness found in young Vermont men by the wartime draft boards, they proposed to study what they saw as the problems of rural degeneracy besetting the state. As Nancy Gallagher has shown in *Breeding Better Vermonters,* her study of this movement, their work mirrored elements of Progressive reformism, particularly in the care and treatment of children and others considered incapable of looking out for their own interests. These concerns, which had already inspired a series of reforms since the turn of the century, reflected a modern, scientific version of the old worry that Vermont was losing its edge, and that the old Yankee stock, depleted by emigration and diluted by alien newcomers, might no longer be capable of producing the sorts of men and women in which the state had earlier taken such pride.

Such ideas, obviously, were in the air well before the flood. In fact, what would become the Commission on Country Life grew out of a proposal for a "Comprehensive Rural Survey of Vermont," drawn up by Perkins in 1927, and designed, as he put it, to clear up "some of the complications of conserving the good old Vermont stock in the rural parts."[23] While the statement betrays something of the nostalgia and sentimental traditionalism of the country life movement at large and echoes the era's nativism, Perkins believed strongly in the need for rigorous and disinterested scientific approaches to social problems. He was not the first to try to apply measures based on the then-popular belief in eugenics, for as early as 1912, Governor Fletcher had vetoed a law passed by the General Assembly to permit sterilization. In 1926, Perkins lobbied hard for a similar measure to improve the state's human breeding stock, only to see it pass the House but fail in the Senate in early 1927. After this setback, he began to float his proposal for the rural survey, using his eugenics findings as a starting point, explaining his ideas to influential Vermonters, and seeking financial support from various foundations. Although at least one of his correspondents—Clarence Dempsey, the commissioner of education—worried that the findings might be "interpreted or misinterpreted as revealing a very deplorable state of affairs in Vermont and the conclusions might very easily be drawn that the State is disintegrating and deteriorating," Perkins forged ahead, and in June 1927, sought the backing of Governor Weeks.[24]

Four months later came the flood. To Perkins and his backers, the immense task of reconstruction not only pointed up the urgency of their work, but also presented them with a heaven-sent opportunity to develop a new and broader framework for their efforts. In February 1928, Perkins again approached the governor, who agreed to lend his name to the enterprise as chairman of the survey committee.[25] Some weeks later, Perkins wrote to a number of other notables, on the letterhead of the Eugenics Survey, asking them to join a group of roughly a hundred other "representative, progressive Vermonters" to discuss the problems of declining rural communities.

"The flood has made a difference to the whole population," he wrote, "and has opened up some new possibilities. You are anxious to see Vermont made—to help make Vermont—a better place in which to live."[26] Most of those invited appear to have responded favorably, although some—Luther Johnson of the *Randolph Herald and News* and Howard Hindley of the *Rutland Herald,* among them—begged off, pleading pressures of time (Hindley later joined). From New Hampshire, William Rossiter, who for years had studied rural decline in northern New England, agreed to serve, while expressing some impatience with the project. "[P]oor Vermont has been studied and classified as a curiosity long enough," he wrote; the problems were obvious, and the money would be better spent training and using experts to advance commerce, industry, and agriculture.[27]

After some delay, the organizational meeting took place in Burlington on 18 May 1928, addressed by, among others, Governor Weeks, Henry Perkins, President Guy Bailey of the University of Vermont, and Henry Israel of the American Country Life Association in New York. "It seems an opportune time for an investigation of this sort," Perkins told the gathering.

> The flood has changed the situation in Vermont more than most of us realized. Any great catastrophe brings a good many changes in its wake and that is true in this case. People are much more open minded and ready to consider calmly suggestions for improvement than they were a year ago. There is an alertness noticeable amongst our country people, a keen and intelligent interest in their particular problems. The inertia amounting almost to torpor of a generation ago is giving way.

Vermont, said the proposal circulated to the meeting, and presumably from Perkins's pen, was at a "critical period in its history," as modern improvements such as the automobile, the telephone, the radio, were all "making the country a less lonesome place to live." Nevertheless, the rural population continued to decline, and many of the young who left for school or college would never return (eighty years later the question of how to keep them in Vermont still concerns the state's government). Still, he was realistic about the goals; important as it was to revitalize rural living conditions, that did not mean trying "to induce people to return to every rural community or to rehabilitate every abandoned farm"; some of them should simply be let go.[28]

Thus was the Vermont Commission on Country Life constituted. As Perkins pointed out, it would not be starting afresh, but building on work already done by the Eugenics Survey, by various state agencies, and by other groups such as the American Medical Association, the Carnegie Foundation, and the Institute of Social and Religious Research, which had already looked into medical facilities, rural schools, and rural churches. But the information needed to be collated, systematized, and augmented. To do this, Perkins proposed dividing the study into eleven separate headings, reflecting various aspects of rural life, including questions of agriculture, politics, medicine, education, and religion, as well as the mental, ethnic or racial, and eugenic aspects of country life.

Funding came from the Social Sciences Research Council, while a three-year grant from the Laura Spelman Rockefeller Memorial provided $84,000 to cover the salary and office expenses of a director. By July 1928, Perkins had succeeded in having Henry Taylor of Northwestern University, a respected rural sociologist and economist, appointed as General Director of the Comprehensive Rural Survey. Taylor was, Perkins remembered later, the one man in the country of whom the Laura Spelman Rockefeller officers would have approved, and his salary was set at $10,000 a year—a substantial amount in those days, although lower than the $12,000 originally budgeted.[29] In 1929, by way of comparison, the governor's salary had just been raised from $3,000 to $5,000.

The strong eugenics component, which comprised three of Perkins's proposed eleven subjects of study, is hardly surprising, given the plan's provenance. The Commission, however, as it began the meetings that would continue over the next three years, took on a life of its own. While eugenics was by no means forgotten (it was subsumed by a committee dealing with "the Human Factor," chaired by President Paul Moody of Middlebury College), other aspects, such as agriculture, education, and a new venture into the study and conservation of Vermont traditions, became important as well. Perhaps the flood and the unfinished business of reconstruction had something to do with this change of emphasis; in any case, as Nancy Gallagher has concluded, most of the participants in the Commission seem to have been little interested in Perkins's eugenics agenda, and used the study instead to pursue other avenues of inquiry.[30]

As time went on, the number of committees varied, changing their names as the Commission changed its focus. There emerged, for example, a committee on a Vermont Foundation, to be established to help finance worthy projects in the state, as well as a very active Committee on the Conservation of Vermont Traditions and Ideals, chaired by Professor Arthur Peach of Norwich University, and containing such luminaries as the writer Dorothy Canfield Fisher and Sarah Cleghorn, the Quaker socialist who combined protest with poems depicting an idyllic Vermont. The number of participants, originally set at roughly a hundred, reached close to three hundred by the time the Commission was ready to report in 1931, though some seem to have lent little more than their names. Most were men prominent in business, public affairs, education, health care, or religion (they included two bishops, for instance, one Episcopal, one Catholic). While a few women held important roles, they were significantly underrepresented and, as Marion Gary of Rutland pointed out later (she chaired the committee on education), the committees on agriculture, on religious forces, and on the Vermont Foundation had no female members, despite the important role played by women in local church affairs, in farm life, and in economic matters.[31]

Not surprisingly, the agricultural committee—or, to give it its proper name, the Committee on the Farm Production and Marketing Program—chaired by Elbert Brigham, was the largest group. Made up of fifty-four men, it spent much time discussing the need to stabilize the economic basis of farming in the face of increased competition. When one member, John Candon of Pittsford, suggested that young men and women could be kept on the farm by "emphasizing the beauty of Vermont, its scenery, the fresh air, the fact that we have plenty of elbow room . . . those things which cannot be bought with dollars and cents," Brigham rather testily reminded him that such talk had gone on for half a century, "and still our young people have been leaving Vermont . . . we must go a step farther and give them a satisfactory economic opportunity."[32] The Committee on Religious Forces, chaired by Bishop Samuel Booth of the Protestant Episcopal Church, discovered, rather to its surprise, how many unchurched there were in certain parts of the state, and looked at ways of revitalizing local congregations. A Committee on Summer Residence and Tourism examined ways to bring in those from beyond the state, while other committees discussed such matters as rural education, health, medical care, and forestry.

And, of course, closest to Perkins's heart, no doubt, was Paul Moody's Committee on the Human Factor, which, among other things, looked at the effects of immigration.

> What sort of Vermonters do the French Canadians or the Finns make? [asked an article of 1929 in the Commission's Newsletter.] What numbers must be added to the United States Census reports on the numbers of French-Canadians, Finns, etc. in order to show the second generation derivations? This question of course implies that in some racial groups more than others there is a tendency to hurry into Americanism, representing themselves as being Americans whereas they have but recently migrated from some other country.[33]

Given the relative paucity of Finns in Vermont, the phrasing seems thoroughly disingenuous, for the real question here evidently had to do with the French-Canadians (who were almost totally unrepresented on the Commission). The suggestion appeared to be that even the native born, if they were of French-Canadian parents, were somehow less than complete Americans ("the whole of the French-Canadian population could be wiped out of Middlebury and no one would miss it," Perkins remembered President Paul Moody once telling him). Such jaundiced attitudes were not uncommon, and Nancy Gallagher has concluded that the unflattering views of Vermonters of Quebec origin put forth by the writer Rowland E. Robinson some years earlier provided part of the defining narrative of the original Eugenics Survey and were carried over into the Commission's work. Perkins, in fact, had hoped to make a special study of French-Canadians part of the rural survey's work, pursuing the suggestions of Charles Davenport of the Carnegie Institute that Vermont's "subnormalcy" might well have been due to the replacement of native stock by this particular alien race, but was unable to find the special funding for it he sought.[34]

Although Perkins, for political reasons, played no overt role in the successful movement to get the new sterilization measure through the legislature in 1931, he had been active behind the scenes. This time, the law's proponents did their homework more carefully, avoiding the legal pitfalls that had tripped them up earlier, and with the full support of Governor Wilson (who had given the move his backing in his opening address to the lawmakers), the bill went through both houses in March 1931 and was signed into law on 1 April.[35]

The Country Life Commission's connections with other American regionalist movements can be seen most clearly in the Committee on the Conservation of Vermont Ideals, one of the most active and best publicized of the subgroups. "Throw out the radio and take the fiddle down from the wall," Andrew Lytle, one of the contributors to *I'll Take My Stand,* the manifesto of the Southern Agrarians, had written.[36] Although no one was quite urging that step in Vermont, something of the same spirit underlay the committee's work—as in its view that Vermont's villages, once among its "chief glories," might once again "come into their own and develop an existence highly distinctive and thoroughly enviable" (379).

Even before the Commission published its final report, Arthur Peach's group had already brought out four volumes of what it called the Green Mountain Series—one each for Vermont prose, Vermont poetry, Vermont ballads and folk songs (compiled by Helen Hartness Flanders, one of the pioneers of the scholarly study of American folk music), and a book of biographies of notable Vermonters, edited by Walter Crockett. In this endeavor, Peach and his colleagues were continuing a long Vermont interest in the preservation of history and tradition, going back at least as far as Zadock Thompson's state history of 1833, and continued by, among others, Walter Crockett himself in his *Vermont: The Green Mountain State,* whose five volumes had appeared in the early twenties. In the mid-nineteenth century, in fact, the redoubtable Abby Maria Hemenway had constituted herself a one-woman committee on the preservation of Vermont ideals, for her collection of *Vermont Poets and Poetry* in 1858 had been followed by the monumental *Vermont Historical Gazetteer,* a five volume compendium of the histories of all the state's towns, undertaken to record the accomplishments of Vermont's earliest generations of white inhabitants.[37]

Reviewers greeted the Green Mountain Series with a mixture of surprise and restrained enthusiasm. Stewart Mitchell's notice in the *New England Quarterly,* for instance, reported his pleasant surprise at finding in *Vermont Poetry* "how much good verse the editors were able to rake into their volume" from a population smaller than that of Boston, but still he reminded his readers of Dr. Johnson's famous comparison of women preaching to dogs walking on their hind legs. A dismissive review of *Vermonters: A Book of Biographies* by Eda Lou Walton in the *Nation*, was notable for the biting rejoinder it drew from Sinclair Lewis, at the time a resident of Barnard. Despite "the inevitable Calvin Coolidge and Robert Frost," Walton rather sniffily suggested, the most interesting passages had to do with the lives of such pioneers as Ethan Allen and Walter H. Crockett. "Here is vivid history."[38]

"Vivid history indeed!" replied Lewis, gleefully pointing out that Crockett, born in 1870, was a professor at the University of Vermont, and wondering (like many wounded authors) whether Walton had even bothered to read the book she was reviewing. What of Chester Arthur, he asked, or Admiral Dewey, and Ira Dutton, who became Brother Joseph of Molokai? What of Thaddeus Fairbanks, Hiram Powers, William Morris Hunt, and various other worthies?

> I should have thought that a writer for a magazine with the purposes of *The Nation* would have had sense enough to see that here was, ready-made, an extraordinary study of the effect on character of living amidst a sturdy and not over-crowded folk. . . .
> Is this no news—not perhaps, for a New York tabloid, but for such an audience as that of *The Nation?* A State, not rich, not boosting and peppy, has made an effort to understand itself better by collecting and recording its own history, with no help whatever from outside millionaire "Foundations."[39]

Almost four years after the flood, and three years after its founding, in mid-June 1931, the Commission celebrated the completion of the first phase of its work by holding a three-day-long public meeting at the University of Vermont's gymnasium in Burlington. The audience of some two hundred people seems rather small, and raises the question of how many others besides the Commission's members were present. Perkins, stepping in for an absent Paul Moody, led off with the report of the Committee on the Human Factor, sounding rather more optimistic than one might expect, pointing out that even though the state's foreign-born were increasing more rapidly than the American-born, there was still "plenty of good stock among the foreign born in the State."[40] Perhaps so, although that is hardly the impression a reader might carry away from the later written report. The summaries of other chairmen followed over the course of the next two days, although there's no evidence that the audience grew any larger. On the other hand, despite a sky threatening rain, some two thousand people turned out for the presentation of Sarah Cleghorn's pageant, "Coming Vermont," at the university's Centennial Field. Set fifty years in the future, "Coming Vermont" had three scenes, depicting life at home, at school, and in church in 1981, in which characters with names such as Mr. and Mrs. Homestead, Grandfather and Grandmother Homestead, Mr. and Mrs. Summerfolk, and various other members of the family, joined by some ghosts from the past, reflected on the enormously beneficial changes that had taken place over the last half-century (Lindbergh, Lenin, and Gandhi were among the out-of-staters favorably mentioned by the author).[41]

Shortly thereafter, the Commission published its work in *Rural Vermont: A Program for the Future,* "by Two Hundred Vermonters." The preface, however, speaks of the Commission as "made up of about three hundred progressive citizens of the state," and gives John Weeks's rather unhelpful definition of "progressive" as meaning "those who strive for 'the furtherance of our present ideals in life and the ideals that may grow out of our activities'" (2). Three hundred and eighty-three pages long, *Rural Vermont* consisted of reports by the eighteen final committees, and usually, but not always, included a set of recommendations from each for the future. Some were eminently practicable, and indeed had been talked about for some time: encouraging summer tourism, improving the state's roads (surprisingly enough there was no mention of the railroads), overhauling the state's educational system, and in particular studying the way it was financed (a subject that continues to roil Vermont eighty years later). Others covered such subjects as the reorganization of medical services, the provision of more and better recreational opportunities, better facilities for agricultural marketing and production, and better facilities for the care of the handicapped and the feeble-minded. Although the recent sterilization act was mentioned here only in passing, a "eugenics addendum" by Perkins called for the "strict enforcement of our laws governing marriage of defectives and other such measures as are calculated to check the multiplication of the unfit" (303–304). Some of the Commission's other recommendations not only appear extraordinary today, but did so at the time. This was particularly true of the Committee on Citizenship, chaired by Charles Plumley, president of Norwich University (and future congressman), which advised that suffrage be restricted to those who had achieved a certain educational level (340). They also recommended a unicameral legislature of roughly fifty members, and this, whether or not a good idea, would have marked an enormous break with tradition (342–43).

On the whole, the notices given to *Rural Vermont,* both in the state and beyond it, were favorable.[42] Inevitably, some readers missed the point, like the reviewers in the *New York Herald-Tribune* and the *New England Quarterly,* both of whom suggested that Vermonters were— commendably—seeking to turn their backs on the last century and a half of history. The *Boston Herald* praised *Rural Vermont* as the work of "two hundred Vermonters" rather than outside experts, but the *Evening Transcript* worried that the failure of Vermonters to breed in adequate numbers might suggest "race suicide . . . down on the farm" (though in fact *Rural Vermont's* concerns had less to do with the failure of Vermonters to reproduce themselves than with the failure of the "old stock" to do so). Writing in the *Journal of the American Association of University Women,* Marion Gary, who had chaired the committee on rural education, praised the exercise as an example of thinking by a group of "serious and progressive" people, studying themselves and their institutions in order to draw up goals based on scientific planning for the future. Vermonters, she concluded, had asked themselves "perplexing questions . . . They have envisioned possibilities which are much more than dreams and which give fresh courage."

Within the state, the report's reception, rather surprisingly, was mixed. Several papers—including Luther Johnson's *Randolph Herald,* as well as the *Bennington Banner*—asked whether the time and expense had been worth it, and suggested that entirely too much money had gone to outside experts (presumably meaning Henry Taylor, the Northwestern professor who had directed the study). The *Brattleboro Reformer,* however, praised it as "one of the most valuable books ever published with regard to Vermont, or in regard to country life," while admitting that the recommendations for limited suffrage and for a unicameral legislature were too radical even to be considered, let alone adopted. The *Burlington Free Press* and *Rutland Herald* praised it, and the *Burlington Clipper* rather nastily suggested that Johnson's criticisms reflected his bitterness in not having been asked to join the commission (in fact he had twice been asked and twice refused).

Perhaps the most searching review came from John P. Clement of the Vermont Historical Society, who found the report "an outstanding contribution to the State and its people, the value of which is beyond any possibility of comprehension." If it were to become outdated because its recommendations had been accepted, its compilers might be well pleased; and if its recommendations were ignored, it would be useless, "because the old Vermont will have sunk into oblivion, beyond all hope of revival."

Not that *Rural Vermont* was beyond criticism. Some of the committee reports, Clement continued, were better than others, some of the recommendations were practical, while others were only "pious hopes." The report failed to grapple with the question of costs. Yet if its recommendations in such fields as education, recreation, and the care of the defective and indigent were put into effect, there would be an enormous and expensive growth of officialdom. Finally, Clement distrusted what he considered the report's unqualified praise for all individuals, all officials and their agencies, and all religious groups, which, in its search to avoid controversy, seemed "to rob the work of much of its critical value." Not that he himself was willing to specify from which groups or individuals the praise should be withdrawn. Elsewhere, Henry Perkins himself admitted that the Commission had steered clear of those aspects of rural life that were "dangerous politically or were already well taken care of by existing agencies."[43]

In retrospect, whatever one thinks of *Rural Vermont* as a piece of state planning, for the historian it gives a snapshot of Vermont, or at least of agrarian and small-town Vermont as seen by a particular, self-selected group of state leaders, taken at a time when it was possible to begin to understand the effects of the flood. In that sense, it is representative, if not of Vermont as a whole, at least of those who defined themselves as "progressives," the ones who were educated, who had access to the state's financial and public relations resources, the ones who were the makers of opinion. What remains unclear, of course, is how far other Vermonters, particularly those rural dwellers for whom the report claimed to speak, would have regarded the picture as one reflecting their own particular realities.

In addition to some of the criticisms made at the time, several other facets of the study strike the reader today. First, there was in *Rural Vermont* virtually no mention of industry, apart from very brief treatments of wood and woodworking. Not surprising, perhaps, given the purposes of the original rural survey. Yet while on the one hand, the Commission tried to be forward looking, denying that it wanted to repopulate every declining village or return every abandoned farm to production, it also reflected the view that Vermont's future would be an agricultural one. Thus it seems never to have considered seriously the ways in which light rural industry might help keep people on the land or at least in the smaller towns. Indeed, the work closes with a quotation from a speech by President John Thomas of Middlebury in 1913, calling for Vermont's return to its agricultural heritage.

Second, while many of the "progressive Vermonters" went their own ways, pursuing their own agendas, the eugenic origins of the Commission remain unmistakable. As others have pointed out, there is more than a hint of nostalgia about the need to revivify the "old stock," and both implicitly and explicitly, *Rural Vermont* reflected the belief that Vermont's regeneration must come from that stock. John Thomas's words eighteen years earlier, with which the report closes (from the Committee on the Conservation of Ideals) give clear evidence of this.

> The old stock is here still, in greater proportion to the total population than in any other commonwealth of the north. The old spirit is by no means dead. All we need is organization, the power and habit of working together for a fixed and determined purpose. And all we need for organization is leadership—leaders who see the goal plain, and who will consecrate themselves to its attaining in high patriotic devotion.[44]

Whether such language represents a crippling defect or not, whether it represents a kind of ethnocentrism or nativism, is a matter of interpretation; the point for the historian is that such a belief was probably a generally accurate representation of the collective mind of the two or three hundred Vermonters who drew up the report.

Third, there are a number of other aspects of the state that one might have expected the Commission to address. The silence about railroads has already been noted, despite their still vital importance in getting Vermont goods to market, and despite all the enthusiasm that had greeted their restoration in 1928 and 1929 (Sarah Cleghorn's pageant of "Coming Vermont," on the other hand, predicted the end of Vermont's railways by 1945). While electricity is mentioned in passing as a desirable aspect of rural home life (162), nothing is said of the slowness of rural electrification in Vermont or the ways in which the process might be hastened. Yet at the time this was a topic of rapidly growing interest to the state's farmers, and particularly to the Vermont Farm Bureau. Only 30 percent of farms had access to power in 1930, and while the number was well above the national average of 13 percent, it was the lowest in

New England, and the real drive for electrification was going to have to wait for the New Deal and the governorship of George Aiken.[45]

Finally, there is in the entire work virtually no mention of the flood. As the Commission was being formed in 1928, Perkins had insisted on the flood's importance, the very extent of the catastrophe forcing Vermonters into new ways of thinking, devising new approaches to old problems. Marion Gary echoed this, pointing to the flood's role in firing Vermonters "with new impulses for progress." Yet Perkins had begun his organizational work before the flood, and even if it had never occurred, would have tried to advance his rural survey as a means of continuing his eugenic studies. Without the flood, however, and the new ways of thinking that it encouraged, the conclusions reached might well have been rather different from those found in *Rural Vermont,* and it may be that the elements of nostalgia and the desire to return to the past might have been even stronger than they were.

Or would they? For if we consider *Rural Vermont* not simply as a planning document standing on its own, but as part of Vermont's post-flood reconstruction, the emphasis on tradition takes on a new meaning. Perhaps it was not simply an exercise in nostalgia or a fear of the changes that modernity might bring. Perhaps it was, rather, a sense of pride, not simply in Vermont's past, but in its present as well. For it had been precisely those traditional qualities that Vermonters valued in themselves and outsiders often valued in them that the state had drawn on in its Herculean efforts at rebuilding. Self-reliance, independence, the ability to cope with the unexpected, the ability to sacrifice, to join with one's neighbors in a common effort—these were precisely the qualities that had made reconstruction possible. In this sense, while the flood by itself may not have called the commission into existence, the memories of those November days run as a subtext beneath the questions that it asked and the ways in which it answered them.

It is beyond the purview of this book to consider how far the the Commission's study did or did not affect the future development of the state. It is easy enough to be critical of some of its assumptions and omissions, and particularly its more than occasional nostalgic backward glances. On the other hand, it surely helped at least to make acceptable the idea of planning (and thus to meet some of the kinds of outspoken criticisms that the urban planner John Nolen, for example, had leveled against the state a year earlier). Richard Judd, in his study of the New Deal in Vermont, has high praise for the Commission's work, even suggesting that its outlook "resemble[d] closely the human-itarian concerns of Franklin and Eleanor Roosevelt, Harry Hopkins, Frances Perkins, Rexford G. Tugwell, and other prominent figures of the first two Roosevelt administrations." Thus, he concludes that, over a year before Roosevelt was swept into power, *Rural Vermont* presented Vermonters with "a sweeping program for social development through political action." Kevin Dann, too, suggests that "to an astonishing ex-tent the recommendations of the VCCL committees prophesied the di-rection the state would take in the next half century," and he cites a land-use law, the banning of billboards, and the considerable development of the tourist industry.[46]

Perhaps so. But perhaps, for all its virtues, *Rural Vermont* cannot bear quite that much weight. It's noteworthy that in 1935, a year after the es-tablishment of the new State Planning Commission (of which Nolen, incidentally, was a member), the *Graphic Survey* issued by that body re-ferred to itself as "a first step in State Planning," and, while traversing much the same ground as the Commission on Country Life, made no mention of *Rural Vermont,* save for a glancing reference to "two hun-dred enlightened Vermont spokesmen" who sought a plan of proper land utilization. Even Henry Perkins, writing a brief notice in *Vermont History* a quarter of a century later, while citing the "incalculable im-portance" of having brought leading Vermonters together to discuss the state's future, in the end seemed hard put to mention any contributions apart from the publication of the Green Mountain Series and the emer-gence of rural bookwagons.[47]

Although Judd shows little interest in the eugenic origins of *Rural Vermont,* to Nancy Gallagher, not surprisingly, that aspect constitutes the Commissions's tragic flaw, a view earlier implied by Kevin Dann.[48] Far from laying out a future course for the state, the Commission, in their eyes, was hampered by its reverence for the "old stock" that had earlier peopled the state, and thus it was at least partly an exercise in nostalgia, calling up a Vermont that in some ways owed more to histori-cal memory than to historical reality. It's worth noting, moreover, that when the State Planning Commission issued its *Graphic Survey* in 1935, this older tone had entirely vanished.

The Commission on Country Life's work and its report need further study from the historians, in particular for the ways in which it af-fected, or failed to affect, the state's later history and development. In any case, the appearance of *Rural Vermont* in the summer of 1931 makes a convenient stopping place for this study. The report was certainly intended to be widely read, a copy given to every library in the state, although a few years later, a project to reprint it came to nothing, presumably for financial reasons. However much the Commission's work was influenced by the experience of reconstruction after the flood, by the time their report came out, the ravages of the Winooski and White rivers had been supplanted by the greater and longer-lasting ravages of the Depression. One can argue over the question of whether the state and the nation that emerged after 1945 owes more to the New Deal or, as Ellis Hawley suggests, to a kind of modernized Hooverism, but that is not our purpose here. For the historian, *Rural Vermont,* whatever may be its shortcomings or its strengths, is above all a historical document that, carefully read, can teach us a great deal about Vermont and views of Vermont as they were held in those first years after the deluge.

7

Conclusion

The Flood of 1927 in History and Memory

"The flood is now ancient history," Edward Rockwood's *Vermont Review* told its readers in the summer of 1928. "Like the World War, it is a catastrophe which all who experienced its hardships are eager to forget . . . What Vermonters now want is that there should rise from the debris of their inundation, a new Vermont, virile with young blood and pregnant with new opportunities."[1] Quite apart from the question of what a "virile pregnancy" might be, the writer overstated the case, for not everywhere was the disaster quite so easily forgotten. Throughout 1928, Vermont newspapers were filled with stories about reconstruction, applauding the speed with which the state took hold of its recovery. Meanwhile, a valuable series of articles began to appear in the *Vermonter*, describing the ravages of the flood in the state's different regions. "Vermont has had a terrible experience in the past year," Stanley Wilson told a group of pilgrims at the Rockingham Meeting House in August 1928, "but it may yet be worth what it cost in lives and money, if it brings a renewal of the pioneer spirit and the casting aside of non-essentials" (he foresaw, he told his listeners, the dawning of a new age of Puritanism). In late February, however, the Peacham-born George Harvey, a former ambassador to London, took issue with Governor Weeks's optimistic view of Vermont's recovery, predicting that the state had "a long pull ahead," and would feel the effects of the flood for a quarter-century.[2]

When these assessments were made, it was still impossible to draw up an accurate balance sheet showing the flood's effects, and even today, some questions remain. The damage surveys were important, of course. But they are incomplete and leave much unsaid. Nor do they tell us about the losses in trade suffered by disrupted farms, businesses, and industries. The toll taken on highway and rail communications is clear enough, as is the rough cost of the repairs to those lines. Given the sketchiness of some of the evidence, if we ask about lasting damage, we are on much shakier ground. Take the farmers, for instance. In December 1927, the Department of Agriculture in Washington, while noting that the flood had been particularly destructive to some of the state's most highly productive farms, predicted that few farmers would leave the land because of it. A year later, Agriculture Commissioner E. H. Jones, estimating farm damage at $2 million, including the losses of houses, barns, outbuildings, livestock, and poultry, warned that "a considerable portion of the flooded land [was a] . . . total and permanent loss." But neither in that report, nor in his next one in 1930, is there any indication of how many farmers actually lost their livelihood for good because of the flood, or went into other lines of work, or left the state entirely.[3]

Of course, we lack certain vital records. Those from the Red Cross, for instance, which would tell us something of the circumstances of people to whom awards were made, seem simply to have vanished. So, apparently, have those of the state's Chamber of Commerce. Still, if permanent destruction and dislocation of Vermont's commercial and industrial establishments were widespread, one might expect more evidence than we actually have. A check of *Walton's Register,* which served, among other things, as a state-wide business directory, shows very little change between 1926 and 1929 in the names of concerns in such badly damaged towns as Waterbury and Johnson, and the same is true of the larger cities of Montpelier and Rutland. The number of applications for help to the Vermont Flood Credit Corporation—thirty-eight—seems surprisingly small, although, as suggested earlier, that may be due to a reluctance to assume more debt, to the efficacy of Red Cross help, or indeed to the vaunted disinclination of Vermonters to accept "charity." A few of the firms that had recourse to the VTFCC ultimately defaulted on their debts, but it would be hard to say whether the flood or the Depression—or, for that matter, changes brought by the automobile—were at fault (one of the defaulters, the Nantanna Woolen Mills of Northfield, was bought in the late 1930s by the Boston entrepreneur Bernard Goldfine, and went on to produce the briefly famous vicuna coat appearing at the center of a minor political scandal of the fifties). Furthermore, the *Burlington Free Press* and the *Rutland Herald,* the state's two main dailies, are virtually silent on the subject of farms, industries, or commercial establishments permanently closed down by the flood's effects.

Perhaps that's not surprising, given the papers' invariably optimistic coverage of reconstruction and rehabilitation, yet the town histories also say little of such matters.

Did people actually flee the state after November 1927? What are we to make, for instance, of the report in the *New York Times*—quoting town officials—that, within days of the flood, fully a quarter of Waterbury's population had left to seek, if not greener, at least drier, pastures? There's no question that posters were put up appealing to people to stay and help rebuild the town; but if 25 percent of them really had left they must have returned or been replaced just as quickly. Vermont's 1930 census figures, though showing the failure of the state's population to grow, tell us nothing; there had been virtually no increase for some decades before that, and the slight decline appearing in 1940 surely had more to do with the Great Depression than the flood.

None of this means that the flood was in fact less destructive than it appeared at the time (the enormous damage done to communication lines is proof of that). Rather, it speaks to the resilience of communities and individuals, particularly in a small and relatively homogeneous setting, to recover from disaster. A little village like Gaysville might in fact never return to its earlier state. But Gaysville was an exception. Elsewhere, Vermonters pulled themselves together, cleaned up the mess, repaired or rebuilt what had been shattered, and though many must have felt like Nettie Nichols of Middlesex, when she wrote in those gloomy November days, "we simply exist, we don't live," they went back to the business of living.

If we turn to what did happen rather than what did not, perhaps we can see more easily the flood's effects. Still, they must be examined with the caveat that in many cases the disaster acted simply as a catalyst for changes already underway. Take, for example, the effects of the vast new highway construction program. With or without the flood, Vermont would have developed a system of modern roads, though surely not with the speed made possible by the injection of almost $12 million of new money in the two years following the disaster. The new highways hastened the decline of small towns and marginal communities, and hastened also the decline of the railways. But such declines were already evident after the Great War, and in any case were national phenomena, by no means restricted to Vermont or New England.

Nor would it be too difficult to suggest that the most tangible political result of the flood—the end of the single-term tradition for the governor—would have taken place in any case. In the minds of many it was already outdated and an obstacle to governmental efficiency. The flood was the occasion, rather than the cause, of its death. Consider also the way that new highway construction, under state auspices, hastened the encroachment of Montpelier's political authority in local affairs. But local town independence was already waning well before 1927. As the *Free Press* noted at the time, the towns had often made a great fuss over losing their autonomy "if the State were allowed to have any finger whatever in the local road mud pie." Now, however, lured by the prospect of modern highways and bridges, they were becoming perhaps almost too anxious to see Montpelier come in and take over such matters, even if it meant accepting the imposition of conditions by outsiders.[4] Ten years earlier, Vermont had been quick to understand the advantages of the Federal Aid Roads Act of 1916, and now within the state itself, Vermont reflected national trends, as power and influence moved from small towns and villages toward a larger center.

Yet when Rockwood suggested that people wanted to put the flood behind them, he was by no means entirely wrong. A brief editorial in the *Burlington Free Press* commemorated the flood's first anniversary in November 1928, but the *Rutland Herald* barely mentioned what had happened, preferring to devote its pages to the national election that would take place three days later ("If Jesus Lived in Rutland, What Would He Do On Election Day?" asked the Rev. Leon B. Randall in his Sunday sermon; although no names were mentioned, it is clear that the Lord would be most unlikely to cast his ballot for Al Smith).[5] One looks in vain through such papers for retrospective articles in 1932, five years after the event, although John Weeks, now a congressman, reminded his audience that just as Hoover's arrival within days of the flood had saved Vermont, so too as president he would now save the country from its economic distress, if only granted a second term. The *Vermonter,* however, let the fifth and tenth anniversaries of the flood pass unnoticed. Both the *Burlington Free Press* and the *Rutland Herald* did rather better in 1937, the former paper taking a careful look at the state's progress since the flood, and concluding that the great surge of road building that followed had brought Vermont as a tourist state into modern times. The *Herald,* for its part, told the dramatic story—nowhere supported by evidence, unfortunately—of a boatload of reporters making their way to Governor Weeks's hotel in Montpelier, and, when asking him what help he needed, being told firmly that Vermont would take care of her own.[6]

Nor, if one leaves the periodicals, is the retrospective look at the flood in the years that immediately followed it much better. When Luther Johnson's invaluable *Vermont in Floodtime* appeared in early 1928, the author made it clear that his book was simply a preliminary gathering of information, a help for future historians, who some day would draw up a more complete record (he thoughtfully included the verbal sketch of a "historical pageant" of the flood that some day would be set forth by "a skilled painter"). Shortly thereafter, Lloyd Squier's record of the flood in Waterbury came out, as did those of Charles Walter about St. Johnsbury and Dean Perry about Barre. To them can be added a few others: brief descriptions of the flood in Springfield and Northfield, for instance, or a collection of photographs of Montpelier under water.

That is about all. "I think the Vermont Historical Society ought to assemble all available material concerning the flood," wrote Walter Crockett to John Spargo two weeks after the event. "I believe that our Society ought to be the authoritative source for material which can be consulted by historical writers in the future." A laudable sentiment; but it was never followed, any more than was the Commission on Country Life's recommendation for a "determined search" through attics and trunks for historical records.[7] Nor have Vermont historians done much better in the eight decades since the waters poured over the state. A handful of articles, often dealing with memories of the flood, have appeared in *Vermont History,* but little analytical work has been done. Far better in trying to arrive at some estimate of the flood's effects are the more recent general histories, such as *The Star that Set,* Samuel Hand's passage through the fortunes of Vermont Republicanism, or *Freedom and Unity,* the survey of Vermont history that appeared in 2004. In 2003, William Minsinger of the Blue Hill Observatory in Massachusetts, and the author of works dealing with such weather disasters as the New England hurricane of 1938, published a brief but valuable book that sought to pull together the various strands of flood history, and to separate fact from fiction.

And, finally, in estimating the flood's effects, we must not forget its literary resonances. "The Whisperer in Darkness," H. P. Lovecraft's account in *Weird Tales* of 1931, records the appearance of "strange shapes . . . that were not human, despite some superficial resemblances," washed down from the hills by the waters, to strike terror into the hearts of Vermonters. Many years later, Howard Frank Mosher's 1978 novella *Where the Rivers Flow North,* its story set against the spread of the giant power companies, reaches its climax with the coming of the flood (although the rains arrive after an unhistorical, if metaphorically apt, five-month drought).

"There was a finality about the 1927 flood that old timers recall and speak of with awe," writes Cora Cheney, "as if it closed a book on an old way of life, balanced the accounts, and began a new series."[8] She was not alone in seeing 1927 as a year that divided Vermont history in two. Even if it is true that in 1928 people wanted to put the flood behind them, public interest in the disaster seemed, if anything, to grow over the years. For the twenty-fifth anniversary in 1952 and the fiftieth in 1977, *Vermont Life* published articles that, short though they were, were more than either it or its predecessor, *The Vermonter,* had done for prior anniversaries. In 1952, the *Free Press* ran only a brief editorial and a short story on a commemorative gathering at Waterbury, but the *Rutland Herald* did rather better, as it did again in 1977, when it gave extensive coverage to anniversary events in Waterbury, Rutland, Barre, and Montpelier (by this time, interestingly enough, the remark that "Vermont can take care of its own" had vanished). The fiftieth anniversary also brought the publication of Patricia Belding's invaluable interviews with flood survivors in Barre, which shed additional light, among other things, on the way that Lieutenant-Governor Jackson had met his death. At the time of the seventy-fifth anniversary in 2002, the Waterbury Historical Society published a series of reminiscences of the flood and held a community dinner in the Congregational church to recall the role played by that institution. Although neither the Burlington nor the Rutland papers saw fit to mention the flood that year, Governor Howard Dean proclaimed 3 November as a day of commemoration, and a large gathering met at the University of Vermont under the sponsorship of the Center for Research on Vermont and the National Weather Service, to examine the ways in which the disaster had affected the state, and the ways in which it had become such a significant part of Vermont's historical memory.

Thus Vermonters have kept the popular memory alive, even if the historians have perhaps not done as much as they might have. Still, it has been one of the burdens of this book to suggest that an event like the flood of 1927 needs to be put not just in the context of the history of a particular state (and a tiny one, at that) but more generally in the history of the United States as it passed through the sometimes turbulent and worrying years of the 1920s. This is true, we have suggested, not just because what was happening in Vermont mirrored national trends at the time, but also because of what "Vermont" meant back then, both to Vermonters and to those other observers who found the state, in an era of uncertainty, a storehouse of traditional American ways and values.

To such people, Vermont remained, every bit as much after the flood as before it, a place where the old values and the old stock lived on, a place to be visited when one needed reassurance that there was at least one part of America remaining faithful to its heritage and tradition, while so much of the rest of the country was caught up in a rootless whirl of urbanization, expansion, and restless change. Vermonters in the 1920s were quite canny enough to see the value of playing the role demanded of them, and remained so in later years. Yet they also wished to live in the modern world, and saw no reason to deny themselves the fruits of progress, such as modern highways and other forms of communication. Like so many modernizers, before and since, they wanted to believe that they could take the tools of modernity and progress—highways, industry, technology, and so forth—pressing them into service to shore up traditional ways and traditional values. "Chinese learning for the base, western learning for utility," ran the slogan of reforming statesmen in Beijing and Shanghai in the later nineteenth century, before it became clear that modern science and technology were not quite as value-free as they had once seemed. In this sense, far from being exceptionalist, Vermont was participating in a story that goes well beyond the borders of the state, or even the nation: the engagement with modernity, the debate over what it means, and how far, if at all, it can be reconciled with tradition.

Such questions remain as difficult as ever today. The flood, however, sweeping over a depressed and stagnant Vermont, by its very force and destructiveness gave people a chance to show the kind of grit and gumption and self-reliance they liked to believe set them apart from so much of the rest of the country. In a famous article many years ago, John William Ward wrote of Lindbergh, the "Lone Eagle," who seemed the very incarnation of the American virtues of individualism and courage, as he battled his way across the stormy North Atlantic in a tiny plane.[9] So too, Vermont seemed to be in those days the incarnation of individualism and courage and self-reliance, in the way it met the devastation caused by the flood and took up the work of rebuilding, calling on the very virtues that were its traditional pride. As Ward points out, though, whatever Lindbergh's individualism, the *Spirit of St. Louis* was the work of many hands all over the country, a triumph of modern American industrial and technological know-how (even encompassing the machine tools of Springfield, Vermont, as the *Rutland Herald* pointed out at the time). So too, Vermont's rebuilding, emblematic as it seemed of the determinedly individualistic character of Vermonters, was the work of many hands and many resources, both inside and outside the state. Here too, in its willingness to seek and accept aid from many different quarters, the reconstruction helped prepare Vermont for the coming of the New Deal.

If the way in which Vermont met the disaster of the flood can tell us something of the nation's passage through the 1920s, what might this sort of retrospective look suggest about the ways with which we cope with such crises today?

First, some obvious points. Rebuilding to a normal level of existence in 1927 was plainly a lot simpler than it is today, when some of our necessities of life would have seemed unimaginable luxuries back then. Loss of electric power, for example, meant little to the many who never had it in the first place, and the disruption of transportation and communication was mitigated by a greater degree of self-sufficiency with regard to commodities like food or fuel. Quite apart from Vermont's much-vaunted traditions of self-reliance and independence, expectations of help from the outside, and particularly from the government, were far lower then than they are today. "The Government is not an insurer of its citizens against the hazards of the elements," Coolidge told Congress in his state of the union speech in December 1927, and while Washington should provide relief when states and municipalities were overburdened, "this, however, does not mean restoration."[10] A few years later, of course, came the beginning of a variety of state and federal programs to meet not only the needs of emergency relief, but of longer term reconstruction and rehabilitation as well. The Housing Act of 1937, for instance, included provisions for rebuilding after disaster; the 1968 Flood Insurance Act offered assistance to homeowners; and in 1974, the Federal Disaster Assistance Program was established, a precursor to the Federal Emergency Management Agency (FEMA) in 1979. These are simply a few examples, cited to illustrate the ways in which, as Ted Steinberg puts it, "the long arm and deep pockets of the federal government assumed an ever greater share of the costs associated with natural calamity," ways simply undreamed of by the actors in the dramas of 1927.[11]

Today, such programs supplement or indeed overshadow the kind of response earlier expected of individuals, who in 1927 looked first to their communities for help, only learning later of what might come from a national organization like the Red Cross, or indeed, the federal government. The existence of such resources also obviously changes considerably the ways in which we prepare for disaster and the expectations we have of help. But other kinds of change besides the institutional also illuminate the differences between then and now. Take, for instance, two items found in the *New York Times* of 26 September 2005. One is a report raising the question of possible abuses in the awarding of contracts for cleanup and reconstruction in the wake of hurricanes Katrina and Rita, which struck the Gulf coast that year. The other is an advertisement from the Washington Legal Foundation, complaining about the "gangs of class action lawyers" descending on New Orleans and the nearby countryside to sue hospitals and nursing homes, preparing "to profit from one of the worst national disasters in American history."[12]

More interesting than the truth of such allegations is the way in which they reflect certain kinds of contemporary responses to disaster, and what these responses tell us about changes in the eighty years since Vermont's great flood. The burden of these two items is that certain people try to profit from the misfortunes of others. Although perhaps no one can be blamed for bringing on hurricanes, floods, tsunamis, or earthquakes, we can and do fault those who fail to prepare adequately for disaster or are deaf to the warnings of experts, who show incompetence and inadequacy in their responses, or who may be engaged in plain and simple profiteering.

The contrast with 1927 could not be more striking. Consider first the sense of trust in institutions: in government, in the churches, in the organizations, formal and informal, national, state, and local, that surrounded us then. Search the newspapers, the journals, the public statements of leaders, and of opinion makers, and you will find little of the kinds of fault-finding evident in 2005. It is easy to say, of course, that such voices back then represented those of the establishment, interested in shoring up the structures that served them so well. Yet if we turn to other voices, to those found in private correspondence, or in the recorded memories of flood survivors, the generalization still holds.

It's not that no one at the time was speaking out against, for instance, the croneyism and corruption of the Harding administration,

the contested executions of Sacco and Vanzetti, or the do-nothing attitude of the Coolidge administration in the face of the Mississippi disaster. It's not even as if the distrust between the small towns and Montpelier suddenly vanished—look at the defeat of Crockett's highway bill in
1929, for instance. But at least as far as Vermont's own catastrophe was
concerned, there was virtually no finger-pointing. There was no attempt
to blame those who had built the dams that gave way that night, sending
the waters rushing down through towns and villages. Although flooding
was hardly unusual in Vermont, there was no attempt to blame Montpelier (or Washington) for a lack of preparedness or an inadequate response. In public, at least, the Red Cross came in for nothing but praise,
and even those who had misgivings about the quality and quantity of
their work generally kept silent—journalists included—or took up the
problems in confidence with Red Cross leaders themselves. No lawyers
drove through the damaged towns of 1927, as they did in Louisiana in
2005, putting up advertisements of their readiness to undertake class-
action lawsuits.[13]

Instead, energies were focussed on the common task of rebuilding
and rehabilitation. That suggests that a second difference between now
and then can be found in Vermont's sense of homogeneity in the
1920s—cultural, religious, intellectual, ethnic, and the particular kinds
of social capital (to use a term borrowed from the social scientists) en-
gendered by that sense. Of course to some extent, this was true of the
United States as a whole, where the term "multicultural" had yet to be
invented, and would not likely have carried the favorable interpretation
it often enjoys today. Yet even in Vermont, this homogeneity was more
perceived than real, and certainly did not reflect social and demographic
fact. One searches almost in vain through the records of reconstruction
for names that are identifiably French-Canadian, or Italian, or Irish, for
example, just as one searches in vain for such names among the two or
three hundred Vermont leaders who made up the Commission on
Country Life. Still, perhaps the self-perception that their absence re-
veals—narrow, provincial, and class-based as it undoubtedly was (reflecting what has been called the "downside" of social capital)—may actually have been a help in getting the job done. So today, some have
argued that the heroic work done by the New York police and fire departments after the attack of 11 September 2001 owed much to the sense
of solidarity among those groups, narrow and parochial though it
might sometimes be. Sinclair Lewis, if we can consider him a Vermont

writer for a moment, captures this ambiguity splendidly. In *Main Street* (1919), the book that made him famous, the stultifying small town culture of Gopher Prairie has almost no redeeming characteristics. But sixteen years later, *It Can't Happen Here,* with its Vermont setting, shows what happens to local community when it is swamped by oppressive national forces.

A third difference between 1927 and today may lie in optimism and in its corollary, a lack of resentment against others. The *Free Press,* the *Rutland Herald,* and the scores of small-town newspapers did not see their task as exposing the folly and evil of others. Professors and students at the University of Vermont and Middlebury College did not take to the streets to insist that Governor Weeks's administration should have been better prepared for the emergency (despite the long history of floods in Vermont) nor did anyone suggest that Fred Howland, president of the huge and powerful National Life Insurance Company, owed his position as emergency finance commissioner to croneyism and corruption in the State House. An obvious fraud, like Matthew Spiero, the self-styled water-pollution expert from the Rockefeller Foundation, could be exposed, and William Tracy, the trouble-making Johnson lawyer, could be bypassed. But the press never suggested that builders and contractors, from the local Vermont firms to the huge American Bridge Company, should be investigated to see if they were profiting unjustly from Vermont's misfortune. Instead, the papers did all they could to paint an optimistic picture of the recovery, seeing it as their duty to rally spirits in the face of terrible hardship.

One can argue, of course, that they and their readers were ingenuous. One can argue that they papered over the dividing lines between various groups and classes in Vermont, and that the apparent homogeneity of Yankee Vermont was in large part a construction of articulate Vermonters and sympathetic outsiders. Yet the sense of commonality emerging from the record nevertheless strikes one as being real, reinforced by the sense that Vermonters were somehow different, even from their immediate neighbors. Regional divisions remained, as the Mountain Rule showed, but they were not strong enough to undermine the common purpose that underlay reconstruction.

To say all this is not an exercise in nostalgia, or a suggestion that we have somehow fallen away from a golden past. But it is the business of the historian to illuminate other times, to understand that while we may have much in common with Americans of the 1920s, they—even

Vermonters of the time—are still in many ways foreign to us. If Jan Albers is correct when she writes that "the Vermonters of 1940 were apparently more self-confident than they had been fifty years before," perhaps the experience of having lived through the flood must be given some of the credit. "The question of whether, fifty years from now, this terrible disaster shall be regarded as a blessing or a death blow will depend upon the intelligence and courage and industry of our people—and you," wrote the Bostonian William Fletcher to Governor Weeks.[14] In this sense, the flood, for all its destruction, can also be seen as an event that helped the state in its own negotiation of modernity. At least for a brief period, it showed that the old values were not simply the irrelevant leavings of the past, but had a solid and tangible usefulness in modern America. The flood and the recovery that followed helped, perhaps, to overcome the fear that a stark choice had to be made between Progress and Tradition, and the even greater fear that Progress must inevitably mean the destruction of Tradition. Rather, in those years immediately after 1927, it was precisely the reliance on tradition that made progress itself possible.

Not, of course, that the conflict was resolved. The trade-offs between the maintenance of rural community and the changes brought by increased affluence and mobility must still be faced in the twenty-first century.[15] Battles over taxation, development, and land use still reflect different visions of Vermont's future, just as they did in Vrest Orton's day. Indeed, his call for Vermont's independence in 1928 has recently been mirrored by the movement for a "Second Vermont Republic" today, and the fears of the state becoming another Florida or New Jersey live on (in 1993, the National Trust for Historic Preservation put Vermont at the top of its list of endangered sites).

Meanwhile, the flood story has played out its own kind of metaphorical role in fixing the state's particular identity. Vermont's disaster was more than simply the old tale of destruction and purification by water, common to flood myths everywhere. The important story was not that of destruction, but rather of reconstruction, a reconstruction that was a very modern American victory over the forces of nature. Not only native human grit, but modern technology and aid from the outside as well did the job—think of the rebuilding of highways, bridges, railways. Yet it has often suited Vermonters, and those who observed Vermont, to tell the story by couching it in the old language of tradition and local self-reliance. This has enabled them, as one historian has remarked, to continue to live with the old myths—"Vermont can take care of its own"—while benefitting from the greater forces of change beyond the state.[16] And, from the story and its mythical aspects, Vermonters and their admirers drew a new strength that would serve them in the difficult years of depression and war that lay ahead.

Notes

Abbreviations

AREA: *Bulletin of the American Railway Engineering Association*
BET: *Boston Evening Transcript*
BFP: *Burlington Free Press*
Governor's Papers: Governor's Correspondence, John Weeks, 1927–1931 (Vermont State Archives)
HFC: Howland Flood Correspondence (Vermont Division of Public Records)
NEFD: American National Red Cross, *The New England Flood Disaster, November, 1927: Official Report of the Relief Work* (Washington, D.C.: American National Red Cross, 1929)
NYT: *New York Times*
RANRC: Records of the American National Red Cross (National Archives)
RH: *Rutland Herald*
VCCL: Records of the Vermont Commission on Country Life (Vermont Division of Public Records)
VTFCC: Records of the Vermont Flood Credit Corporation (Vermont Historical Society)

1. Rising Waters (pp. 1–29)

1. Myrtie Caldwell Redmond, "The Vermont Flood in the Mountains," *Vermonter* 33, no. 2 (1928): 32; Charles T. Walter, *Lights and Shadows of the Flood of 1927: Vermont at Its Worst; Vermonters at Their Best* (St. Johnsbury, Vt.: Cowles Press, 1928), 7; Robert C. Jones, *The Central Vermont Railway: A Yankee Tradition*, vol. 3, *Austerity and Prosperity, 1911–27* (Silverton, Colo.: Sundance Books, 1981), 123.

2. U.S. Congress, *Congressional Record: Proceedings and Debates of the First Session of the Seventieth Congress of the United States of America,* vol. 69, part 5, 4878.

3. *Burlington Free Press* (hereafter *BFP*) 4 November 1928, 2.

4. H. B. Kinnison, *The New England Flood of November 1927* (Washington, D.C.: Government Printing Office, 1929); newspaper sources include the *Boston Globe, Boston Evening Transcript* (hereafter *BET*), *Boston Post, Burlington Free Press, La Presse* (Montreal), *New York Times* (hereafter *NYT*), *New York Herald–Tribune, Philadelphia Evening Bulletin,* and *Rutland Herald* (hereafter *RH*).

5. *BFP*, 31 December 1927, 1.

6. Lawrence Mills, "The Avalanche of Waters at Gaysville, Nov. 3, 1927," *Vermonter* 34, no. 3 (March 1929): 44.

7. U.S. Department of Agriculture, Weather Bureau, *Climatological Data, New England Section* 39, no. 11 (November 1927): 43. See also Kinnison, *New England Flood*, 53–57, for more reports.

8. Winooski Historical Society, "1927 Flood Memories" (videotape, 23 November, 1994); *NYT*, 5 November 1927, 2; Consuelo Northrop Bailey, *Leaves Before the Wind: The Autobiography of Vermont's Own Daughter* (Burlington, Vt.: George Little Press, 1976), 134.

9. Mary E. Whitney, "Royalton's Flood," *Vermonter* 34, no. 7 (July 1929): 111; Luther Burnham Johnson, *Floodtide of 1927; A Gathering of Reports and Pictures Which Tell Their Story Graphically of the Great November Flood in Vermont State* (Randolph, Vt.: Roy L. Johnson Co. 1927), 78, 146.

10. *Norwich Guidon*, 11 November, 18 November 1927; *Norwich University Record* 19, no. 11 (19 November 1927): 121–23.

11. *NYT*, 8 November 1927, 20.

12. *BFP*, 6 November 1927, 1; Lloyd E. Squier, *When the Water Came to Waterbury: A Tragedy in Three Acts Depicting Scenes of the Great Flood of November, 1927, As They Occurred on the Panoramic Stage of Vermont's Most Devastated Valley* (Waterbury,Vt.,: The Record Print, 1928), 52–55.

13. Roy L. Johnson, *The Challenge: A Recountal of the Great Flood of 1927 in the Upper White River Valley and of the Destruction and Restoration of the White River Railroad* (Randolph, Vt.: Roy L. Johnson Co., 1928), 12–13.

14. *BFP*, 8 November 1927, 3; Rose Lindley Kent, "Flood–tides of Bennington," *Vermonter* 33, no. 4 (1928): 61; Florence A. Kendall, "The Flood of 1927 in Orleans County," *Vermonter* 33, no. 1 (1928): 9.

15. *Boston Post*, 6 November 1927, 3; *NYT*, 8 November 1927, 20; Leon S. Gay, "Black River Valley and Cavendish Flood," *Vermonter* 32, no. 12 (Special Edition, 1927): 14.

16. *Boston Post*, 8 November 1927, 1; E. H. Jones to Clyde Jones, 9 November 1927, letter in Moretown (Vermont) Public Library.

17. *RH*, 6 November 1927, 5; *BFP*, 11 November, 1927, 7; Jim Shaughnessy, *The Rutland Road*, 2nd ed. (San Diego: Howell North Books, 1981), 140–42.

18. Walter, *Lights and Shadows*, 64; *BFP*, 4 November 1927, 1; 12 November 1927, 8; 15 November 1927, 7; Earle, "Dispatcher's Office" in *Train Dispatcher*, January 1928, 30 (Berwyn, Illinois; in UVM Flood folder); Robert C. Jones, *The Central Vermont Railway: A Yankee Tradition,*, vol. 4, *Flood and Depression, 1927–1940* (Silverton, Colo.: Sundance Books, 1981), 11, 21; Luther B. Johnson, *Vermont in Floodtime* (Randolph, Vt.:Roy L. Johnson Co., 1928), 51; Robert A. Clough, "Restoring the Mails in Vermont," *Vermonter* 32, no. 9 (1927): 156.

19. Differing accounts can be found in Jones, *Central Vermont*, vol. 4, 13; *RH*, 7 November 1927, 2; *BFP*, 7 November 1927, 2.

20. *La Presse*, 9 November 1927, 31; Florence Kendall, "Orleans County," 17–19; William Minsinger, *The 1927 Flood in Vermont and New England, November 3–7, 1927: An Historical and Pictorial Summary* (East Milton, Mass.: Blue Hill Meteorological Observatory, 2002), 101.

21. *NYT*, 5 November 1927, 1; 4 November 1927, 14; *BET*, 5 November 1927, 4.

22. *RH*, 4–6 November 1927; "The Flood at Rutland," *Vermonter* 33, no. 5 (1928): 70–76.

23. *RH*, 5 November 1927, 4; Shaughnessy, *Rutland Road*, 131–38; *BFP*, 14 November 1927, 1; 12 November 1927, 2; Robert E. Atwood, *Stories and Pictures of the Vermont Flood: November of 1927* (Burlington, Vt.: n.p., 1927), 20–21.

24. E. E. Sears to Mrs. Joseph Peck, 11 November 1927, Susan Peck Collection, Sheldon Museum, Middlebury, Vermont.

25. Johnson, *Vermont in Floodtime*, 128.

26. Gay, "Black River Valley and Cavendish Flood," 19.

27. Johnson, *Vermont in Floodtime*, 153, 156; Hyde Park *News and Chronicle*, 9 November 1927, 1, 4; 16 November 1927, 1; 20 November 1927, 1; Oread Literary Club, *History of Johnson, Vermont* (Essex Junction, Vt.: Essex Publishing, 1962), 71–2; J. M. French, "The Flood of 1927 in Lamoille County," *Vermonter* 35, no. 3 (March 1930): 56–60.

28. French, "Flood in Lamoille County," 56–58; Oread Literary Club, *History of Johnson*, 71.

29. Dean H. Perry, *Barre in the Great Flood of 1927: A History of Tragic Events and of Great Loss Sustained in a Vermont City, November 3–4* (Barre, Vt.: n.p., 1928), 7–9, 21–22; *BET*, 7 November 1927, 13.

30. Perry, *Barre*, 52–59; *BFP*, 9 November 1927, 9.

31. Patricia W. Belding, *Through Hell and High Water in Barre, Vermont: Twenty-five Eyewitness Accounts of the Flood of 27* (Barre, Vt.: Potash Book Publishing, 1998), 56–65; Sarsfeld McNulty to Cecil Dowers, 21 August 1967, Vermont Historical Society Misc File Add. Belding's invaluable book includes the memories of both Carlson and Harley Decouteau, who also had been in the Thomas house.

32. *Vermont Review* 2, no. 4 (March–April 1928): 88–89; Perry, *Barre*, 42–43.

33. Belding, *Hell and High Water*, 45–47; Perry, *Barre*, 40–46; *BFP*, 7 November 1927, 1; *BET*, 8 November 1927, 4.

34. Perry, *Barre*, 72–75; *BET*, 7 November 1927, 13.

35. R. G. Dun Report, 14 March 1928, in Records of the Vermont Flood Credit Corporation, Vermont Historical Society, MSC 40. R. G. Dun, the predecessor of Dun and Bradstreet, was the nation's first commercial reporting agency.

36. Joseph G. Abair, *The Flood, Nov. 3, 4, 1927, Montpelier, Vermont* (Montpelier, Vt.: Capital City Press, 1928), 2; *BFP*, 6 November 1927, 2.

37. Hattie Weeks to Catherine Marion Wood, 18 November 1927, Weeks Papers, University of Vermont.

38. Montpelier *Evening Argus*, 5 November 1927; *BFP*, 6 November 1927, 1; *RH*, 7 November 1927, 1.

39. Clara Harvey to Dorothy Harvey, 15 November 1927, Harvey Papers, Vermont Historical Society Misc File add.

40. *NYT*, 5 November 1927, 1–2; 13 November 1927, section 10, 14; 20 November 1927, section 3, 7; Boyden Sparkes, "Some Attic Adventures," *Saturday Evening Post* 201, no. 3 (21 July 1928): 134.

41. *BFP*, 6 November 1927, 1–2.

42. Minnie Nelson to Bessie, 21 November 1927, in Waterbury Historical Society, *75th Anniversary: November 3–4, 1927 Flood* (Waterbury, Vt.: Waterbury Historical Society, 2002), 1.

43. *BFP*, 6 November 1927, 1; Della LeBaron Swasey, "When Waterbury Was Under the Deluge," *Vermonter* 31, no. 8 (1927): 125.

44. *BFP*, 6 November 1927, 1; Squier, *Waterbury*, 11–21, 36.

45. *RH*, 10 November 1927, 9; Squier, *Waterbury*, 30–33; "Trials and Heroisms of the New England Flood," *Literary Digest* 95, no. 9 (26 November 1927): 38; Rutherford H. Moore, "Intimate Experiences of Waterbury Refugees," *Vermonter* 32, no. 8 (1927): 138.

46. Waterbury Historical Society, *75th Anniversary*, 1–2.

47. Flora S. Carpenter, "The Flood of November 3 & 4, 1927," ms. in possession of Caleb Pitkin, Marshfield, Vermont.

48. *NYT*, 9 November 1927, 16.

49. Swasey, "Waterbury," 122–23; Jones, *Central Vermont*, vol. 4, 14, 19; James Sabin, et al., eds., *History of Waterbury Vermont, 1915–1991* (Waterbury, Vt.: Waterbury Historical Society, 1991), 92.

50. *NYT*, 10 November 1927, 8.

51. R. W. Germain to "Dear Friends," 4 December 1927, in Fred Howland Flood Correspondence (hereafter HFC), Vermont Division of Public Records (Middlesex), PRA 585.

52. *RH*, 9 November 1927, 2.

53. *RH*, 10 December 1927, 9.

54. Johnson, *Vermont in Floodtime*, 45; Whitney, "Royalton's Flood," 110.

55. Squier, *Waterbury*, 49–50.

56. Minnie Metcalf, "The Flood at South Royalton, White River Valley," *Vermonter* 34, no. 11 (November 1929): 175.

57. Middlebury College *Campus*, 9 November 1927, 4.

58. Johnson, *Vermont in Floodtime*, 85; Wade Keyes to Fred Howland (undated), HFC; Gay, "Black River Valley and the Cavendish Flood," 19, 35.

59. Mills, "Gaysville," 43–47; French, "Lamoille County," 56–60.

2. *"Her Great Product Is Character"* (pp. 30–58)

1. *BFP*, 21 July 1927, 4.

2. David M. Ludlum, *The Vermont Weather Book* (Montpelier, Vt.: Vermont Historical Society, 1985), 217–49; Lemuel B. Eldridge, *The Torrent: Or, An Account of a Deluge Occasioned by an Unparalleled Rise of the New-Haven River, in which Nineteen Persons Were Swept Away, Five of Whom Only Escaped, July 26th, 1830* (Middlebury, Vt.: Printed at the Office of the Free Press, by E. D. Barber, 1831).

3. Ted Steinberg, *Acts of God: The Unnatural History of Natural Disaster in America* (New York: Oxford University Press, 2000), 69–71.

4. Figures for the Florida hurricane have been revised upward in recent years; see Russell Pfost, "Reassessing the Impact of Two Historical Florida

Hurricanes," *Bulletin of the American Meteorological Society* 84 (October 2003): 1367–72.

5. American National Red Cross, *The Mississippi Valley Flood Disaster of 1927: Official Report of the Relief Operations* (Washington, D.C.: American National Red Cross, 1929), 9.

6. American National Red Cross, *The New England Flood Disaster, November, 1927: Official Report of the Relief Work* (hereafter *NEFD*) (Washington, D.C.: American National Red Cross, 1929), 7; H. B. Kinnison, *The New England Flood of 1927* (Washington, D.C.: Government Printing Office, 1929), 82; William E. Minsinger, *The 1927 Flood in Vermont and New England, November 3–7, 1927: An Historical and Pictorial Summary* (East Milton, Mass.: Blue Hill Meteorological Observatory, 2002), 107.

7. Vermont Public Service Commission, *Report of Advisory Committee of Engineers on Flood Control, Public Service Commission, State of Vermont*, to Hon. John E. Weeks, Governor, December 15, 1928. The report can be found in the *Journal of the House of the State of Vermont, Biennial Session, 1929 and Special Session, 1927* (Montpelier, Vt., 1929), 38–52.

8. Vermont Department of Agriculture, *Agriculture of Vermont: Fourteenth Biennial Report of the Commissioner of Agriculture of the State of Vermont, 1926–1928*, E. H. Jones, Commissioner, 6; "The New England Flood of November, 1927," *Bulletin of the American Railway Engineering Association* (henceforth *AREA*) 30, no. 308 (August 1928): 102; "The Mississippi Valley Flood—1927," *AREA* 29, no. 303, part 2 (January 1928): 104.

9. *BFP*, 14 March 1928, 6; *Congressional Record*, 10 May 1928, 8333.

10. Prof. Alan Wolfe, addressing a gathering at the University of Vermont on 3 November 2002, commemorating the seventy-fifth anniversary of the flood.

11. *Congressional Record*, 9 February 1928, 2799–2800.

12. U.S. Department of Commerce, Bureau of Foreign and Domestic Commerce, *Statistical Abstract of the United States, 1928* (Washington, D.C.: Government Printing Office, 1928), 7–8, 612.

13. Samuel B. Hand, *The Star that Set: The Vermont Republican Party, 1854–1974* (Lanham, Md.: Lexington Books, 2002), 127.

14. *RH*, 29 July 1927, 4.

15. Hand, *Star that Set*, 109–11; Richard Munson Judd, *The New Deal in Vermont, its Impact and Aftermath* (New York: Garland Publishing, 1979), 9; Michael Sherman, Gene Sessions, and P. Jeffrey Potash, *Freedom and Unity: A History of Vermont* (Montpelier: Vermont Historical Society, 2004), 415–17.

16. Christopher McGrory Klyza and Stephen C. Trombulak, *The Story of Vermont: A Natural and Cultural History* (Hanover, N.H.: University Press of New England, 1999), 87–91; Edwin C. Rozwenc, *Agricultural Policies in Vermont, 1860–1945* (Montpelier, Vt.: Vermont Historical Society, 1981), 139–40, 161.

17. *RH*, 16 May 1928, 1; see also 25 September 1928, 3, and Klyza and Trombulak, *Story of Vermont*, 90–91. *BFP*, 23 April 1928, 8.

18. For a general overview of Vermont's rail lines, see Robert C. Jones, *The Railroads of Vermont*, 2 vols. (Shelburne, Vt.: New England Press, 1993).

19. Roy. L. Johnson, *The Challenge: A Recountal of the Great Flood of 1927 in the Upper White River Valley and the Destruction and Restoration of the White River Railroad* (Randolph, Vt.: Roy L. Johnson Co., 1928), 7.

20. *BFP*, 20 January 1928, 2; Robert C. Jones, *The Central Vermont Railway: A Yankee Tradition*, vol. 3, *Austerity and Prosperity, 1911–27* (Silverton, Colo.: Sundance Books, 1981), 92.

21. Jim Shaughnessy, *The Rutland Road*, 2nd ed. (San Diego: Howell-North Books, 1981), 129–30; R. W. Nimke, *The Rutland: Betterments, Statistics, Traffic, Equipment, Plans, Structures, Fixtures* (Walpole, N.H.: published by the author, 1989), 30–33.

22. Jones, *The Central Vermont*, vol. 3, 92–94, 121–30, 135, 158–59, 173.

23. Klyza and Trombulak, *Story of Vermont*, 113; Shaughnessy, *The Rutland Road*, 114; *BFP*, 3 June 1927, 1.

24. Wallace Nutting, *Vermont Beautiful* (Framingham, Mass.: Old America Co., 1922), 7; *BFP*, 13 December 1928, 2.

25. *BFP*, 22 March 1927, 7.

26. Benjamin Gates, "Holding Hands with Speed," *Vermonter* 26, no. 11 (1921): 219.

27. Putney Haight, "Vermont Finds Itself Hampered by Poor Roads; Neighboring States Offer More to Tourists," *Chicago Tribune*, 15 July 1928, A6.

28. Robert H. Ferrell, *The Presidency of Calvin Coolidge* (Lawrence: University of Kansas Press, 1998), 95.

29. Lois Goodwin Greer, "John E. Weeks, 64th Governor of Vermont," *Vermonter* 33, no. 1 (1928): 4.

30. Roosevelt's quotation is in John Barrett to Weeks, 15 September 1928; Brigham to Weeks, 26 March 1927, Weeks Papers, Middlebury College, Box I.

31. *BFP*, 28 March 1927, 4.

32. *BFP*, 4 November 1937, 6; Hand, *The Star that Set*, 123.

33. U.S. *Congressional Record*, 16 March 1928, 4880.

34. Vermont Sesqui-centennial Commission, *Bennington, Vermont, 1777–1927: A Record of the Celebration held at Bennington August 13–16, 1927, in Honor of the One Hundred and Fiftieth Anniversary of the Battle of Bennington and the One Hundred and Fiftieth Year of the Separate Existence of the State of Vermont* (Burlington, Vt.: Sesqui-centennial Commission, 1927), 66; Vermont Sesqui-centennial Commission, *The Battle of Hubbardton, 1777–1927: Report of the Celebration of the One Hundred and Fiftieth Anniversary at Hubbardton* (Burlington, Vt.: Vermont Sesqui-centennial Commission, 1927), 10; *BFP*, 17 August 1927, 3; 8 July 1927, 4.

35. John Bodnar, *Remaking America: Public Memory, Commemoration, and Patriotism in the Twentieth Century* (Princeton, N. J.: Princeton University Press, 1992), 171.

36. Christopher Morley, "Blythe Mountain, Vermont," *Saturday Review of Literature* 6, no. 52 (19 July 1930): 1206.

37. "Postage Stamps of the United States First Issued in 1927," http://www.1847usa.com/identify/YearSets/1927.htm, accessed 14 July 2005; *NYT*, 17 August 1927, 28; *BFP*, 17 August 1927, 1; 31 August 1927, 4.

38. Herbert Corey, "The Green Mountain State," *National Geographic* 51, no. 4 (March 1927): 344; *RH*, 18 November 1927, 4; *Vermont Review*, March–April 1928, 92.

39. See Peter Bishop, *The Myth of Shangri-La: Tibet, Travel Writing and the Western Creation of Sacred Landsape* (Berkeley: University of California Press, 1989).

40. Michael Sherman, Jennie Versteeg, Samuel B. Hand, and Paul Gillies, *The Character of Vermont: Twentieth-Anniversary Reflections* (Center for Research on Vermont, Occasional Paper no. 19 (Burlington: University of Vermont, 1996), 14.

41. Nolen's address of 5 June 1930 is found in James Taylor to Henry Taylor, 18 July, 1930, in Vermont Commission on Country Life Papers (hereafter VCCL), Vermont Division of Public Records, Box PRA 24.

42. Reprinted as Shane Leslie "Vermont: A Memory," in *Vermonter* 33, no. 4 (1928): 65.

43. Lynn Dumenil, *The Modern Temper: American Culture and Society in the 1920s* (New York: Hill and Wang, 1995), 4. For more on the causes of American nervousness in the period, see, for instance, David J. Goldberg, *Discontented America: The United States in the 1920s* (Baltimore: Johns Hopkins University Press, 1999); Roderick Nash, *The Nervous Generation: American Thought 1917–30* (Chicago: Rand McNally and Company, 1970); Lawrence W. Levine, *The Unpredictable Past: Explorations in American Cultural History* (New York: Oxford University Press, 1993), 189–205; and John Braeman, "The American Polity in the Age of Normalcy: A Reappraisal," in John Earl Haynes, ed., *Calvin Coolidge and the Coolidge Era: Essays on the History of the 1920s* (Washington, D.C.: Library of Congress, 1998), 39.

44. Yves Roby, *Les Franco–américains de la Nouvelle–Angleterre (1776–1930)* (Sillery, Quebec: Septentrion, 1990), 18; Sherman et al., *Freedom and Unity*, 348.

45. Millard W. Newcomb, "The Land of Opportunity," *Vermont Review*, July–August 1927, 35; President John M. Thomas, "The Idealization of the Near: A Plea for the Small Towns of Vermont," Baccalaureate Sermon preached at the 113th Commencement of Middlebury College, 15 June 1913, *Middlebury College Bulletin* 7, no. 6 (July 1913): 18–22.

46. Dorothy Canfield Fisher, *The Vermont Tradition: The Biography of an Outlook on Life* (Boston: Little, Brown, 1953): 283–84.

47. Harold Fisher Wilson, *The Hill Country of Northern New England: Its Social and Economic History, 1790–1930* (New York: Columbia University Press, 1936; reprinted, New York: AMS Press, 1967); H. Nicholas Muller, "From Ferment to Fatigue? 1870–1900: A New Look at the Neglected Winter of Vermont," (Burlington: Center for Research on Vermont, Occasional Paper no. 7, University of Vermont, 1984); Sherman et al., *Freedom and Unity*, 309.

48. Hal S. Barron, *Those Who Stayed Behind: Rural Society in Nineteenth-Century New England* (Cambridge: Cambridge University Press, 1984), 40.

49. Paul M. Searls, *Two Vermonts: Geography and Identity, 1865–1910* (Lebanon, N.H.: University Press of New England), 2006.

50. John A. Jakle, *The American Small Town: Twentieth-Century Place Images* (Hamden, Conn.: Archon Books, 1982), chap. 6; Searls, *Two Vermonts*, chap. 4;

Dona Brown, *Inventing New England: Regional Tourism in the Nineteenth Century* (Washington, D.C.: Smithsonian Institution Press, 1995), 143–145.

51. Levine, *Unpredictable Past*, 191.

52. Searls, *Two Vermonts*, 99–111.

53. *NYT*, 6 January 1927, 19.

54. Dorothy Canfield Fisher, "Our Rich Little Poor State," *The Nation* 114, no. 2969 (31 May 1922): 643–44; Morley, "Blythe Mountain," 1206.

55. William Allen White, *Calvin Coolidge: The Man Who Is President* (New York: Macmillan, 1925), 238.

56. R. L. Duffus, "The Republic of the Green Mountains," *New York Times Magazine*, 7 August 1927, SM12.

57. Bruce Bliven, "Rock-Ribbed," *New Republic* 32, no. 429 (21 February 1923): 344–46; H. P. Lovecraft, "Vermont—a First Impression," *Driftwind* 2, no. 5 (March 1928): unpaged.

58. Dumenil, *Modern Temper*, 202; *RH*, 25 July 1928, 5; Ferrell, *The Presidency of Calvin Coolidge*, 37–38; Hand, *The Star that Set*, chap. 6, "Alien Elements," 96–116, deals with these aspects of Vermont.

59. *NYT*, 22 June 1924, E4; Vermont Commission on Country Life, *Rural Vermont: A Program for the Future, by Two Hundred Vermonters* (Burlington: Vermont Commission on Country Life, 1931), 355.

60. Hand, *The Star that Set*, 86–87; Nancy L. Gallagher, *Breeding Better Vermonters: The Eugenics Project in the Green Mountain State* (Hanover, N.H: University Press of New England, 1999), 44; John M. Lund, "Vermont Nativism: William Paul Dillingham and U.S. Immigration Legislation," *Vermont History* 63, no. 1 (Winter 1995): 15–29.

61. Joseph-André Sénécal, "Nos Ancêtres les Gaulois: Ethnicity and History in Vermont," *Vermont History* 71 (Winter/Spring 2003): 62–70; William S. Rossiter, "Three Sentinels of the North," *Atlantic* 132 (July 1923): 97; Searls, *Two Vermonts*, 67–73. For the humorous view of French-Canadians, see Rowland E. Robinson, *Danvis Tales: Selected Stories,* edited by David Budbill (Hanover and London: University Press of New England, 1995).

62. Joseph A. Conforti, *Imagining New England: Explorations of Regional Identity from the Pilgrims to the Mid-Twentieth Century* (Chapel Hill: University of North Carolina Press, 2001), 266.

63. Maudean Neill, *Fiery Crosses in the Green Mountains: The Story of the Ku Klux Klan in Vermont* (Randolph Center, Vt.: Greenhills Books, 1989) looks at aspects of the story; see also Sherman, *Freedom and Unity*, 404–407; *BFP*, 6 July 1927, 7; *Barre Times*, 5 July 1927, 1.

64. Walter Lippmann, "The Causes of Political Indifference To-Day," *Atlantic* 140 (February 1927): 261–68, reprinted in Alan Bilton and Philip Melling, *America in the 1920s: Literary Sources and Documents*, vol. 1, *The Cultural Condition* (Mountfield, East Sussex: Helm Information, 2004), 205–13.

65. Gallagher, *Breeding*, 95–97; François Weil, *Les Franco-américains* (Paris: Belin, 1989), 75, 90–98; Roby, *Franco-américains*, 123.

66. Besides the appearance in the *Vermonter*, already cited, see also *BFP*, 6 December 1927, 11; *RH*, 5 December 1927, 4.

67. *BFP*, 2 June 1927, 4.

68. *BFP*, 12 January 1929, 6.

69. Michael C. Steiner, "Regionalism in the Great Depression," *Geographical Review* 73, no. 4 (October 1983): 434.

70. Arthur Patten Wallace, "'Progress' in Vermont," *Drift-Wind* 2, no. 6 (May 1928): unpaged; Alberton Blanchard, "Vermont Redivivus," *Drift-Wind* 3, no. 1 (July 1928): 12–14; Vrest Orton, "Vermont for Vermonters," *Drift-Wind* 3, no. 1 (July 1928): 26–28; Vrest Orton, "How to Make Vermont Free," *Drift-Wind* 3, no. 4 (January 1929): 146; Vrest Orton, "A Declaration of Independence for Vermont," *Drift-Wind* 3 no. 5 (March 1929): 197–201.

71. Paul Searls, "America and the State that 'Stayed Behind': An Argument for the National Relevance of Vermont History," *Vermont History* 71 (Winter/Spring 2003): 76.

72. E. S. Martin, editorial, *Life* 90, no. 2354 (15 December, 1927): 16.

73. Searls, *Two Vermonts*, 99; see also 3.

3. *"Sympathy Flowed in from the Hills"* (pp. 59–87)

1. Ethel Colby to Mildred, 17 November 1927, in Waterbury Historical Society *75th Anniversary: November 3–4, 1927 Flood* (Waterbury, Vt.: Waterbury Historical Society, 2002), 9.

2. Hyde Park *News and Citizen*, 9 November 1927, 1; *RH*, 7 November, 7; 8 November, 2.

3. *Randolph Herald*, 10 November 1927; *Vergennes Enterprise & Vermonter*, 2 December 1927, 4.

4. *BFP*, 8 November 1927, 8; *RH*, 15 November 1927, 7.

5. *BFP*, 12 November 1927, 1; 13 February 1928, 8; Charles S. Ferrin, "Military Reminiscences of the Flood of 1927," *Vermont History*, 43 (Spring 1975): 153–54.

6. Vergennes *Enterprise & Vermonter*, 2 December 1927, 8; *Washington Post*, 13 November 1927, 10.

7. R. W. Germain to "Dear Friends," 4 December 1927, HFC.

8. Ida Morgan Anderson, "Early History of Cambridge," Cambridge *Town Crier*, 26 March 1936, np; Clara Harvey to Dorothy (Harvey?), 15 November 1927, Harvey Papers.

9. Harvey to "My Dears," 21 November 1927, Harvey Papers.

10. *RH*, 14 November 1927, 4; 11 November 1927, 7.

11. *RH*, 6 November 1927, 2 ; Montpelier *Evening Argus*, 9 November 1927.

12. Glover Bicentennial Committee, *History of the Town of Glover, Vermont (1783–1983)*, Burlington, Vt.: Queen City Printers, 1983, 96; interview with Raymond DeForge, Montpelier, 23 January 1987, Vermont Folk Life Center; *NYT*, 8 November 1927, 1.

13. *NYT*, 9 November 1927, 16; interview with Ruby Dalley and Clara Pratt, 30 May 1991, Vermont Folk Life Center.

14. Peter H. Haraty, ed., *Put the Vermonters Ahead: A History of the Vermont National Guard, 1764–1978* (Burlington, Vt.: Queen City Printers, 1979), 184; *RH*, 5 November 1927, 1; *BFP*, 7 November 1927, 1.

15. Barbara Carpenter, interview with Arecca Urban, 1989 (private collection); *NYT*, 9 November 1927, 16.

16. Craig O. Burt, *We Lived In Stowe: A Memoir* (Middlebury, Vt.: Ranch Camp Publishers, 2003), 144–67.

17. *Waterbury Register*, 16 November 1927, 2; Waterbury Historical Society, *75 th Anniversary*, 1.

18. Hyde Park *News and Citizen*, 9 November 1927, 1; Mrs. Harry Noyes to Kramer (John Cremer?), 10 November 1927, National Archives, RG 200, Records of the American National Red Cross, 1917–1934, DR251, November Flood, 11/27, Box 747, folder DR251.11. References to this group henceforth cited as RANRC, with the appropriate folder number.

19. Hyde Park *News and Citizen*, 23 November 1927, 1; Noyes to Cremer, 20 November 1927, RANRC, folder 251.11; Oread Literary Club, *History of Johnson, Vermont* (Essex Junction, Vt,: Essex Publishing, 1962), 156.

20. Arecca Urban interview; Oread Literary Club, *History of Johnson*, 73.

21. Anderson, "Early History of Cambridge," Cambridge *Town Crier*, 2 April 1936.

22. *BET*, 10 November 1927, 4; Karen Hansen, *A Very Social Time: Crafting Community in Antebellum New England* (Berkeley: University of California Press, 1994), 9, 108.

23. Clara Harvey to Dorothy Harvey, 15 November 1927, Harvey Papers.

24. *Waterbury Record*, 16 November 1927, 1, 4; 23 November 1927, 1; *Norwich University Record*, 3 December 1927, 138.

25. George Mead, "Flood Days: an Account of the Work Done by the College Community in the Statewide Flood of 1927," ms. in Middlebury College archives; *BFP*, 15 November 1927, 6; *NYT*, 20 November 1927, 5; *Cynic* (University of Vermont), 18 November, 1927, 1; Robert A. Clough, "Restoring the Mails in Vermont," *Vermonter* 32, no. 9 (1927): 155.

26. *History of Newbury, Vermont, 1900 to 1977, with Genealogical Records of Many Families* (Bradford, Vt.: Fox Publishers, 1978), 245; *NYT*, 19 November 1927, 9; 11 November, 1927, 1; *BFP*, 11 November 1927, 1.

27. Mead, "Flood Days," 3.

28. Mead, "Flood Days," 2; Middlebury College *Campus*, 23 November 1927, 2.

29. D. C. Ormsbee to Ann McColl Ormsbee, 10 November 2003, private collection.

30. Middlebury College *Campus*, 23 November 1927, 2; *Norwich Guidon*, 11 November 1927.

31. *BFP*, 15 November 1927, 6; *RH*, 18 November 1927, 2.

32. Herrle to DeWitt Smith, 21 November 1927, RANRC Box 747, folder DR 251.11.

33. *RH*, 19 November 1927, 2; Ruth Estelle Slack to "Dear People," 15 November 1927, Ruth Estelle Slack Papers, Vermont Historical Society, MSC 209:29; Lamb to Chase, 25 August 1955, in Waterbury Historical Society, *75th Anniversary*, 11.

34. *NYT*, 5 November 1927, 2; *RH*, 6 November 1927, 2; *BFP*, 6 November 1927, 3; 8 November 1927, 2; *NEFD*, 9.

35. *RH*, 3 November 1937, 3; 5 November 1952, 8; 2 November 1963, 5; 6 November 1977, sec. III.

36. George D. Aiken, *Speaking from Vermont* (New York: Frederick A. Stokes Co., 1938), 199; James M. Jeffords, *An Independent Man: Adventures of a Public Servant* (New York: Simon and Schuster, 2003), 72–73; Consuelo Northrop Bailey, *Leaves Before the Wind: The Autobiography of Vermont's Own Daughter* (Burlington: George Little Press, 1976), 134.

37. *Boston Post*, 8 November 1927, 1, 14.

38. *BFP*, 7 November 1927, 7.

39. Earle S. Kinsley, *Recollections of Vermonters in State and National Affairs* (Rutland, Vt.: privately printed, 1946), 141.

40. Ferrin, "Military Reminiscences," 149–50.

41. Greene to Weeks, 9 November 1927, Vermont State Archives, Governor's Correspondence, John Weeks, 1937–1941 (hereafter cited as Governor's Papers), reel S–1384.

42. Memorandum by Harry Chadwick, 6 November 1927, in Papers of Frank L. Greene, 1895–1930, Library of Congress, Box 40, 3rd folder.

43. *BFP*, 6 November 1927, 1.

44. Vermont Adjutant General, *Biennial Report of the Adjutant, Inspector and Quartermaster General of the State of Vermont for the Two Years Ending June 30, 1928* (Rutland, Vt.: Tuttle, 1928), 24–26.

45. *BFP*, 7 November 1927, 7; Vermont Adjutant General, *Biennial Report*, 25–26.

46. *BFP*, 7 November 1927, 1; John M. Barry, *Rising Tide: The Great Mississippi Flood of 1927, and How it Changed America* (New York: Simon and Schuster, 1997), 371–72.

47. Weeks to Greene, 23 November 1927, Greene Papers, Box 40, 3rd folder.

48. *Boston Globe* 13 November 1927, 1; *RH*, 9 November 1927, 1; 10 November 1927, 2.

49. John Lawrence to Howland, 5 November 1927, HFC; *NYT*, 7 November 1927, 3; 8 November 1927, 20. *BFP*, 8 November 1927, 1.

50. *NYT*, 10 November 1927, 1, 8; *RH*, 11 November 1927, 1; Kinsley, *Recollections*, 141; *BET*, 10 November 1927, 8.

51. *BET*, 14 November 1927, II, 2.

52. *BET*, 19 November 1927, III, 1–2. The letter quoted to him actually was written by Greene's secretary, as the senator later pointed out to Howland, in a letter of 25 November (Greene Papers).

53. Kinsley, *Recollections*, 140–41.

54. Barry, *Rising Tide*, 286–89, 372–75; Bruce Lohof, "Herbert Hoover, Spokesman of Humane Efficiency: The Mississippi Flood of 1927," *American Quarterly* 22, no. 3 (Autumn 1970): 690–700.

55. *NYT*, 13 November 1927, 1; Barry, *Rising Tide*, 270. George H. Nash, "The 'Great Enigma' and the 'Great Engineer':The Political Relationship of Calvin Coolidge and Herbert Hoover," in *Calvin Coolidge and the Coolidge Era: Essays in the History of the 1920s,*ed. John Earl Haynes, 149–80 (Washington, D.C.: Library of Congress, 1998), discusses the general difficulties between the two.

56. *BET*, 14 November 1927, II, 1.

57. *BET*, 17 November 1927, 6; *BFP*, 18 November 1927, 4; James Sabin et al., *History of Waterbury, Vermont, 1915–1991* (Waterbury, Vt.: Waterbury Historical Society, 1991), 185.

58. Hoover to Weeks, 17 November 1927, Hoover Papers, University of Vermont; *BFP*, 18 November 1927, 1.

59. Recollections of former State Senator Melvin Mandigo, in *Randolph Herald*, 1 October 2002, in University of Vermont Library Special Collections, box marked Flood, 1927.

60. *BFP*, 3 November 1932, 3.

61. Charles T. Walter, *Lights and Shadows of the Flood of 1927: Vermont at Its Worst; Vermonters at Their Best* (St. Johnsbury: Cowles Press, 1928), 9; *BFP*, 17 November 1927, 1.

62. Dorothy Harvey's comment is in James Taylor to Henry Baker, 11 February 1928, RNARC, box 747, folder DR 251.9.

63. *NYT*, 27 November 1927, III, 2.

64. *RH*, 19 November 1927, 1; Herbert Comings to Howland, 20 November 1927, in HFC. Barry, *Rising Tide*, 366–75, discusses credits arranged by Hoover in the Mississippi Valley.

65. *BFP*, 12 November 1927, 3; 15 November 1927, 4.

66. *BFP*, 15 November 1927, 4.

67. Crockett to Weeks, 8 November 1927, Governor's Papers.

68. Howland to W. A. Hallett, 11 November 1927; E. A. Davis to Howland, 15 November 1927, HFC.

69. *BFP*, 8 November 1927, 4; 11 November 1927, 1; 19 November 1927, 4; 22 November 1927, 4.

70. *BET*, 29 November 1927, 14.

71. *RH*, 1 December 1927, 1.

72. Edward Rockwood, "Notes on the Governor's Message," *Vermont Review* 2, no. 4 (March–April 1928): 91. The text of Weeks's speech can be found in *Journal of the Senate of the State of Vermont*, Special Session, 1927 Biennial Session, 1929 (Montpelier: Capital City Press, 1929), 33–36. Thomas's letter to Weeks of 22 November 1927 is in the Weeks Papers, Middlebury College archives.

73. *BET*, 19 November 1927, III, 2; 29 November 1927, II, 2. The text of the proclamation is in *State of Vermont Executive Records*, vol. xvii (1927–29): 157.

74. *Waterbury Record*, 23 November 1927, 4.

75. *Waterbury Record*, 28 December 1927, 1.

76. *Waterbury Record*, 28 December 1927, 1–3; Waterbury Historical Society, *75th Anniversary*, 10; *NYT*, 27 December 1927, 6.

4. *"New Experiences in Disaster Relief"* (pp. 88–118)

1. Lloyd E. Squier, *When the Water Came to Waterbury; A Tragedy in Three Acts Depicting Scenes of the Great Flood of November, 1927, as They Occurred on the Panoramic Stage of Vermont's Most Devastated Valley, Compiled from Marion's Workshop* (Waterbury, Vt.: The Record Print, 1928), 49–50; Nellie V. Canning, "Bolton Memorial School," Vermont Historical Society, Misc File addenda; *BFP*, 18 November 1927, 4, 22 November 1927, 11.

2. Canning, "Bolton"; *Christian Science Monitor*, 6 January 1928, 3; *BFP*, 29 December 1927, 2.

3. *RH*, 14 January 1928, 2.

4. *BFP*, 22 December 1927, 4; 9 July 1928, 6; Smilie Memorial School website, http://www.smilie.k12.vt.us/handbook.htm, accessed 9 September 2005.

5. *BFP*, 5 November 1928, 6.

6. *Boston Globe*, 13 November 1927, 1.

7. Much correspondence relative to gifts can be found in Vermont Auditor of Accounts, Records Relating to Gifts to Vermont Following the Flood of 1927, Vermont Historical Society MS Box A18. See also *Knickerbocker Press* to Weeks, 3 December 1927, Governor's Papers, reel S–3184; *BET*, 4 November 1927, 4; 10 November 1927, 8.

8. *NEFD*, 10.

9. *NYT*, 12 November 1927, 2; 11 November 1927, 10; 19 November 1927, 8; 28 November 1927, 23.

10. Vermont Auditor, A. H. Lyons to Weeks, 12 December 1927; C. F. Harrington to Weeks, 19 November, 1927; E. A. Davis to Howland, two letters of 15 November 1927, all in HFC; Barrett to Weeks, 15 November 1927, Governor's Papers, reel S–3184.

11. *NYT*, 13 January 1928, 6.

12. Addie Nichols to Frank Nichols, 14 November 1927; Nettie Nichols to Frank Nichols, 26 November 1927. Copies of these letters, from a "Special Issue" of the "Burbank Family News," a newsletter put out by John R. Burbank of St. Johnsbury, can be found in the Moretown Library. Savage's letter to Weeks of 27 November 1927 is in the Governor's Papers, reel S–3184.

13. Merrill to Weeks, 29 November 1927, 4 December 1927, in Governor's Papers, reel S–3184; *RH*, 20 November 1927, 4; 19 December 1927, 4.

14. Parkhurst to Howland, 2 December 1927; see also the comment of the *New York World*, quoted in *BFP*, 14 December 1927, 2.

15. Brigham to Hindley, 26 January 1928, Brigham Papers, folder Ha–Hoo, 1928.

16. Howland to W. Stickney, 6 December 1927; to J. Grissingham, 21 January 1928, HFC, and undated clipping, presumably mid–January, in HFC.

17. *Boston Globe*, 13 November 1927, 1; *Washington Post*, 30 November 1927, 2.

18. Herrle to DeWitt Smith, 6 December 1927, DR 251, New England Flood 11/27, RANRC, box 746.

19. Foster Rhea Dulles, *The American Red Cross: A History* (New York: Harper and Bros., 1950), 226–41.

20. Dulles, *Red Cross*, 269; Ted Steinberg, *Acts of God: The Unnatural History of Natural Disaster in America* (New York: Oxford University Press, 2000), 57. On professional associations, see Ellis Hawley, *The Great War and the Search for a Modern Order: A History of the American People and Their Institutions, 1917–1933* (New York: St. Martin's Press, 1979), esp. 90–99.

21. Dulles, *Red Cross*, 236–37, 169.

22. John M. Barry, *Rising Tide: The Great Mississippi Flood of 1927, and How It Changed America* (New York: Simon and Schuster, 1997), 364.

23. S. D. Johnson to Fieser, 3 December 1927; G. Crane to E. Dix, 8 December 1927, folder DR 251.11, New England Flood 11/27 Vermont, RANRC, Box 747.

24. G. Crane to K. Monroe, 1 March 1928, folder DR 251.11, RANRC, box 747.

25. *BET*, 7 November 1927, 7; 10 November 1927, 8; J. B. Payne to Red Cross chapters, 10 November 1927, folder DR251.2 New England Flood 11/27, Finance and Accounts, RANRC, box 747.

26. Howland to J. M. Thomas, 11 November 1927; Howland to H. Comings, 16 November 1927, HFC.

27. J. Cremer memorandum of 9 November 1927; Baker to Fieser, 23 February 1928, DR251.11, RANRC, box 747.

28. Payne to J. Lawrence, 22 November 1927, folder DR251.6 New England Flood 11/27 Relief Other Than Health, RANRC, box 747; *BFP*, 17 November 1927, 13; 20 December 1927, 6; 9 January 1928, 2; 18 January 1928, 7. See also the exchange of wires between Lawrence and Payne, 18–21 November 1921 in Hoover Papers, University of Vermont.

29. Weeks wire to Fieser, 19 December 1927 (date uncertain); Baker to Fieser, 3 January 1928, 7 January 1928, DR 251.6, RNARC, box 747; Howland to Ratshesky, 29 December 1927, HFC.

30. Baker to Fieser, 1 February 1928, DR 251.11; K. Monroe to H. Baker, 4 February 1928 DR 251.08, New England Flood 11/27 Progress Reports, RNARC, box 747.

31. W. Rossiter to Hoover, 17 January 1928, Hoover Papers; Mrs. B. R. Demeritt to Howland, 18 December 1927; R. Proctor to Weeks, 20 December 1927, Governor's Papers, reel S-3184; memorandum of C. Carr, 9 November 1927; memorandum of H. J. Hughes, 16 December 1927, DR 251.11, RNARC, box 747.

32. Howland to D. Howe, 13 December 1927; Howland to Ratshesky, 29 December, HFC; Weeks to Proctor, 2 January 1928, Governor's Papers, reel S-3184; Howland memorandum of 14 June 1928, Greene Papers, box 40.

33. *NYT*, 10 November 1927, 1; *Montpelier Evening Argus*, 11 November 1927; 16 November 1927, 2; C. Harvey to "My Dears," 21 November 1927, Harvey Papers.

34. W. Barton to J. Haigis, 18 November 1927, RANRC, DR 251.11 New England Flood 11/27 Vermont, RANRC, box 747; *BFP*, 23 November 1927, 2.

35. *Middlebury Register*, 27 January 1928, 4; *BFP*, 19 January 1928, 7; *Burlington Daily News*, 28 January 1928.

36. *BFP*, 16 May 1927, 5; *NYT*, 24 April 1927, 1.

37. D. Howe to Howland, 14 January 1928, Howland Correspondence MSS 21 #21, Vermont Historical Society.

38. *Burlington Daily News,* 28 January 1928; 30 January 1928; *RH,* 31 January 1928, 4.

39. Howland to Hindley, 13 January 1928, HFC; Earle S. Kinsley, *Recollections of Vermonters in State and National Affairs* (Rutland, Vt.: privately printed, 1946), 96–97.

40. Vermont Flood Credit Corporation Record Book, minutes of directors' meeting of 18 January 1928, Vermont Historical Society, MS A1; *RH,* 17 December 1927, 1; 9 February 1928, 6; *BFP,* 31 December 1927, 2.

41. *RH,* 28 February 1928, 1; 23 February 1928, 1; VTFCC Annual Report, 27 March 1928, Vermont Historical Society, MS A1.

42. *NYT,* 20 May 1928, III, 2; Bullard to Howland, 28 April 1928; Fitzgerald to Bullard, 5 May 1928, HFC.

43. M. D. Dimick to Greene, 30 May 1928, Greene Papers, Box 40. The records of the VTFCC, Vermont Historical Society, MSC 40, has the correspondence and claims of loss by applicants, including that of Bashaw; see also Comings to W. W. Russell, 4 April 1928, in the same collection.

44. Memorandum by K. Monroe, 10 March 1928; Herrle to Baker, 17 February 1928, DR 251.11, RNARC, box 747; Oread Literary Club, *History of Johnson,* 88.

45. Baker to Fieser, 23 February 1928, DR 251.2, Finance and Accounts, RNARC, box 747.

46. *BFP,* 1 May 1928, 9.

47. Baker to Fieser, 7 May 1928, memorandum "The Attitude of the Governor of Vermont," R 251.9, New England Flood 11/27 Misc., RANRC, box 747; Baker to Fieser, 21 May 1928, DR 251.6, Relief Other Than Health, RANRC, box 747.

48. C. B. Adams to Weeks, 15 May 1928, Governor's Papers, reel S–3186.

49. Fieser to Hoover, 6 June 1928; see also Minutes of the Meeting of the Vermont State Red Cross Advisory Committee, 1 June 1928, DR 251.04, New England Flood, 11/27, Committees and Conferences, RANRC, box 746.

50. Baker to Weeks, Howland, et al., 23 July 1928; Baker to Smith 2 August 1928, DR 251.1 New England Flood, 11/27 Organization and Administration, RANRC, box 747; Baker and Jones to Weeks, 3 August 1928; Weeks to Baker, 7 August 1928, Governor's Papers, reel S–3186.

51. Baker to Smith, 3 August 1928, DR 251.1, New England Flood 11/27 Organization and Administration, RANRC, box 747; Weeks to Payne, 7 August 1928, Governor's Papers, reel S–3186. The Jones and Gates statements appear in the Red Cross *Courier* 7, no. 17: 12, a copy of which is in the HFC.

52. Howland to Payne, 6 August 1928; Howland to Ratshesky, 6 August 1928, HFC.

53. *NEDF,* 19–20; *BFP,* 16 November 1928, 8; *Christian Science Monitor,* 28 August 1928, 7.

54. Nancy L. Gallagher, *Breeding Better Vermonters: The Eugenics Project in the Green Mountain State* (Hanover, N.H.: University Press of New England, 1999), 60.

55. *RH,* 28 September 1928, 1; *BFP,* 28 September 1928, 3.

56. *NYT*, 9 November 1927, 8; *BFP*, 29 March 1929, 3; VTFCC Annual Meeting, 26 March 1929.

57. VTFCC questionnaire folder, MSC 40, Vermont Historical Society; Minutes of meeting of 9 May 1928, VTFCC Record Book.

58. Annual Report of the VTFCC, 26 March 1929.

59. Barry, *Rising Tide*, 375–76.

60. *BFP*, 17 January 1928, 2.

61. *BFP*, 12 January 1928, 4; *BET*, 16 November 1927, 12.

62. R. W. Nimke, *The Rutland: Betterments, Statistics, Traffic, Equipment, Plans, Structures, Fixtures* (Walpole, N.H.: published by the author, 1989), 30–31; *RH*, 19 December 1927, 3; Vermont State Chamber of Commerce, *Vermont Progress: Official Publication of the Vermont State Chamber of Commerce* (St. Albans, Feb. 1928; *BFP*, 17 January 1928, 1; 10 February 1928, 2; John S. Kendall, *The History of the St. Johnsbury and Lake Champlain Railroad* (St. Johnsbury, Vt.: published by the author, 1974, revised from original articles in *The Morrisville Messenger*, 11 October 1939 and 25 October 1939; Robert C. Jones, *The Railroads of Vermont*, vol. 2 (Shelburne, Vt.: New England Press, 1993), 230.

63. *BFP*, 24 December 1927, 8.

64. Jones, *Railroads of Vermont*, vol. 2, 230.

65. E. H. Jones to Clyde Jones, 9 November 1927, Moretown Library.

66. *BFP*, 6 January 1928, 2; American National Red Cross, *The New England Flood Disaster, November, 1927. Official Report of the Relief Work* (Washington, D.C.: American National Red Cross, 1929), 80.

67. American National Red Cross, *New England Flood*, 67.

68. Robert C. Jones, *The Central Vermont Railway: A Yankee Tradition*, vol. 4, *Flood and Depression, 1927–1940* (Silverton, Colo.: Sundance Books, 1981), 11; *Barre Times*, 10 November 1927, 1; *BFP*, 12 November 1927, 3.

69. D'Arcy Marsh, *The Tragedy of Henry Thornton* (Toronto: Macmillan, 1935), 130; *NYT*, 15 March 1933, 17.

70. Squier, *Waterbury*, 74.

71. Brigham to Howland, 21 December 1927, Brigham Papers, box 2441, folder H–2; *NYT*, 13 December 1927, 50; 18 December 1927, E2.

72. *BFP*, 6 January 1928, 7; 14 January 1928, 2; 16 December 1927, 3; *NYT*, 14 December 1927, 46; 15 December 1927, 42.

73. *Waterbury Record*, 1 February 1928, 1.

74. Squier, *Waterbury*, 78; Waterbury Historical Society, *75th Anniversary: November 3–4, 1927 Flood* (Waterbury, Vt.: Waterbury Historical Society, 2002), 22.

75. *BFP*, 6 February 1928, 1; Charles T. Walter, *Lights and Shadows of the Flood of 1927: Vermont at Its Worst, Vermonters at Their Best* (St. Johnsbury: Cowles Press, 1928), 87.

76. *BFP*, 6 February 1928, 1; *NYT*, 4 February 1928, 17; *Boston Globe*, 5 February 1928, 1.

77. *BFP*, 30 May 1928, 2; 9 August 1928, 7; 14 December 1928, 2.

78. Wes Herwig, Miriam Herwig, and Robert C. Jones, *A Whistle Up the Valley: The Story of the Peavine, Vermont's White River Railroad* (Burlington, Vt.:

Evergreen Press, 2005), 75–83, has the most recent account of the line's destruction and reconstruction.

79. *RH*, 14 February 1928, 4.

80. Paul Winfield Masten, "A History of the White River Valley Road," *Vermont History* 32, no. 4 (October 1964): 214; Roy L. Johnson, *The Challenge: A Recountal of the Great Flood of 1927 in the Upper White River Valley and of the Destruction and Restoration of the White River Railroad* (Randolph, Vt.: Roy L. Johnson Co., 1928), 4–5, 23.

81. Middlebury College Trustee Records, meetings of 16 April and 30 April 1928, Middlebury College archives.

82. *RH*, 20 June 1928, 3; 13 July 1928, 1; *BFP*, 4 July 1928, 2; 10 July 1928, 2; Johnson, *Challenge*, 21–23.

83. *BFP*, 10 July 1928, 2.

84. Kendall, *History of the St. Johnsbury and Lake Champlain Railroad*, 19.

85. *RH*, 22 November 1927, 1 [or 2?]; 13 March 1929, 2; Jones, *Railroads of Vermont*, 346.

86. *RH*, 21 June 1928, 4; *BFP*, 10 July 1928, 2.

87. Walter, *Lights and Shadows*, 87–88.

5. *"Squeezed Through after Many Hairbreadth Escapes" (pp. 119–42)*

1. *BFP*, 24 January 1928, 3; 10 March 1928, 2; "Metal, Truss, Masonry, and Concrete Bridges in Vermont," Multiple Property Documentation Form, 12 April 1990. E–10, United States Department of the Interior, National Park Service, National Register of Historic Places. We are indebted to Glenn Andres of Middlebury College, and to the Vermont Division of Historic Preservation for pointing out to us the existence of this study.

2. *BFP*, 1 June 1927, 4.

3. Morgan Brainard to Howland, 2 December 1927; Howland to Brainard, 6 December 1927, HFC.

4. Brigham to Allen Plumley, 11 November 1927; Plumley to Brigham, 14 November 1927, 16 November 1927, Brigham Papers, Congress File: 2 1927; *BFP*, 30 December 1927, 4; Brigham to Austin, 14 December 1927, Congress File: A 1927.

5. *BFP*, 12 November 1927, 4.

6. *BET*, 3 November 1927, 5; *RH*, 1 December 1927, 2.

7. Brigham to Howland, 30 November 1927, HFC; *BET*, 6 December 1927, II, 19.

8. Brigham to Partridge, 20 December, 1927; Partridge to Brigham, 17 December 1927, which encloses undated clipping from the *Brattleboro Reformer*, "Opposition to Aiding Vermont," in Frank Partridge Papers (uncatalogued), Vermont Historical Society.

9. *BFP*, 12 January 1928, 1–3; *RH*, 12 January 1928, 1.

10. *NYT*, 15 March 1928, 16.

11. *RH*, 25 January 1928, 3; 9 February 1928, 6; *BFP*, 26 January 1928, 4.

12. Extension of the remarks of Elbert S. Brigham and Ernest S. Gibson, *Congressional Record*, Appendix, 16 March 1928, 5090–93, in Hoover Papers, University of Vermont.

13. Brigham to F. Howe, 22 March 1928, Congressional File Hop–Hy 1928; Brigham to Partridge, 14 March 1928, Congressional File Pa–Pl, Brigham Papers.

14. Brigham to Howe, 31 October 1928; Brigham to Howland, 3 April 1928, Congress File Hop–Hy 1928, Brigham Papers.

15. *RH*, 7 May 1928, 4; 8 May 1928, 1; 11 May 1928, 1; wire, delegation to Weeks, 10 May 1928, Greene Papers, Box 40, 3rd folder.

16. Brigham to Partridge, 28 May 1928, Congress File Pa–Pl 1928; Brigham to Howe, 31 October 1928, Congress File Hop–Hy, Brigham Papers.

17. *BFP*, 13 March 1928, 4; 25 April 1928, 4; John M. Barry, *Rising Tide: The Great Mississippi Flood of 1927, and How It Changed America* (New York: Simon and Schuster, 1997), 405.

18. William E. Leuchtenburg, *Flood Control Politics: The Connecticut River Valley Problem, 1927–1950* (Cambridge, Mass.: Harvard University Press, 1953), 30–32.

19. H. Chadwick memorandum, 10 May 1928, Greene Papers, Box 40, 3rd folder.

20. Samuel B. Hand, Jeffrey D. Marshall, and Gregory D. Sanford, "'Little Republics': The Structure of State Politics in Vermont, 1854–1920," *Vermont History* 53 (Summer 1985): 152–54.

21. *BFP*, 14 March 1928, 6; 4 April 1928. An interesting editorial reflecting such views in the aftermath of Hurricane Katrina appeared in the *NYT*, 3 October 2005, 20.

22. *BFP*, 4 April 1928, 2.

23. *RH*, 7 April 1928, 1; 10 April 1928, 1; *BFP*, 9 April 1928, 2.

24. *RH*, 7 April 1928, 2, 4.

25. Vermont State Highway Board, *Fifth Biennial Report of the State Highway Board for the Two Years Ending June 30 1930* (Rutland, Vt.: The Tuttle Company, 1930), 30.

26. *BFP*, 10 January 1929, 2; Letter of Transmission, Third Biennial State Budget of Commissioner of Finance Including Recommendations for Appropriations for Two Years Ending June 30, 1931, undated and unpaged.

27. Samuel B. Hand, *The Star that Set: The Vermont Republican Party, 1854–1974* (Lanham, Md.: Lexington Books, 2002), 124; memorandum by Thomas MacDonald, 6 January 1928; Greene to Weeks, 7 January 1928, Greene Papers, box 40.

28. *RH*, 11 June 1928, 1.

29. *RH*, 15 May 1928, 4; 25 July 1928, 1; *BFP*, 28 July 1928, 5; L. B. Shonyo to James Taylor, 14 July 1928, James Taylor Papers, Doc T7, folder 37, Vermont Historical Society.

30. *RH*, 24 July 1928, 4.

31. *NYT*, 20 May 1928, III, 2; *BET*, 3 July 1928, II, 9; *RH*, 23 August 1928, 2.

32. *Hyde Park News and Citizen,* 4 July 1928, 2; 29 August 1928, 4; *Woodstock Standard,* 11 October 1928, 7; *BFP,* 25 August 1928, 6; *RH,* 10 July 1928, 1.

33. *BFP*, 4 August 1928, 11.

34. *RH*, 14 June 1928, 1; 15 June 1928, 1, 4; *BFP*, 6 August 1928, 6; 12 August 1928, 4.

35. George H. Nash, "The 'Great Enigma' and the 'Great Engineer': The Political Relationship of Calvin Coolidge and Herbert Hoover," in *Calvin Coolidge and the Coolidge Era: Essays on the History of the 1920s,* ed. John Earl Haynes, 167–69 (Washington, D.C.: Library of Congress, 1998).

36. Brigham to Hindley, 12 April 1928; Hindley to Brigham, 13 April 1928, Brigham Papers, Congress File Ha–Hoo 1928; Rossiter to Howland, 14 January 1928, Howland Papers, MSS 21#21,Vermont Historical Society.

37. *Washington Post*, 28 July 1927, 3.

38. Samuel B. Hand, "The Mountain Rule Revisited," *Vermont History* 71 (Summer/Fall 2003): 139–51; Hand, *Star that Set*, 36–37.

39. Smith is quoted in Hand, *Star that Set*, 37; for Hartness, see Hand et al., "Little Republics," 164.

40. Howard Wardner to Weeks, 17 March 1928, Weeks Papers, Middlebury College, box 2.

41. *BFP*, 28 October 1927, 4; *Middlebury Register*, 14 October 1927, 2.

42. Hand, *Star that Set*, 140n12.

43. Hand, *Star that Set*, 124; Crockett to Greene, 7 December 1927, Greene Papers, box 40.

44. *RH*, 14 March 1928, 4; Rice to Weeks, 28 January 1928, Weeks Papers, Middlebury College.

45. *NYT*, 11 March 1928, 52; *BFP*, 30 March 1928, 4; 21 July 1928, 6.

46. Howland to Brigham, 30 March 1928, Congress File Hop–Hy 1928, Brigham Papers; Partridge to Weeks, 5 April 1928, Middlebury College, Weeks Papers, box 2, Campaign 1928, folder 1.

47. *Vermont Review* 2, no. 4 (March–April 1928): 75–76; *BFP*, 7 March 1928, 4; *RH*, 28 July 1928, 1. The wire from the Fascisti is in the Weeks Papers, Middlebury College, box 2, folder "Governorship second term."

48. *NYT*, 13 May 1928, 48.

49. *BFP*, 18 May 1928, 1; Weeks to J. Spargo, 25 July 1928, John Spargo Papers, University of Vermont; *RH*, 19 May 1928, 4.

50. *RH*, 19 May 1928, 1; *BFP*, 26 May 1928, 2; Bailey to Billings, 3 August 1928, in Middlebury Weeks Papers, box 2, Campaign 1928, folder 1.

51. *Vermont Review* 2, no. 5 (May–June 1928): 100.

52. Hand, *Star that Set*, 125–26; *Brattleboro Reformer*, quoted in *Woodstock Standard*, 16 July 1928, 1.

53. *Waterbury Record*, 25 July 1928, 6; Bailey to Billings, 3 August 1928; Billings to Weeks, 8 August 1928, Middlebury Weeks Papers, box 2; Weeks to Spargo, 25 July 1928, Spargo Papers, correspondence with John Weeks.

54. *BFP*, 13 September 1928, 6.

55. *Vermont Review* 2, no. 2 (July–August 1927): 27; *Waterbury Record*, 28 March 1928, 2; see also *RH*, 2 April 1928, 4.

56. Robert H. Ferrell, *The Presidency of Calvin Coolidge* (Lawrence: University of Kansas Press, 1998), 197–98.

57. *NYT*, 21 September 1928, 1; 22 September 1928, 13.

58. *BET*, 21 September 1928, 12.

59. Craig O. Burt, *We Lived in Stowe: A Memoir* (Middlebury, Vt.: Ranch Camp Publishers, 2003), 152.

60. Text taken from http://www.calvin-coolidge.org/html/1927_flood.html, accessed 14 November 2006.

61. *Boston Globe*, 21 September 1928, 1, 21.

62. *Montpelier Evening Argus*, 3 November 1928, 2; *RH*, 8 September 1928, 1; 14 September 1928, 4; *NYT*, 13 September 1928, 26.

63. *NYT*, 18 September 1928, 20; *RH*, 18 September 1928, 4.

64. Quoted in Hand, *Star that Set*, 105; Lawrence W. Levine, *The Unpredictable Past:Explorations in American Cultural History* (New York: Oxford University Press, 1993), 200.

65. Ronald Edsforth, "Made in the U.S.A: Mass Culture and the Americanization of Working-Class Ethnics in the Coolidge Era," in Haynes, *Coolidge*, 244–45; Hand, *Star that Set*, 126.

66. *BFP*, 1 January 1929, 16; *Senate Journal, Biennial Session 1929*, 413–14.

67. *RH*, 16 March 1929, 1.

68. *BFP*, 21 March 1929, 2.

69. *RH*, 9 March 1929, 4; *BFP*, 14 March 1929, 2.

70. *BFP*, 18 March 1929, 6.

6. *"Any Great Catastrophe Brings a Good Many Changes in Its Wake"*
(pp. 143–65)

1. William E. Leuchtenburg, *Flood Control Politics: The Connecticut River Valley Problem, 1927–1950* (Cambridge, Mass.: Harvard University Press, 1953) 30; *BFP*, 9 November 1927, 1; 14 December 1927, 4; 9 December 1927, 4.

2. *BFP*, 5 December 1927, 4; 30 December 1927, 4.

3. *RH*, 29 February 1928, 6; *BFP*, 30 December 1927, 4; 28 March 1928, 4; Leuchtenburg, *Flood Control*, 32.

4. *BFP*, 14 March 1928, 6.

5. Vermont Public Service Commission, Advisory Committee of Engineers on Flood Control, *Report of Advisory Committee of Engineers on Flood Control, Public Service Commission, State of Vermont, to Hon. John E. Weeks, Governor, December 15, 1928* (Montpelier, Vt : Vermont Public Service Commission, 1928). The report can also be found in the *Journal of the House of the State of Vermont, Biennial Session, 1929 and Special Session, 1927* (Montpelier, 1929), 38–52. Hereafter cited in text.

6. *RH*, 14 January 1929, 1.

7. Vermont Public Service Commission, Advisory Committee of Engineers on Flood Control, *Report of the Advisory Committee of Engineers on Flood Control, Public Service Commission, State of Vermont, to Hon. John E. Weeks, Governor* (Montpelier, Vt.: Vermont Public Service Commission, 1930).

8. Lee Webb, "A History of Electric Utility Regulation in Vermont, 1880–1965" (master's thesis, Goddard College, 1974; copy at the University of Vermont).

9. Vermont General Assembly, *Journal of the Joint Assembly, Biennial Session, 1931* (Montpelier, Vt.: General Assembly, 1931), 624–36 for Weeks's address, and 640–48 for Wilson's.

10. *BFP*, 18 March 1931, 17; Vermont General Assembly, House of Representatives, *Journal of the House of the State of Vermont* (Montpelier: House of Representatives, 1931), 98.

11. George D. Aiken, *Speaking from Vermont* (New York: Frederick A. Stokes, 1938), 167–68.

12. *Black River Tribune* 17 July 1991, clipping in University of Vermont Special Collections folder, "Flood Control"; Samuel B. Hand, *The Star that Set: The Vermont Republican Party, 1854–1974* (Lanham, Md.: Lexington Books, 2002), 130–33; Leuchtenberg, *Flood Control*, 35–36; Richard Munson Judd, *The New Deal in Vermont, its Impact and Aftermath* (New York: Garland Publishing, 1979), 63.

13. Webb, "Utility Regulation," 50.

14. Leuchtenberg, *Flood Control*, 45–49.

15. Thomas W. Patton, "When the Veterans Came to Vermont: The Civilian Conservation Corps and the Winooski River Flood Control Project," *Vermont History* 73 (Summer/Fall 2005): 160–89.

16. Leuchtenberg, *Flood Control*, 34.

17. *BFP*, 2 January 1928, 2.

18. Hand, *Star that Set*, 109.

19. J. Taylor to H. Taylor, 18 July 1930, VCCL, Box PRA 24, unnamed folder.

20. William L. Bowers, *The Country Life Movement in America, 1900–20* (Port Washington, N.Y.: Kinnikat Press, 1974); Hal S. Barron, *Those Who Stayed Behind: Rural Society in Nineteenth-Century New England* (Cambridge: Cambridge University Press, 1984), 41–48.

21. On regionalism in this period, see Robert L. Dorman, *Revolt of the Provinces: The Regionalist Movement in America, 1920–1945* (Chapel Hill: University of North Carolina Press, 1993); and Joseph A. Conforti, *Imagining New England: Explorations of Regional Identity from the Pilgrims to the Mid-Twentieth Century* (Chapel Hill: Univesity of North Carolia Press, 2001).

22. Ellis W. Hawley, *The Great War and the Search for a Modern Order: A History of the American People and Their Institutions, 1917–1933* (New York: St. Martin's Press, 1979), 50–51; Warren I. Susman, *Culture as History: The Transformation of American Society in the Twentieth Century* (New York: Pantheon Books, 1984), 116–17; Barry Karl, *The Uneasy State: The United States from 1915 to 1945* (Chicago: University of Chicago Press, 1983), 71–72.

23. H. F. Perkins, "Contributory Factors in Eugenics in a Rural State," reprinted from *A Decade of Progress in Eugenics, Scientific Papers of the Third International Congress of Eugenics, 1932,* 183–89; offprint, VCCL PRA 23, folder "History of survey."

24. Perkins to "Dear Friend," 23 May 1927; VCCL PRA 23, folder, Vermont Commission on Country Life Meetings, 1929; Dempsey to Perkins, 2 June 1927; Perkins to Weeks, 4 June 1927, folder Executive Committee Correspondence.

25. Perkins to Weeks, 24 February 1928, VCCL PRA 23, folder Executive Committee Correspondence.

26. Perkins to Brigham, 2 April 1928, Brigham Papers, Congress File 1928, Pa–Pl.

27. Rossiter to Perkins, 15 June 1928; to Taylor, 10 October 1928, VCCL PRA 24, folder Committee on Country Life Correspondence.

28. Notes for first meeting, 18 May 1928; "Plan for a Comprehensive Survey of Rural Areas in Vermont," distributed to first meeting, in VCCL PRA 23, folder VCCL Addresses.

29. Perkins to Weeks, 22 May 1928; Gallagher, *Breeding*, 96; Henry Perkins, "The Vermont Commission on Country Life," *Vermont History* 23, no. 4 (October 1955): 336.

30. Gallagher, *Breeding*, 121.

31. Marion Gary, "Vermonters Study Themselves," *Journal of the American Association of University Women* (June 1932): 92. Offprint in VCCL, PRA 02385, box 106331, looseleaf folder entitled Clippings.

32. "Vermont Commission on Country Life 1929 Meeting October 9th, Issued as the December News Letter," VCCL PRA 23.

33. VCCL Meeting October 9, 1928, 43–44.

34. Kevin Dann, "From Degeneration to Regeneration: The Eugenics Survey of Vermont, 1925–1936," *Vermont History* 59, no. 1 (Winter 1991): 16; Gallagher, *Breeding*, 45–46, 95–96.

35. Dann, "Degeneration," 23–24.

36. Quoted in Dorman, *Revolt*, 102.

37. Zadock Thompson, *History of the State of Vermont, from Its Earliest Settlement to the Close of the Year 1832* (Burlington, Vt.: Edward Smith, 1833); Walter Crockett, *Vermont: the Green Mountain State* (New York: Century History Company, 1921); Deborah Pickman Clifford, *The Passion of Abby Hemenway: Memory, Spirit, and the Making of History* (Montpelier, Vt.: Vermont History Society, 2001).

38. Stewart Mitchell review in the *New England Quarterly* (April 1932): 390–93, copy in VCCL, PRA 02385, box 106331; Eda Lou Walton, *The Nation* 133, no. 3450 (19 August 1931): 189.

39. Sinclair Lewis, "Letter to Critics," *The Nation* 133, no. 3454 (16 September 1931): 280–81.

40. *BFP*, 17 June 1931, 3.

41. Sarah Cleghorn, "Coming Vermont: A Pageant," copy in VCCL, PRA 23.

42. The reviews, as well as other news clippings, are conveniently gathered in two folders found in VCCL PRA 02385, box 106331.

43. Henry F. Perkins, "The Comprehensive Survey of Rural Vermont, Conducted by the Vermont Commission on Country Life," reprint from *New England's Prospect: 1933*, American Geographical Society Special Publication No. 16, New York, 1933, 206 (offprint in VCCL PRA 23, folder, "History of Survey)".

44. Vermont Commission on Country Life, *Rural Vermont: A Program for the Future, by Two Hundred Vermonters* (Burlington Vt.: Vermont Commission on Country Life, 1931), 385.

45. Leuchtenberg, *Flood Control*, 13; Michael Sherman, Gene Sessions, and D. Jeffrey Potash, *Freedom and Unity: A History of Vermont* (Montpelier:

Vermont Historical Society, 2004), 449; Webb, "Utility Regulation," 42–45; Edwin C. Rozwenc, "The Group Basis of Vermont Farm Politics, 1870–1945," *Vermont History* 25, no. 3 (October 1957): 268–87.

46. Judd, *New Deal*, 2–4; Dann, "Degeneration," 22.

47. Vermont State Planning Board, *Graphic Survey: A First Step in State Planning for Vermont. A Report Submitted to the Vermont State Planning Board and National* [sic] *Resources Board* (Montpelier: n.p., 1935); Perkins, "Eugenics," 337–38.

48. Gallagher, *Breeding*, 115 and *passim*.

7. Conclusion (pp. 166–78)

1. *Vermont Review* 2, no. 6 (July–August, 1928): 123–24.

2. *RH*, 4 August 1928, 2; *NYT*, 21 February 1928, 22.

3. *Christian Science Monitor*, 21 December 1927, 2; Vermont Department of Agriculture, *Agriculture of Vermont: Fourteenth Biennial Report of the Commissioner of Agriculture of the State of Vermont, 1926–1928*, E. H. Jones, Commissioner. No publication information.

4. *BFP*, 12 April 1928, 4.

5. *BFP*, 5 November 1928, 6; *RH*, 3 November 1928, 3; 5 November 1928, 7.

6. *BFP*, 3 November 1932, 2; 3 November 1937, 6; 4 November 1937, 6; *RH*, 3 November 1937, 2.

7. Crockett to Spargo, 22 November 1927, Spargo Papers; Vermont Commission on Country Life, *Rural Vermont: A Program for the Future, by Two Hundred Vermonters* (Burlington: Vermont Commission on Country Life, 1931), 378.

8. Cora Cheney, *Profiles from the Past: An Uncommon History of Vermont* (Taftsville, Vt.: Countryman Press, 1976), 211.

9. John William Ward, "The Meaning of Lindbergh's Flight," *American Quarterly* 10, no. 1 (Spring 1958): 3–16.

10. The speech can be found at http://janda.org/politxts/State%20of%20Union%20Addresses/1923–1928%20Coolidge/Coolidge27.html, accessed 1 November 2005.

11. Ted Steinberg, *Acts of God: The Unnatural History of Natural Disaster in America* (New York: Oxford University Press, 2000), xxii.

12. *NYT*, 26 September 2005, 1, 12.

13. *Baltimore Sun*, 10 October 2005, 1A.

14. Jan Albers, *Hands on the Land: A History of the Vermont Landscape* (Cambridge, Mass.: MIT Press, 2000), 267; Fletcher to Weeks, 6 November 1927, Governor's Papers, reel S–1384.

15. This is the burden of much of Joe Sherman's *Fast Lane on a Dirt Road: A Contemporary History of Vermont* (White River Junction, Vt.: Chelsea Green Publishing, 2000).

16. Paul Searls, private conversation.

Select Bibliography

Newspapers and Periodicals

Barre Daily Times (1927)
Boston Evening Transcript (1927–1928)
Boston Globe (1927–1928)
Boston Post (1927)
Burlington Daily News (1927–1928)
Burlington Free Press (1927–1931)
Campus (Middlebury College, 1927)
Chicago Tribune (1927–1929)
Christian Science Monitor (1927–1930)
Cynic (University of Vermont, 1927)
The Drift-Wind (North Montpelier, Vermont, 1926–1930)
La Presse (Montreal, 1927)
Middlebury Register (Middlebury, Vermont, 1926–1931)
New York Times (1926–1931)
New York Herald-Tribune (1927)
News and Citizen (Hyde Park, Vermont, 1927–1928)
Rutland Herald (1927–1931)
Vergennes Enterprise (1927–1928)
Vermonter (1927–1937)
Vermont History
Vermont Progress: Official Publication of the Vermont State Chamber of Commerce. (St. Albans 1927–1928)
Vermont Review (1927–1928)
Walton's Vermont Register, Almanac and State Year Book, 1927–1928, compiled and edited by Berenice R. Tuttle. Rutland: Tuttle, annual.
Washington Post (1927–1930)
Waterbury Record (1927–1928)
Woodstock Standard (1927–1928)

Books and Articles

A. W. P. "Breaking the Black Silence: A Sketch of the work of the Norwich University Radio Station 1 YD during the flood period," by the Officer in Charge. *Vermonter* 32, no. 10 (1927): 185–88.
Abair, Joseph G. *The Flood, November 3, 4, 1927, Montpelier, Vermont.* Montpelier, Vt.: Capital City Press, 1928.

Aiken, George D. *Speaking from Vermont*. New York: Frederick A. Stokes Co., 1938.

Albers, Jan. *Hands on the Land: A History of the Vermont Landscape*. Cambridge, Mass.: MIT Press, 2000.

American National Red Cross. *The Mississippi Valley Flood Disaster of 1927: Official Report of the Relief Operations*. Washington, D.C.: American National Red Cross, 1929.

———. *The New England Flood Disaster, November, 1927: Official Report of the Relief Work*. Washington, D.C.: American National Red Cross, 1929.

Anderson, Ida Morgan. "Early History of Cambridge." Cambridge *Town Crier*, 12 March, 19 March, 26 March, 2 April 1936.

Anderson, S. Axel, and Florence M. Woodard. "Agricultural Vermont." *Economic Geography* 8, no. 1 (January 1932): 12–42.

Atwood, Robert E. *Stories and Pictures of the Vermont Flood: November of 1927*. Burlington, Vt.: n.p., 1927.

Bailey, Consuelo Northrop. *Leaves Before the Wind: The Autobiography of Vermont's Own Daughter*. Burlington, Vt.: George Little Press, 1976.

Bailey, Harold L. "Flood Days in a Tavern." *Vermonter* 32, no. 12 (1927): 22–30.

Barron, Hal S. *Those Who Stayed Behind: Rural Society in Nineteenth-Century New England*. Cambridge: Cambridge University Press, 1984.

Barry, John M. *Rising Tide: The Great Mississippi Flood of 1927, and How It Changed America*. New York: Simon and Schuster, 1997.

Belding, Patricia W. *Through Hell and High Water in Barre, Vermont: Twenty-five Eyewitness Accounts of the Flood of '27*. Barre: Potash Brook Publishing, 1998.

Bigelow, Walter J. *Vermont: Its Government*. Montpelier, Vt.: The Historical Publishing Company, annual, 1927–1930.

Black, John Donald. *The Rural Economy of New England: A Regional Study*. Cambridge, Mass.: Harvard University Press, 1950.

Blanchard, Alberton M. "Vermont Redivivus." *The Drift-Wind* 3, no. 1 (July 1928): 12–14.

Bliven, Bruce. "Rock–Ribbed." *New Republic* 32, no. 429 (21 February 1927).

Bodnar, John. *Remaking America: Public Memory, Commemoration, and Patriotism in the Twentieth Century*. Princeton, N.J.: Princeton University Press, 1992.

Booraem, Hendrik. *The Provincial: Calvin Coolidge and His World, 1885–1895*. Lewisburg, Penn.: Bucknell University Press, 1994.

Bowers, William L. *The Country Life Movement in America, 1900–20*. Port Washington, N.Y.: Kinnikat Press, 1974.

Braeman, John. "The American Polity in the Age of Normalcy: A Reappraisal." In *Calvin Coolidge and the Coolidge Era: Essays on the History of the 1920s*, ed. John Earl Haynes. Washington, D.C.: Library of Congress, 1998.

Brown, Dona. *Inventing New England: Regional Tourism in the Nineteenth Century*. Washington, D.C.: Smithsonian Institution Press, 1995.

Bullard, Lauriston F. "Vermont Is Different—and It Means to Stay So." *New York Times*, 1938. Reprinted in Michael Sherman, et al., *The Character of Vermont:*

Twentieth Anniversary Reflections, Occasional Paper no. 19. Burlington: University of Vermont, 1996.

Burt, Craig O. *We Lived in Stowe: A Memoir*. Middlebury, Vt.: Ranch Camp Publishers, 2003.

Cabot Oral History Committee. *A Collection of Memories from the Century Past*. Cabot, Vt.: Oral History Committee, 1999.

Cady, Daniel L. "The Vermont Flood." *Vermonter* 32, no. 8 (1927): 113.

Cate, Weston A. *Forever Calais: A History of Calais, Vermont*. Calais, Vt.: Calais Historical Society, 1999.

Chadwick, Harold H. "Flood." *Vermont Life* 7 (Autumn 1952): 8–13.

Chelsea Historical Society. *A History of Chelsea, Vermont, 1784–1984, Authorized by the Town in March 1980 and Compiled by a Committee from the Chelsea Historical Society, Inc.* Chelsea, Vt.: The Society, 1984.

Cheney, Cora. *Profiles from the Past: An Uncommon History of Vermont*. Taftsville, Vt.: Countryman Press, 1976.

Clarendon Vermont: 1761–1976. Rutland, Vt.: Academy Books, 1982.

Clifford, Deborah Pickman. *The Passion of Abby Hemenway: Memory, Spirit, and the Making of History*. Montpelier, Vt.: Vermont Historical Society, 2001.

Clifford, Susannah. *Village in the Hills: A History of Danville, Vermont, 1786–1995*. West Kennebunk, Maine: Published for the Danville History Committee by Phoenix Publications, 1995.

Clough, Robert A. "Restoring the Mails in Vermont." *Vermonter* 32, no. 9 (1927): 152–57.

Coates, Walter John, and Frederick Tupper, eds. *Vermont Verse: An Anthology*. Green Mountain Series. Brattleboro, Vt.: Stephen Day Press, 1932.

Colton, F. B. "Bridge Reconstruction in Vermont." *Vermonter* 33, no. 3 (1928): 39–41.

Comings, Herbert C. *Years of an Old Vermonter: Some Biographical Jottings*. Privately Printed, 1939.

Conforti, Joseph A. *Imagining New England: Explorations of Regional Identity from the Pilgrims to the Mid–Twentieth Century*. Chapel Hill, N.C.: University of North Carolina Press, 2001.

"Continuing the Flood Record." *Vermonter* 33, no. 12 (1928): 202–203.

Corey, Herbert. "The Green Mountain State." *National Geographic* 51, no. 4 (March 1927): 333–69.

Crane, Charles Edward. *Let Me Show You Vermont*. New York: Alfred A. Knopf, 1937.

———. *Pendrift: Amenities of Column Conducting, by the Pendrifter*. Brattleboro, Vt.: Stephen Daye Press, 1931.

———. *Winter in Vermont*. New York: Alfred A. Knopf, 1941.

Crockett, Walter. *Vermont: The Green Mountain State*. New York: Century History Company, 1926.

———, ed. *Vermonters: A Book of Biographies*. Green Mountain Series. Brattleboro, Vt.: Stephen Daye Press, 1932.

Dann, Kevin. "From Degeneration to Regeneration: The Eugenics Survey of Vermont, 1925–1936." *Vermont History* 59, no. 1 (Winter 1991): 5–29.

Dorman, Robert L. *Revolt of the Provinces: The Regionalist Movement in America, 1920–1945.* Chapel Hill: University of North Carolina Press, 1993.

Doyle, William T. *The Vermont Political Tradition and Those Who Helped Make It.* Montpelier, Vt.: W. Doyle, 1990.

Duffus, R. L. "Old Maine and Vermont—There They Stand." *New York Times Magazine,* 30 May 1937, 6–7, 16.

———. "The Republic of the Green Mountains." *New York Times Magazine,* 7 August 1927, SM12.

Duffy, John, and Vincent Feeney. *Vermont: An Illustrated History.* Sun Valley, Calif.: American Historical Press, 2000.

Dulles, Foster Rhea. *The American Red Cross: A History.* New York: Harper and Bros., 1950.

Dumenil, Lynn. *The Modern Temper: American Culture and Society in the 1920s.* New York: Hill and Wang, 1995.

Dupigny-Giroux, Lesley-Ann. "Climate Variability and Socioeconomic Consequences of Vermont's Natural Hazards: A Historical Perspective." *Vermont History* 70 (Winter/Spring 2002): 19–39.

Edsforth, Ronald. "Made in the U.S.A.: Mass Culture and the Americanization Ethics in the Coolidge Era." In *Calvin Coolidge and the Coolidge Era: Essays on the History of the 1920s,* ed. John Earl Haynes. Washington, D.C.: Library of Congress, 1998.

Eldridge, Lemuel B. *The Torrent: Or, An Account of a Deluge Occasioned By An Unparalleled Rise of the New-Haven River, in Which Nineteen Persons Were Swept Away, Five of Whom Only Escaped, July 26th, 1830.* Middlebury, Vt.: Printed at the Office of the Free Press, by E. D. Barber, 1831.

Evans, Timothy. "A Last Defense against the Dark: Folklore, Horror, and the Uses of Tradition in the Works of H. P. Lovecraft." *Journal of Folklore Research* 42, no. 1 (2005): 100–35.

F. L. S. "Around the Flood with a Rural Carrier," *Vermonter* 32, no. 9 (1927): 158–63.

Fairfax Bicentennial Committee. *Fairfax, Vermont, Its Creation and Development.* St. Albans, Vt.: Regal Art Press, 1980.

Ferrell, Robert H. *The Presidency of Calvin Coolidge.* Lawrence: University Press of Kansas, 1998.

Ferrin, Charles S. "Military Reminiscences of the Flood of 1927," ed. Robert V. Daniels. *Vermont History* 43 (Spring 1975): 149–54.

Fisher, Dorothy Canfield. "Our Rich Little Poor State." *The Nation* 114, no. 2969 (31 May 1922): 643–44.

———. *The Vermont Tradition: The Biography of an Outlook on Life.* Boston: Little, Brown, 1953.

———. "Vermonters." In *Vermont: A Guide to the Green Mountain State.* Federal Writers' Project. Boston: Houghton Mifflin, 1937.

Flanders, Helen Hartness, and George Brown, eds. *Vermont Folk-Songs and Ballads.* Green Mountain Series. Brattleboro, Vt.: Stephen Daye Press, 1932.

"The Flood at Rutland: A Letter by an Eye Witness." *Vermonter* 33, no. 5 (1928): 70–60.

French, J. M. "The Flood of 1927 in Lamoille County." *Vermonter* 35, no. 3 (March 1930): 56–60.

Frost, Francis. "Flood Episode in Vermont." *Vermonter* 32, no. 7 (1927): 97.

Gallagher, Nancy L. *Breeding Better Vermonters: The Eugenics Project in the Green Mountain State.* Hanover, N.H.: University Press of New England, 1999.

Gary, Marion. "Vermonters Study Themselves." *Journal of the American Association of University Women* (June 1932): 90–92.

Gates, Benjamin. "Holding Hands with Speed." *Vermonter* 26, no. 11 (1921): 216–20.

Gay, Leon S. "Black River Valley and the Cavendish Flood." *Vermonter* 32, no. 7 (1927): 104–107.

———. "Black River Valley and Cavendish Flood." *Vermonter* 32, no. 12 (Special edition, 1927): 9–21.

Gillies, Paul. "The Evolution of the Vermont State Tax System" *Vermont History* 65 (Winter/Spring 1997): 26–44.

Glover Bicentennial Committee. *History of the Town of Glover, Vermont.* Burlington, Vt.: Queen City Printers, 1983.

"Going Thro Hell and High Water." *Vermonter* 32, no. 6 (1927): 88–95.

Goldberg, David J. *Discontented America: The United States in the 1920s.* Baltimore: Johns Hopkins University Press, 1999.

Graff, Nancy Price, ed. *Celebrating Vermont: Myths and Realities.* Middlebury, Vt.: Christian A. Johnson Memorial Gallery, Middlebury College, 1991.

Graffagnino, J. Kevin. "It Did Happen Here: Sinclair Lewis and the Image of Vermont." *Vermont History* 49 (Winter 1981): 31–38.

Graffagnino, J. Kevin, Samuel B. Hand, and Gene Sessions, eds. *Vermont Voices, 1609 through the 1990s: A Documentary History of the Green Mountain State.* Montpelier: Vermont Historical Society, 1999.

Greer, Lois Goodwin. "John E. Weeks, 64th Governor of Vermont." *Vermonter* 33, no. 1 (1928): 3–7.

Hand, Samuel B. "The Mountain Rule Revisited." *Vermont History* 71 (Summer/Fall 2003): 139–51.

———. "The 1927 Flood: Watershed Event." In *In a State of Nature: Readings in Vermont History*, ed. H. Nicholas Muller, III, and Samuel B. Hand, 338–40. Montpelier, Vt.: Vermont Historical Society, 1982.

———. "Potholes and Watersheds: Perspectives on 1920–60." In *Lake Champlain: Reflections on Our Past*, ed. Jennie Versteeg, 21–41. Burlington: Center for Research on Vermont, 1987.

———.*The Star that Set: The Vermont Republican Party, 1854–1974.* Lanham, Md.: Lexington Books, 2002.

Hand, Samuel B., Jeffrey D. Marshall, and D. Gregory Sanford. "'Little Republics': The Structure of State Politics in Vermont, 1854–1920." *Vermont History* 53 (Summer 1985): 141–66.

Hansen, Karen. *A Very Social Time: Crafting Community in Antebellum New England.* Berkeley: University of California Press, 1994.

Haraty, Peter H., ed. *Put the Vermonters Ahead: A History of the Vermont National Guard, 1764–1978.* Burlington, Vt.: Queen City Printers, 1979.

Harvey, Carrie K., and Clara M. Kellogg. *History of Bristol, Vermont, 1862–1940.* Omaha: W. Gail, 1941.

Haskins, Harold W. *A History of Bradford, Vermont, Covering the Period from Its Beginning in 1765 to the Middle of 1968.* Littleton, N.H.: Courier Print Co., 1968.

Hawley, Ellis W. *The Great War and the Search for a Modern Order: A History of the American People and Their Institutions, 1917–1933.* New York: St. Martin's Press, 1979.

Hayes, Lyman Simpson. *High Water at Bellows Falls and North Walpole, November, 1927; With a Record of Previous High Water Periods.* Bellows Falls, Vt.: F. H. Gobie Press, 1927.

Haynes, John Earl, ed. *Calvin Coolidge and the Coolidge Era: Essays on the History of the 1920s.* Washington, D.C.: Library of Congress, 1998.

Herwig, Wes. "A Whistle Up the Valley," *Vermont Life* 18, no. 1 (Autumn 1963): 44–48.

Herwig, Wes, Miriam Herwig, and Robert C. Jones. *A Whistle Up the Valley: The Story of the Peavine, Vermont's White River Railroad.* Burlington, Vt.: Evergreen Press, 2005.

Hicks, John D. *Republican Ascendancy 1921–1933.* New York: Harper and Row, 1963.

Hill, Ellen C., and Marilyn S. Blackwell. *Across the Onion: A History of East Montpelier, Vermont, 1781–1981.* East Montpelier, Vt.: East Montpelier Historical Society, 1983.

Hill, Ralph Nading. *Contrary Country: A Chronicle of Vermont.* New York: Rinehart Publishing Co., 1950.

History of Newbury, Vermont, 1900 to 1977, with Genealogical Records of Many Families. Bradford, Vt.: Fox Publishing, 1978.

Hugill, Peter J. "Good Roads and the Automobile in the United States, 1880–1929." *Geographical Review* 72, no. 3 (July 1982): 327–49.

Hungerford, Edward, David W. Sargent, Jr., Lawrence Doherty, and Charles E. Fisher. *Vermont Central–Central Vermont: A Study in Human Effort.* Issued by the Railway and Locomotive Historical Society, Inc. Boston: Baker Library, Harvard Business School, 1942.

"I was there." *Vermont Historical Society News & Notes* 11, no. 3 (November 1957): 17–28.

Jakle, John A. *The American Small Town: Twentieth-Century Place Images.* Hamden, Ct.: Archon Books, 1982.

Jeffords, James M. *An Independent Man: Adventures of a Public Servant.* New York: Simon and Schuster, 2003.

Johnson, Luther Burnham. *Floodtide of 1927; A Gathering of Reports and Pictures Which Tell Their Story Graphically of the Great November Flood in Vermont State.* Randolph, Vt.: Roy L. Johnson Co., 1927.

———. *Vermont in Floodtime.* Randolph, Vt.: Roy L. Johnson Co., 1928.

Johnson, Roy L. *The Challenge: A Recountal of the Great Flood of 1927 in the Upper White River Valley and of the Destruction and Restoration of the White River Railroad.* Randolph, Vt.: Roy L. Johnson Co., 1928.

Jones, Robert C. *The Central Vermont Railway: A Yankee Tradition.*Vol. 3, *Austerity and Prosperity, 1911–27*; vol. 4, *Flood and Depression, 1927–1940*. Silverton, Colo.: Sundance Books, 1981.

———. *The Railroads of Vermont*. 2 vols. Shelburne, Vt.: New England Press, 1993.

Judd, Richard Munson. *The New Deal in Vermont, Its Impact and Aftermath*. New York: Garland Publishing, 1979.

Kammen, Michael. *Mystic Chords of Memory: The Transformation of American Culture*. New York: Alfred A. Knopf, 1991.

Karl, Barry. *The Uneasy State: The United States from 1915 to 1945*. Chicago: University of Chicago Press, 1983.

Kelley, Jerome E. "Flood! Vivid Memories of the 1927 Catastrophe." *Vermont Life* 32 (August 1977): 30–55.

Kendall, Florence A. "The Flood of 1927 in Orleans County." *Vermonter* 33, no. 1 (1928): 9–20.

Kendall, John S. *The History of the St. Johnsbury & Lake Champlain Railroad*. St. Johnsbury, Vt.: published by the author, [1974].

Kent, Dorman B. E. "Vermont in Agriculture and Industry." *Vermont Highways* (June 1930): 19–20.

Kent, Rose Lindley. "Flood–tides of Bennington." *Vermonter* 33, no. 4 (1928): 55–62.

Kinnison, H. B., *The New England Flood of November 1927*. U.S. Geological Survey Water-Supply Paper, 636–C. Washington, D.C.: Government Printing Office, 1929.

Kinsley, Earle S. *Recollections of Vermonters in State and National Affairs*. Rutland, Vt.: privately printed, 1946.

Klyza, Christopher McGrory, and Stephen C. Trombulak. *The Story of Vermont: A Natural and Cultural History*. Hanover, N.H.: University Press of New England, 1999.

La Pierre, George. *51 Views of the Vermont Flood, November 3–6, '27*. Burlington, Vt.: G. W. LaPierre, 1927.

Leinwand, Gerald. *1927: High Tide of the Twenties*. New York: Four Walls Eight Windows, 2001.

Leslie, Shane. "Vermont: A Memory." *Vermonter* 33, no. 4 (1928): 65 (reprinted from the London *Observer*).

Leuchtenburg, William E. *Flood Control Politics: The Connecticut River Valley Problem, 1927–1950*. Cambridge, Mass.: Harvard University Press, 1953.

Levine, Lawrence W. *The Unpredictable Past: Explorations in American Cultural History*. New York: Oxford University Press, 1993.

Lindsell, Robert M. *The Rail Lines of Northern New England*. Pepperell, Mass.: Branch Line Press, 2000.

Lipke, William C., and Philip N. Grime, eds. *Vermont Landscape Images, 1775–1976*. Burlington, Vt.: Robert Hall Fleming Museum, 1976.

Lippmann, Walter. "The Causes of Political Indifference To-Day." *Atlantic* 140 (February 1927): 261–68.

Lohof, Bruce. "Herbert Hoover, Spokesman of Humane Efficiency: The Mississippi Flood of 1927." *American Quarterly* 22, no. 3 (Autumn 1970): 690–700.

Lovecraft, H. P. "Vermont—a First Impression." *The Drift-Wind* 2, no. 5 (March 1928): n.p.

———. "The Whisperer in the Darkness." *Weird Tales* 18, no. 1 (August 1931): 32–73.

Ludlum, David M. *The Vermont Weather Book.* Montpelier, Vt.: Vermont Historical Society, 1985.

Lund, John M. "Vermont Nativism: William Paul Dillingham and U.S. Immigration Legislation." *Vermont History* 63, no. 1 (Winter 1995): 15–29.

Lyndes, E. J., and Theo Menard. *The Black River's Rampage, 1927: Springfield, Vermont.* Springfield, Vt.: Springfield Post No. 18, American Legion, [1927].

Mail Story of the Flood. Concord, N.H.: The Concord Press, 1928.

Marsh, D'Arcy. *The Tragedy of Henry Thornton.* Toronto: Macmillan, 1935.

Martin, E. S. Editorial. *Life* 90, no. 2354 (15 December 1927): 16.

Masten, Paul Winfield. "A History of the White River Valley Road." *Vermont History* 32, no. 4 (October 1964): 213–21.

McCullough, David. *The Johnstown Flood.* New York: Simon and Schuster, 1968.

Meeks, Harold A. *Time and Change in Vermont: A Human Geography.* Chester, Ct.: Globe-Pequot Press, 1986.

Metcalf, Minnie. "The Flood at South Royalton, White River Valley." *Vermonter* 34, no. 11 (November 1929): 172–76.

Miller, H. S. "As It Was in the Days of Noah." *Vermonter* 34, no. 5 (May 1929): 73–74.

Mills, Lawrence. "The Avalanche of Waters at Gaysville, November 3, 1927, with interpolations by the editor." *Vermonter* 34, no. 3 (March 1929): 43–7.

Minsinger, William E. *The 1927 Flood in Vermont and New England, November 3–7, 1927: An Historical and Pictorial Summary.* East Milton, Mass.: Blue Hill Meteorological Observatory, 2002.

"The Mississippi Valley Flood—1927." *Bulletin of the American Railway Engineering Association* 29, no. 303, part 2 (January 1928).

Moore, Rutherford H. "Intimate Experiences of Waterbury Refugees." *Vermonter* 32, no. 8 (1927): 136–39.

Morissey, Charles T. *Vermont: A Bicentennial History.* New York: W. W. Norton, 1981.

Morley, Christopher. "Blythe Mountain, Vermont." *Saturday Review of Literature* 6, no. 52 (19 July 1930): 1206.

Morrissey, Charles. "Living Heritage: Cal Coolidge's Indomitable People." *Vermont Life* 33, no. 1 (Autumn 1978): 12–13.

Morse, Victor L. *36 Miles of Trouble; The Story of the West River R.R.* Brattleboro, Vt.: Book Cellar, 1959.

Muller, H. Nicholas. *From Ferment to Fatigue? 1870–1900: A New Look at the Neglected Winter of Vermont.* Burlington: Center for Research on Vermont, Occasional Paper no. 7. Burlington: University of Vermont, 1984.

Nash, George H. "The 'Great Enigma' and the 'Great Engineer': The Political Relationship of Calvin Coolidge and Herbert Hoover." In *Calvin Coolidge and the Coolidge Era: Essays on the History of the 1920s,* ed. John Earl Haynes, 149–180. Washington, D.C.: Library of Congress, 1998.

Nash, Roderick. *The Nervous Generation: American Thought, 1917–30.* Chicago: Rand McNally and Company, 1970.

Neill, Maudean. *Fiery Crosses in the Green Mountains: The Story of the Ku Klux Klan in Vermont.* Randolph Center, Vt.: Greenhills Books, 1989.

Newcomb, Millard W. "The Land of Opportunity." *Vermont Review* 3, no. 2 (July–August 1927): 28–35.

"The New England Council." *Vermonter* 35 no. 5 (May 1930): 125–27.

"The New England Flood of November, 1927." *Bulletin of the American Railway Engineering Association* 30, no. 308 (August 1928).

Nimke, R. W. *The Rutland: Betterments, Statistics, Traffic, Equipment, Plans, Structures, Fixtures.* Walpole, N.H.: published by the author, 1989.

———. *The Rutland: Sixty Years of Trying.* 9 vols. Walpole, N.H.: published by the author, 1987–1990.

Nutting, Wallace. *Vermont Beautiful.* Framingham, Mass.: Old America Co., 1922.

Oread Literary Club. *History of Johnson, Vermont.* Essex Junction, Vt.: Essex Publishing, 1962.

Orton, Vrest. "A Declaration of Independence for Vermont." *The Drift–Wind* 3, no. 5 (March 1929): 197–201.

———. "How to Make Vermont Free." *The Drift–Wind* 3, no. 4 (January 1929): 145–48.

———. "Vermont—for Vermonters." *The Drift–Wind* 3, no. 1 (July 1928): 26–28.

Parrish, Michael E. *Anxious Decades: America in Prosperity and Depression, 1920–1941.* New York: W. W. Norton and Co., 1992.

Patton, Thomas W. "When the Veterans Came to Vermont: The Civilian Conservation Corps and the Winooski River Flood Control Project." *Vermont History* 73 (Summer/Fall 2005): 160–89.

Peach, Arthur Wallace, and Harold Goddard Rugg, eds. *Vermont Prose: A Miscellany.* Green Mountain Series. Brattleboro, Vt.: Stephen Daye Press, 1932.

Perkins, Henry. "The Vermont Commission on Country Life." *Vermont History* 23, no. 4 (October 1955): 335–40.

Perry, Dean H. *Barre in the Great Flood of 1927: A History of Tragic Events and of Great Loss Sustained in a Vermont City, November 3–4.* Barre, Vt.: privately printed, 1928.

Petersen, Max. *Salisbury: From Birth to Bicentennial.* Salisbury, Vt.: privately printed, 1991.

Quimby, Lorna. "The 75th Anniversary: Peacham in the 1927 Flood." *The Peacham Patriot* [publication of the Peacham Historical Association] (Fall/Winter 2002): 1–3.

Rebek, Andrea. "The Selling of Vermont: From Agriculture to Tourism." *Vermont History* 44, no. 1 (Winter 1976): 13–27.

Redmond, Myrtie Caldwell. "Inroads of the Flood on Old Waterbury Landmarks." *Vermonter* 32, no. 8 (1927): 115–21.

———. "The Vermont Flood in the Mountains." *Vermonter* 33, no. 2 (1928): 32–33.

Roby, Yves. *Les Franco-américains de la Nouvelle-Angleterre (1776–1930).* Sillevy, Quebec: Septentrion, 1989.

Rockwood, Edward. "Notes on the Governor's Message." *Vermont Review* 2, no. 4 (March–April 1928): 91.

Rossiter, William S. "Three Sentinels of the North." *Atlantic* 132 (July 1923): 87–97.

Rozwenc, Edwin C. *Agricultural Policies in Vermont, 1860–1945.* Montpelier, Vt.: Vermont Historical Society, 1981.

———. "The Group Basis of Vermont Farm Politics, 1870–1946." *Vermont History* 25, no. 3 (October 1957): 268–87.

Sabin, James, et al., eds. *History of Waterbury Vermont, 1915–1991.* Waterbury, Vt.: Waterbury Historical Society, 1991.

Sanford, D. Gregory. "You Can't Get There From Here: The Presidential Boomlet for Governor George D. Aiken, 1937–1939." *Vermont History* 49, no. 4 (Fall 1981): 197–208.

Searls, Paul. "America and the State That 'Stayed Behind': An Argument for the National Relevance of Vermont History." *Vermont History* 71 (Winter/Spring 2003): 75–87.

———. *Two Vermonts: Geography and Identity, 1865–1910.* Lebanon, N.H.: University Press of New England, 2006.

———. *Yankee's Kingdom: The Imagined Community of Vermonters and the American Struggle with Modernity, 1865–1915.* Ph.D. dissertation, New York University, January 2002. Ann Arbor, Mich.: University Microfilms.

Sénécal, Joseph-André. "Nos Ancêtres les Gaulois: Ethnicity and History in Vermont." *Vermont History* 71 (Winter/Spring 2003): 62–70.

Shaughnessy, Jim. *The Rutland Road,* 2nd ed. San Diego: Howell-North Books, 1981.

Sherman, Joe. *Fast Lane on a Dirt Road: A Contemporary History of Vermont.* White River Junction, Vt.: Chelsea Green Publishing, 2000.

Sherman, Michael, Gene Sessions, and P. Jeffrey Potash. *Freedom and Unity: A History of Vermont.* Montpelier, Vt.: Vermont Historical Society, 2004.

Sherman, Michael, Jennie Versteeg, Samuel B. Hand, and Paul Gillies. *The Character of Vermont: Twentieth-Anniversary Reflections.* Center for Research on Vermont, Occasional Paper no. 19. Burlington: University of Vermont, 1996.

Sobel, Robert, and John Raimo. *Biographical Directory of the Governors of the United States, 1789–1978.* Westport, Ct.: Meckler Books, 1978.

Soule, Bradley, M.D. "Recollections of the Vermont Flood of November, 1927." *Vermont History* 45, no. 4 (Fall 1977): 229–35.

Sparkes, Boyden. "Some Attic Adventures." *Saturday Evening Post* 201, no. 3 (21 July 1928): 36–39, 134, 138.

Squier, Lloyd E. *When the Water Came to Waterbury; A Tragedy in Three Acts Depicting Scenes of the Great Flood of November, 1927, as They Occurred on the Panoramic Stage of Vermont's Most Devastated Valley, Compiled from Marion's Workshop.* Waterbury, Vt.: The Record Print, 1928.

Stanley, E. A. "A Graphic Account of How the Flood Situation Was Met at the Vermont State Hospital." *Vermonter* 32, no. 8 (1927): 141–43.

Steinberg, Ted. *Acts of God: The Unnatural History of Natural Disaster in America.* New York: Oxford University Press, 2000.

Steiner, Michael C. "Regionalism in the Great Depression." *Geographical Review* 73, no. 4 (October 1983): 430–46.

Stetson, Frederick W. "The Civilian Conservation Corps in Vermont." *Vermont History* 46, no. 1 (Winter 1978): 24–42.

Stewart, John R. "Saving the Lamoille Mail Service." *Vermonter* 32, no. 9 (1927): 167–69.

Stone, Arthur F. *The Vermont of Today: With Its Historical Backgrounds, Attractions, and People.* 4 vols. New York: Lewis Historical Publishing Co., 1929.

Susman, Warren I. *Culture As History: The Transformation of American Society in the Twentieth Century.* New York: Pantheon Books, 1984.

Swasey, Della LeBaron. "When Waterbury Was Under the Deluge." *Vermonter* 32, no. 8 (1927): 122–35.

Thomas, President John M. "The Idealization of the Near: a Plea for the Small Towns of Vermont." Baccalaureate Sermon preached at the 113th Commencement of Middlebury College, 15 June 1913. *Middlebury College Bulletin* 7, no. 6 (July 1913): 18–22.

Thompson, Zadock. *History of the State of Vermont, From Its Earliest Settlement to the Close of the Year 1832.* Burlington, Vt.: Edward Smith, 1833.

Tinkham, Jessie Briggs, and Blanche Dunham Hubbard. "The Upper White River Valley in Flood." *Vermonter* 34, no. 2 (February 1929): 29–32.

"Train Ride Home from School, 1927." *Vermonter* 5 (August 1967): 32–33.

"Trials and Heroisms of the New England Flood." *Literary Digest* 95, no. 9 (26 November 1927): 38–44.

Truettner, William H., and Roger B. Stein. *Picturing Old New England: Image and Memory.* National Museum of American Art; Smithsonian Institution. New Haven: Yale University Press, 1999.

U.S. Congress. *Congressional Record: Proceedings and Debates of the First Session of the Seventieth Congress of the United States of America,* 1928.

U.S. Department of Agriculture, Weather Bureau. *Climatological Data, New England Section.* Monthly, 1927–1928.

U.S. Department of Commerce, Bureau of Foreign and Domestic Commerce. *Statistical Abstract of the United States, 1928.* Washington, D.C.: Government Printing Office, 1928.

U.S. Department of the Interior, National Park Service, National Register of Historic Places. "Metal, Truss, Masonry, and Concrete Bridges in Vermont." Multiple Property Documentation Form, 12 April 1990, E–10.

U.S. Railway Mail Service. *Mail Story of the Flood.* Concord, N.H.: Printed by the Concord Press [1928].

Vermont, State of. *Public Documents: Being Reports of State Officers, Departments, and Institutions for the Two Years Ending June 30 . . . .* Rutland, Vt.: The Tuttle Co., biennial, 1922–1932.

Vermont Adjutant General. *Biennial Report of the Adjutant, Inspector and Quartermaster General of the State of Vermont for the Two Years Ending June 30, 1928.* Rutland, Vt.: Tuttle, 1928.

Vermont Century: Photographs and Essays from the Green Mountain State. Rutland, Vt.: Rutland Herald/Barre Montpelier Times-Argus, 1999.

Vermont Commission on Country Life. *Rural Vermont: A Program for the Future, by Two Hundred Vermonters.* Burlington: Vermont Commission on Country Life, 1931.

Vermont Department of Agriculture. *Agriculture of Vermont: Fourteenth Biennial Report of the Commissioner of Agriculture for the State of Vermont, 1926–1928,* E. H. Jones, Commissioner.

Vermont Flood Survey Committee. "Vermont Flood Loss and Damage Survey: Statement of Returns to March 1, 1928." Montpelier, Vt.: The Committee, 1928.

Vermont General Assembly. *Journal of the Joint Assembly, Biennial Session, 1931.* Montpelier, Vt.: General Assembly, 1931.

Vermont General Assembly, House of Representatives. *Journal of the House of the State of Vermont.* Montpelier, Vt.: House of Representatives, 1926–1932.

Vermont General Assembly, Senate. *Journal of the Senate of the State of Vermont.* Montpelier, Vt.: Senate, 1926–1932.

Vermont Public Service Commission, Advisory Committee of Engineers on Flood Control. *Report of Advisory Committee of Engineers on Flood Control, Public Service Commission, State of Vermont, to Hon. John E. Weeks, Governor, December 15, 1928.* [Montpelier, Vt.:] 1928.

———. *Report of Advisory Committee of Engineers on Flood Control, Public Service Commission, State of Vermont to Hon. John E. Weeks, Governor.* [Montpelier, Vt.: The Commission, 1930].

Vermont Sesqui-centennial Commission. *The Battle of Hubbarton, 1777–1927: Report of the Celebration of the One Hundred and Fiftieth Anniversary at Hubbardton.* Vermont Sesqui-centennial Commission, 1927.

———. *Bennington, Vermont 1777–1927: A Record of the Celebration, Held at Bennington August 13–16, 1927, in Honor of the One Hundred and Fiftieth Anniversary of the Battle of Bennington and the One Hundred and Fiftieth Year of the Separate Existence of the State of Vermont.* Burlington, Vt.: Sesqui-centennial Commission, 1927.

Vermont State Highway Board. *Fifth Biennial Report of the State Highway Board, for the Two Years Ending June 30, 1930, Being the Sixteenth Biennial Report of this Department.* Rutland, Vt.: The Tuttle Company, 1930.

Vermont State Planning Board. *Graphic Survey: A First Step in State Planning for Vermont. A Report Submitted to the Vermont State Planning Board and National Resources Board.* Montpelier ,Vt.: 1935.

Wallace, Arthur Patten. "'Progress' in Vermont." *The Drift-Wind* 2, no. 6 (May 1928): n.p.

Walter, Charles T. *Lights and Shadows of the Flood of 1927: Vermont at Its Worst; Vermonters at Their Best.* St. Johnsbury, Vt.: Cowles Press, 1928.

Ward, John William. "The Meaning of Lindbergh's Flight." *American Quarterly* 10, no. 1 (Spring 1958): 3–16.

Warden, Robert L. *Robert Remembers: Rural Life Memories of Robert L. Warden of Barnet Center, Vermont,* ed. Dave Warden. Barnet Center, Vt.: Warden Family Collections, 2003.

Waterbury Historical Society. *75th Anniversary: November 3–4, 1927 Flood.* Waterbury, Vt.: Waterbury Historical Society, 2002.

Wheeler, Lois. *History of Cavendish, Vermont.* Proctorsville, Vt.: privately printed, 1952.

Wheelock, Alan S. "Dark Mountain: H. P. Lovecraft and the 'Vermont Horror.'" *Vermont History* 45, no. 4 (Fall 1977): 221–28.

White, Georgia. "The Rebellion of 'The Long River.'" *Vermonter* 33, no. 6 (1928): 86–93.

White, William Allen. *Calvin Coolidge: The Man Who Is President.* New York: Macmillan, 1925.

———. *A Puritan in Babylon: The Story of Calvin Coolidge.* New York: Macmillan, 1938.

Whitney, Mary E. "Royalton's Flood." *Vermonter* 34, no. 7 (July 1929): 110–11.

Wilgus, William J. *The Role of Transportation in the Development of Vermont.* Montpelier, Vt.: Vermont Historical Society, 1945.

Wilson, Harold Fisher. *The Hill Country of Northern New England: Its Social and Economic History, 1790–1930.* New York: Columbia University Press, 1936, rep. New York: AMS Press, 1967.

Winooski Historical Society. "1927 Flood Memories." Videotape. 23 November 1994.

Wright, Ruth. *History of the Town of Colchester.* Burlington, Vt.: Queen City Printers, 1963.

Wrobel, David M. *The End of American Exceptionalism: Frontier Anxiety from the Old West to the New Deal.* Lawrence: University Press of Kansas, 1993.

Manuscripts and Unpublished Sources

American National Red Cross. Records, New England Flood, 1927: Vermont. United States National Archives.

Brigham, Elbert S. Papers. Special Collections, University of Vermont.

Canning, Nellie V. "Bolton Memorial School." Vermont Historical Society, Misc File addenda.

Carpenter, Flora S. "The Flood of November 3 & 4, 1927." Ms. in possession of Caleb Pitkin, Marshfield, Vermont.

Crockett, Walter H. Papers. University of Vermont, Special Collections.

Greene, Frank, L. Papers of Frank L. Greene. Library of Congress, Washington.

Haskins, Beatrice. Account of flood in Montpelier. Vermont Historical Society, Misc File addenda.

Harvey, Dorothy. Letters, November 1927. Vermont Historical Society, Misc. File addenda.

Hindley, Harold. Papers. University of Vermont, Special Collections.

Hoover, Herbert. See under University of Vermont.

Howes, Philip S. Papers. Vermont Historical Society. MSA 133 Diaries, 1896–1939.

Howland, Fred. Howland Flood Correspondence. Vermont Division of Public Records, Middlesex, PRA 585.

———. Vermont State Flood Bond registers. Vermont Division of Public Records, Middlesex, PRA 2245.

———. Papers. Vermont Historical Society MS 21 #21.

Jones, Edward H. "Account of the Great Vermont Flood in November, 1927, in a letter written by Edward H. Jones, Commissioner of Agriculture in the State of Vermont, to his Son, Clyde E. Jones, then in the employ of the New England Telephone and Telegraph Company," 9 November 1927. Copy in possession of the Moretown Historical Society.

McColl, Dorothy Claflin, to Ann McColl Ormsbee, 10 November 2003. Private collection.

McNulty, Sarsfield E., Letter to C. J. Dowers (1967). Vermont Historical Society, Misc. File addenda.

Mead, George, "Flood Days: An Account of the Work Done by the College Community in the Statewide Flood of 1927." Middlebury College Archives.

Middlebury College Trustee Records. Middlebury College Archives.

"More University Students Join Relief Army," typescript, no author given, Peacham Historical Society, mss-fl.

Partridge, Frank. Papers. University of Vermont, Special Collections.

Peck, Susan. Collection. Sheldon Museum, Middlebury, Vermont.

Severance, Haward M. "Green Mountain Gateway: The Story of the Rutland." Bound carbon copy of a ms. dated 1960. University of Vermont, Special Collections.

Simpson, Mary Jean. Papers, Special Collections, University of Vermont.

Slack, Ruth Estelle. Papers. Vermont Historical Society MSC 209:29.

Spargo, John. Papers. Special Collections, University of Vermont.

Taylor, John. Papers. Vermont Historical Society.

University of Vermont, Special Collections. Folder labeled "Flood Control."

———. Folder labeled "Flood 1927."

———. Folder marked "Hoover, Herbert. Re: Flood of 1927."

Urban, Arecca. Recollections of 1927 Flood by Arecca Urban. Transcript of interview of 1989 by Barbara Carpenter.

Vermont Auditor of Accounts, Records Relating to Gifts to Vermont following the Flood of 1927. Vermont Historical Society, MS Box A18.

Vermont Commission on Country Life. Papers. Vermont Division of Public Records, Middlesex, PRA 23–25, PRA 02385, box 106331.

Vermont Flood Credit Corporation. Records. Vermont Historical Society, MS A1, MSC 40.

Webb, Lee. "A History of Electric Utility Regulation in Vermont, 1880–1965," Master's Thesis, Goddard College, 1974. Special Collections, University of Vermont.

Weeks, John E. Governor's Correspondence, John Weeks, 1927–1931. Vermont State Archives.

———. Papers, 1912–1937. One box, University of Vermont, Special Collections.

———. Two boxes, Middlebury College Archives.

Index

Adams, C. B., 101, 102

Adams, Edward, 8

Addison County, 96, 128

Advisory Committee of Engineers: established (1928), 144; proposals, 145–47. *See also* Barrows, H. W.; Votey, J. W.

Aetna Life Insurance, 120

Agan, Will, 8

agrarianism, 151

agriculture. *See* farms and farming

Aiken, Governor George, 73; and electrification, 163; and flood control proposals, 148–49; opposition to Washington, 149

Alabama, 88

Albany Evening News, 127

Albany, New York, 3, 76, 90

Albers, Jan, 177

Alburg, 12

Allen, Ethan, 158

Ambassador (train), 1, 2, 10, 37, 61, 115

American Bridge Company, 119, 176

American Country Life Association, 153

American Legion, 3, 65

American Library Association, 92

American Medical Association, 154

American National Red Cross. *See* Red Cross

American Railway Engineering Association, 32

American Woolen Company, 34

Amsterdam, New York, 3

Anderson, Ida Morgan, 66

Annis, Warren, 15

Arkansas, 5, 41, 108

Arlington, Vermont, 49

Army, U.S., 21, 61, 74–76; dam construction in Vermont, 150. *See also* Fort Ethan Allen

Arthur, Chester, 158

"articulate Vermonters," 57; defined, 47; position of, 54

Associated Press, 89

Austin, Warren, 121, 136

authenticity, 55, 151

automobile, effects of, 38, 48

aviation, 141

Babbitts and Babbittry, 56

Bailey, Consuelo Northrup, 7

Bailey, Frank, 20

Bailey, Guy, 134, 153

Baker, Henry M., 97, 98, 106; Howland on, 105; photograph, 104; Red Cross work in Vermont, 100–103

Baldwin, Herbert, 73

Ballou, William, 4

Barker, Harry, 144

Barnard, 158

Barre, 52, 78; anniversaries of flood, 171; Democratic Party, 140; flood in, 15–17, 170; industry, 33–34; Red Cross, 97; relief and rescue, 8, 15–16, 64, 68; resumption of rail traffic, 109

Barrett, John, 91–92

Barron, Hal, 47

Barrows, H. W., 144–46, 147, 148–50

Barry, John, 31, 108

Bashaw, Henry, 101, 106–7

Bates, Stoddard, 108, 142

Beatty, Edward, 10

Becket, Massachusetts, 4, 10

Belding, Patricia, 171

Bellows Falls, 14, 34, 36

Bennington Banner, 124, 160

Bennington, xiii, 6, 8–9, 34, 36, 107, 132; and Coolidge speech (1928), 137–39; sesquicentennial, 42–43, 135

Berkshires, 3

Bethel, 10, 36, 37; flood damage, 75, 93, 109–10, 115; photograph, 83; resumption of rail traffic, 116

Billings, Governor Franklin, 46, 53, 147; on Mountain Rule, 130; on Weeks candidacy, 134

Binghamton, New York, 21
Black Hills, South Dakota, 43, 129
Black River, 9, 14, 34, 146
Black River Academy, 137
Bliven, Bruce, 50–51
Bloom, Sol, 127
Bolton, 71; flood and flood damage, 8, 21, 25, 28, 64; photograph, 25; relief and rescue, 68, 75. *See also* Pinneo Flats school
Bolton Mountain, 21
bond issue (1927, 1929), 84–85, 94, 119, 126
Booth, Bishop Samuel, 156
Borglum, Gutzon, xi
Boston, 1, 9, 10, 37, 57, 90, 109; aid to Vermont, 76, 90; bankers, 82; milk market, 34–36; resumption of Vermont rail traffic, 109, 111–12, 115
Boston and Albany Railway, 10, 109
Boston and Maine Railway, 10, 36, 109, 117
Boston Evening Transcript: on aid to Vermont, 76; and Coolidge visit (1928), 137; on emergency relief, 66–67; on Hoover visit, 79; interview with Fred Howland, 78; on tourism after flood, 127; on *Rural Vermont*, 160; on Weeks, 86
Boston Globe, 94, 139. *See also* Lyons, Louis
Boston Herald, 160
Boston Post, 9, 73
Bradlee, Thomas, 106
Brainard, Morgan, 120
Brandon, 38, 61
Brattleboro, 14, 136
Brattleboro Reformer, 131–32, 160
Braytonsville, Massachusetts, 3
Briand, Aristide, xi
bridges: damage, 6–7, 9; rebuilding, 82, 119
Brigham, Congressman Elbert, 34; and Central Vermont, 112; damage estimates, 32; flood control distinguished from flood relief, 121, 143; and highway appropriation, 42, 82, 93, 122–24; photograph, 35; presidential campaign (1928), 140; and Vermont Commission on Country Life, 155–56; on Weeks, 41
Bristol, 146
Brown, Major-General Preston, 74, 75
Brule River, Wisconsin, 135
Bullard, F. Lauriston, 81, 100, 127

Bureau of Public Roads (Federal), 41, 121
Burgoyne, General John, 42
Burlington, 6, 36, 46, 59; aid to flood victims, 66, 68, 71; aid to Johnson, 66; aid to Waterbury, 86–87; bridges to Winooski, 6–7, 61, 109, 128; Coolidge visits, 135, 136; Democratic Party, 140; effects of flood, 6, 11, 60, 61; and flood control, 146; highways, 125–26; industry, 34; photograph, 62; population, 33; rail service, 37, 109, 115
Burlington Clipper on *Rural Vermont*, 160
Burlington Daily News, 17, 98
Burlington Free Press, 30, 54, 140; on effects of flood, 128, 167, 144; on federal aid, 120, 121, 124, 125; on legislature, 41, 83, 142; on Mountain Rule and Weeks candidacy, 130, 132, 135; on relief and reconstruction, 89, 98, 114; on *Rural Vermont*, 160. *See also* Southwick, John
Burnor, Arthur, 107
Burt, Craig, 64–65, 139
Butterfield, Mrs., 63–64

Cabot, 66
California, 50, 122
Cambridge, 29, 66, 107
Camel's Hump, 21
Canada, 3, 111, 114
Canadian National Railway, 37, 81, 127; and Central Vermont, 110–12, 141–42
Canadian Pacific Railway, 10, 36, 109, 117, 127
Candon, John, 155
Carlson, Helge, 16
Carnegie Foundation, 92, 154
Carnegie Institute, 156
Carpenter, Flora, 23, 64
Carr, Charles, 72
Cashman, Grace, 128
Caspian Lake, 6
Castleton, 30
Catholic church, 45, 51, 52; and Klan, 52
Cavendish, 97; Coolidge visit (1928), 137; flood damage, 14, 28; as tourist attraction, 128
Cebula, John, 11
celebrations, public, 42–43, 113–14, 128
Center for Research on Vermont, 171

Central Vermont Public Service Corpora-
tion, 147
Central Vermont Railway, 1, 22, 36, 37, 126;
bankruptcy, 112; and Canadian National,
110–12, 141–42; damage, 2, 7, 10, 25, 61, 63,
110; photographs, 111, 112, 113; reconstruc-
tion, 109–18; resumption of service,
111–14; West River Railroad, 116, 141
Champlain canal, 3
Champlain Valley, 36, 146
Chase, Flora, 8, 14
Chateaugay, 61
Chatham, New York, 36
Chelsea, 131
Cheney, Cora, 171
Chicago, 54, 109
Chicago Flyer, 10
Chicago Tribune, 38
Chicoine, Philbert, 8
Chicopee, Massachusetts, 3
Chittenden County, 66, 140
Chittenden Dam, 6, 12
Christmas (1927), 86–87
Church, Catherine Adams, 114
Civilian Conservation Corps, 150
Clark, Edward, 88
Clark University, 4
Cleghorn, Sarah, 155, 159, 162
Clement, John P., 160–61
Coates, Walter, 55
Colby, Ethel, 59
"Coming Vermont," 155, 159, 162
Comings, Herbert, 40, 99, 101
communications, destruction of, 63
Comprehensive Rural Survey, 152
Concord, New Hampshire, 27, 83
Congregationalism, 45
Connecticut, 14, 91
Connecticut River, xiii, 3, 14, 30, 147, 149
Connecticut Valley, 6, 36
Coolidge, Grace, 129, 136
Coolidge, President Calvin, xi, 14, 33, 46, 158;
administration, 39, 175; Bennington
speech, 137–39; swearing in and inaugu-
ration, 50, 139; flood control in Vermont,
143; flood relief, 90, 95, 120, 122, 124, 133,
144; and Hoover, 79, 136; and noncandi-
dacy (1928), 129–35; photographs, 137,

138; role of federal government, 173;
signs highway appropriation (1928), 123;
as Vermonter, 50; and Vermont sesqui-
centennial, 43; visits Vermont, 135–36;
and Weeks, 73, 86, 135
Corey, Herbert, 44
Cornwall, 146
Country Life movement, 151–52. *See also*
Vermont Commission on Country Life
credits, business, 80, 81, 108
Crockett, Walter, 57, 170; on bond issue, 82;
and Green Mountain Series, 157–58;
highway bill (1929), 142, 175; on Weeks
candidacy, 131
Cross, Mrs. P., 91
Crown Point, New York, 128
Cutting family, 22
Cuttingsville, 9

Dale, Senator Porter, 129, 133, 134
Dann, Kevin, 164
Dartmouth College, 68–69, 76
Daughters of Vermont, 90
Davenport, Charles, 156
Davis, Mrs., 64
Dawes, Charles, 129
Dean, Governor Howard, 45, 171
Deavitt, Edward A., 20, 114; candidacy
(1928), 134–35; seeks water regulation
districts, 148–50
Declaration of Independence for Vermont, 56
Deere, John, 46
Deerfield River, 144, 145, 147
degeneracy, 52, 152–53. *See also* eugenics
movement
Delaware, 61
Delaware and Hudson Railway, 36, 61
Demeritt, B. R., 100, 101–2
Demeritt, Roy, 113
Democratic Party (Vermont), 55, 91, 135, 140
Dempsey, Clarence, 89, 152–53
Depression, 168, 178
Dewey, Admiral George, 46, 158
Dewey, Harold, 4
Dillingham, Senator William, 52, 76
Dimick, M. D., 100–101
District of Columbia, 122
Dog River, 7

Dohm, Marie, 72
Dorset, 11
"downhill Vermont," 47–48
Drift-Wind, The, 55, 57, 151
Drummondville, Quebec, 4
Duffus, R. L., 50
Dumenil, Lynn, 45, 51
Dutton, Ira, 158
Duxbury, 21, 22, 24

East Wallingford, 9
Eastern Magnesia Talc Company, 116
education funding, 159
Eldredge, Reverend Samuel, 30
electrical generation, 144, 149, 162–63
Elks, 71, 90
Elmore Hotel (Johnson), 98
Emergency committees and Red Cross, 71
emigration, from Vermont, 46, 47, 52, 154
Equinox Hotel, 90
Essex Junction, 10, 79, 146; resumption of
    rail traffic, 111, 113, 115
ethnocentrism, 162
eugenics movement, 52, 53, 57, 152–56; and
    Klan, compared, 53; and Vermont Com-
    mission on Country Life, 154–55, 162. *See
    also* Perkins, Henry

Fairbanks, Thaddeus, 158
farms and farming, 34–36, 151, 155, 159; dam-
    age to, 32, 92, 167; decline of, 47, 52; and
    electric power, 147, 162–63; relief and re-
    construction, 101–3, 106–7. *See also* Red
    Cross; Vermont Commission on Coun-
    try Life; Vermont Flood Credit
    Corporation
federal aid in disasters, 82, 124, 173–74; and
    highways, 120–24; and Mississippi, 76,
    120; and Vermont, 80, 93, 121
Federal Aid Roads Act (1916), 38, 121, 169
Federal Disaster Assistance Program (1974),
    173
Federal Emergency Management Agency
    (FEMA), 120, 173
Federal Highway Bureau, 80
Ferrell, Robert, 39, 136
Ferrin, Captain Charles, 74–75
Field, Mrs., 71

Fieser, James, 72, 90, 101–3
Fisher, Dorothy Canfield, 46–47, 52, 155; on
    Town Meeting, 49; image of Vermont, 57
Flanders, Helen Hartness, 157
Fletcher, Governor Allen, 152
Fletcher, William, 177
flood, in Vermont (1927). *See* Vermont flood
    (1927)
Flood, Roger, 60
flood control, 121, 123, 124, 150; Connecticut
    River, 149; and flood relief, 121; and legis-
    lature, 142, 144, 145; Mississippi, 120–21,
    144; New England and Mississippi com-
    pared, 143; power generation, 143, 144,
    145–46. *See also* Advisory Committee of
    Engineers, 144
Flood Insurance Act (1968), 173
Florida, 56, 88, 151, 177; hurricanes, xiv, 31,
    95, 106, 136,
folklore, 51
Ford, Henry, 55
forestry, 156
Forshay power interests, 147
Fort Ethan Allen, 61, 68, 74
Fortune family, 8
Fowler, J., 130
Franklin County, 66, 140
Freemasons, 90
French, E. S., 116
French, Philip, 15
French-Canadians, 45, 46, 52, 54, 175; and
    eugenics movement, 53, 156
Frost, Robert, 158
Fuller, Governor Alvin, 10

Gallagher, Nancy, 53, 105, 152, 155; on French-
    Canadians, 156; on *Rural Vermont*, 164
Gandhi, 159
Gary, Marion, 155, 160, 163
Gates, Benjamin, 38, 103
"Gateway Road," 128
Gay, Leon, 14, 28–29, 97, 137
Gaysville, 29; flood control, 146; flood dam-
    age, 5, 8, 13–14, 93, 168; and Red Cross, 72;
    as tourist attraction, 128
General Assembly. *See* Vermont State
    Legislature
George III, King, 43, 44

Germain, R. W., 26, 62, 76

Gibson, Congressman Ernest, 1, 33, 41–42, 121–23

Gilman, 125

Glover, 63

Goddard Seminary, 15–16

Goldfine, Bernard, 167

Grafton, Vermont, 91

Grand Trunk Railway, 111

Granville Gulf, 13

Graphic Survey (1935), 164

Great Eastern Railroad, 110

"Greater Vermont," 47, 56, 57, 150–51

Green Mountain Boys, 43

Green Mountain Flyer (train), 9, 12

Green Mountain Power Company, 147

Green Mountain Series, 157–58, 164

Green Mountains, 3, 6, 21, 110

Greene, Senator Frank, 75, 78, 189n; and aid of Army, 74; and highway funds, 122; and Red Cross, 100

Greenfield Village, Michigan, 55

Greensboro, 6

Greer, Lois, 40

Grissingham, John, 94

Groves, Lieutenant Leslie R., 61

Haight, Putney, 38

Hammett, J. L., 89

Hancock, 13

Hand, Samuel: on flood, 170; on highway reconstruction, 126; on Weeks candidacy (1928), 131

Hanscome Ladies Nest of Owls, 90

Hansen, Karen, 67

Harding administration, 174

Hardwick, 29, 36

Harrington, C. F., 91

Harris, William, 72, 96, 97, 98

Harrison Granite Company, 16

Hartford, Connecticut, 3

Hartford, Vermont, 69

Hartness, Governor James, 34, 130, 150

Harvey, Clara, 20, 63, 67–68, 80–81

Harvey, George, 66

Haverhill, Massachusetts, 4

Hawley, Ellis, 95, 152, 165

Hawley, Frank, 20

Hayes family, 25

Hearst press, 95

Heath, Eldon, 17

Hemenway, Abby, 157

Henry, J. B., 116

Herrle, Colin, 66, 71, 94, 101

Hicks family, 7, 27

highways and bridges, 37–38, 41, 56, 159, 168, 169; damage, 9, 22, 82, 92, 125–26; repair, 82, 85–86, 119–20; state and town responsibility, 82, 142, 175

Himalayas, 44

Hindley, Howard, 134, 153

Hitchcock School, 8

Holland, 52

Holyoke, 3

Hoosick River, 3

Hoover, Herbert, 78; in Mississippi, 79, 99, 107–8, 129; presidential candidacy, 80, 129, 136, 140; photograph, 91; visits Vermont (1927), 32, 73, 79–82, 85, 121, 129, 140, 169

Hooverism, 165

Hopkins, Harry, 164

Hotel Coolidge, 2

Hotel Everett (Johnson), 15

Housing Act (1937), 173

Howe, Frank, 124

Howland, Fred, 28, 100, 113, 176, 189n; background, 76–78; bond negotiations, 93; on federal aid, 120; financial commissioner, 78; interview with Boston Evening Transcript, 78–79; photograph, 77; and Red Cross, 96–97, 98, 103–5

Hubbardton, battle of, 42

Hudson Valley, 3

Hunt, William Morris, 158

Husband, Walter, 127

Hyde Park, 59, 65–66, 71

Ide, Marjorie, 45

I'll Take My Stand, 55, 157

Illinois, 5, 46, 88

immigration and immigrants, 46, 51, 52, 156, 158; Finnish, 52; French-Canadian, 46; Irish, 46, 175; Italian, 46; Polish, 52; Russian, 52; Scotch, 46; Swedish, 52; Welsh, 46. *See also* French-Canadians

industry, 15, 33, 34, 46, 161–62
Institute of Social and Religious Research, 154
Insull electrical interests, 97, 147
International Paper Company, 34, 116
Irasburg, 107
Israel, Henry, 153

Jackson, Major Horatio Nelson, 17
Jackson, S. Hollister: candidacy, 133; drowning of, 16–17, 131, 171
Jail Branch, 15
James, Henry, 46
Jeffords, James, 73
Jennings, Alice, 61–62
Johnson, 59, 146, 176; flood and flood damage, xii, 14–15, 92, 167; and Red Cross, 94, 98, 101; rescue and relief, 65–66, 68, 71, 86, 107
Johnson, Adjutant-General Herbert, 20, 64, 74–75
Johnson, Luther, 7, 27, 28, 170; and Commission on Country Life, 153, 160; opposition to Weeks candidacy, 132
Johnson, Samuel, 158
Jones, Edward H., 9, 34; on flood damage, 21, 110, 167; and Red Cross, 100–103; and Vermont Flood Credit Corporation, 100
Jones, H. F. M., 20, 75
Jones-Reid flood control bill, 123
Jonesville, 21, 26, 62, 68, 125
Judd, Richard, 163–64

Kansas City, 136
Katrina, Hurricane, 174
Keay, Charles, 7
Keene, New Hampshire, 38
Kellogg, Frank, xi
Kellogg-Hubbard Library, 92
Kentucky, flooding in, 31, 123–24
Keyes, Wade, 28
Kingsley, Mrs. P. E., 89
Kinsley, Earl, 73
Kiwanis, 56
Knickerbocker Press (Albany), 90
Knights of Columbus, 71
Ku Klux Klan, 52–53, 57, 63; and Democrats, 55; and eugenics movement, 53; photograph, 53

La Parle, Henry, 12
Lake Champlain, 1, 6, 11, 36, 46; bridge linking New York and Vermont, 128
Lake Okeechobee, 31, 106
Lamoille County, 94; Red Cross, 65, 66, 94
Lamoille River, 5, 14–15, 145
Lamoille Valley, 6, 15, 36, 75
Langill, Samuel, 12
Laura Spelman Rockefeller Memorial, 154
Lawrence, Massachusetts, 4
lawsuits, 174, 175
Leavitt, Henry, 8
Lebanon Valley, 3
Lehigh University, 126
Leinwand, Gerald, xi
Lenin, V. I., 159
Leslie, Shane, 45, 54
Levine, Lawrence, 48
Lewis, Sinclair, 56, 132, 175–76; on Green Mountain Series, 158; *It Can't Happen Here*, 176
libraries, public, 92
Life, 58
Lindbergh, Charles A., xi, 34, 159, 172–73
Lions Club, 56, 71
Lippman, Walter, 53
Little River, 21
Long Island Railroad, 110
Los Angeles, 31
Louisiana, 5, 41, 108, 175
Lovecraft, H. P., 51, 56, 170
Lowell, Massachusetts, 4, 14, 64, 136
Lyndonville, 2, 10, 125
Lyons, Louis, 90, 114, 139–40
Lytle, Andrew, 157

MacDonald, W. H., 78–79
Mad River Valley, 1, 9, 21, 68
Maine, xiii, 33
Maine Central Railway, 36, 109
Manchester, New Hampshire, 4
Manchester, Vermont, 6, 49, 90
Marshfield, 144
Martin, E. S., 58
Massachusetts, 14, 51, 52, 122; flood damage, 3; highways, 38
May family, 8
Mayer, Captain William, 74–75

McColl, Dorothy Claflin, 69–70
McNary-Haugen plan, 129
McNulty, Sarsfield, 16
Memphis, 79
Mencken, H. L., 51
Merrimac River, 4, 150
Metcalf, Minnie, 28
Miami, 31, 95
Middlebury, 6, 9, 18, 40, 46, 86, 134, 146;
    Coolidge visit, 136; French-Canadians,
    156; rail service, 61, 109
Middlebury College, 18, 28, 34, 46, 61, 84,
    116, 155, 176; and student aid in recovery,
    68–70
Middlebury Register, 130–31
Middlesex, 21, 83, 92, 110, 168
Middlesex Notch, 80
Miller, Lawrence, 5, 13, 29
Mineral Spring Brook, 8
Minneapolis, 78
Minsinger, William, 31, 170
Mississippi (state), 5, 41, 92, 108
Mississippi River: flood control and flood
    relief, 76, 90, 120–21, 123–24, 143–45;
    flooding (1927), xii, xiv, 3, 5, 31–32, 41, 72,
    98, 175; and Hoover, 99, 108; and Ver-
    mont, 5, 41, 93, 120–23
Mitchell, Stewart, 157–58
modernity, 51, 151; and tradition, 172
Molly's Falls dam, 6, 144
Molokai, 158
Monroe, Kathryn, 101
Montpelier, 36, 38, 46, 60, 64, 79, 108, 171;
    flood and flood damage (1927), xii, 6,
    17–18, 21, 28, 61, 63, 67, 72, 78, 83–84, 92,
    109, 110, 167, 170, 171; flooding (1928), 125;
    Klan rally, 53; photographs, 20, 67; and
    Red Cross, 72, 75, 94, 96, 97; relief and
    rescue, 8, 17–18, 20, 74, 75, 76, 92, 107; re-
    sumption of rail traffic, 109, 112–14. *See
    also* Vermont State Government
Montpelier and Wells River Railway, 36, 83,
    109
Montpelier Junction, 112, 136
Montreal, 1, 2, 10, 31, 37, 60, 122; and flood, 4;
    rail traffic with Vermont resumes, 109,
    111–12, 115; and tourism, 127
Montrealer (train), 37, 115

Moody, Paul, 28, 70; on French-Canadians,
    156; and Vermont Commission on
    Country Life, 154–55, 156, 158
Moore, Helen, 4
Moose Jaw, Saskatchewan, 127
Moretown, 1, 2, 68, 83
Morgan, J. P., and Company, 93–94
Morley, Christopher, 43, 49
Morrisville, 59; aid to Johnson, 66; aid to
    Waterbury, 65; resumption of rail traffic,
    109
Mosher, George, 15, 17
Mosher, Howard Frank, 170–71
Mount Holly, 9–10
Mount Mansfield, 22
Mount Mansfield Electric Railway, 36
Mountain Rule, 129–31, 168–69, 176; election
    (1928), 133–35;
Mussolini, Benito, 132

Nantanna Mills, 107, 167
Nashua, 4, 90
Nation, 52, 158
National Geographic, 44
National Housing Act, 120
National Life Insurance Company, 28, 67, 78,
    176
National Trust for Historic Preservation, 177
National Weather Service, 171
nativism, 52, 162
Nelson, Minnie, 22, 23, 65
New Brunswick, Canada, 4
New Deal, 31, 120, 140, 165, 173; in Vermont,
    106; and *Rural Vermont*, 163–64
New England, 3, 33; population growth, 46, 47
New England Council, 76; Hoover ad-
    dresses, 80–81; and Vermont Flood
    Credit Corporation, 99
New England Dairy Conference Board, 34
New England Milk Producers Association, 36
New England Power Company, 144, 147
New England Quarterly, 157–58, 160
New Englander (train), 37
New Hampshire, xii, 38, 46, 60; and flood
    control and relief, 123, 149; General
    Court, special session, 83; highways, 38;
    population growth, 33; rail damage, 109;
    water resources, 150

New Haven River, 30, 146
New Jersey, 56, 151, 177
New London, Connecticut, 36
New Orleans, 5, 174
New Republic, 51
New Rochelle, New York, 60
"new Vermont," 47
New York, 3, 57; aid to Vermont, 76, 90; and flood's effects on tourism, 127; flood control and river regulation, 145–46, 148; National Guard, 76; newspapers, 54; resumption of Vermont rail traffic, 109; and Vermont Flood Credit Corporation, 99
New York Central Railroad, 37
New York Herald-Tribune, 43, 160
New York Sun, 124–25
New York Times, 10; on flood and recovery, 100, 114, 127; on Mississippi flood control costs, 124; on Mountain Rule, 130; on Weeks, 132, 140
Newbury, 68
Newcomb, Millard, 46
Newfane, 146
Newport, xiii, 10, 27
Newton, John, 10
Nicaragua, xii
Nichols family, 92–93, 168
Nolen, John, 45, 151, 163, 164
North Carolina, 122
North Walpole, New Hampshire, 14
Northern Pacific Railway, 46
Northfield, 6, 7, 61, 107, 167; highways, 125–26; relief and rescue, 27, 68, 70; resumption of rail traffic, 112
Northwestern University, 154, 155
Norwich University, 155; student aid in rescue and recovery, 7–8, 27, 68, 70–71
nostalgia, 163, 164, 176
Nova Scotia, 31
Noyes, Mrs. Harry, 65–66, 71
Nutting, Wallace, 37, 45, 48, 51, 52

Observer (London), 45
Ogdensburg, New York, 36
Ohio, 5
Ohrstrom power interests, 147
O'Kane, William, 26–27

old stock, 45, 51, 54, 152, 162, 164; decay of, 52, 53
Orange County, 135
Orleans County, 66
Ormsbee, Carrie, 60–61
Orne, Frank, 107
Orton, Vrest, 51, 56–57, 151, 177
Orvis, Anna Louise, 90
Otter Creek, 5, 6, 9, 11, 146

Page, H. J., 81
Page, John B., 141
Palm Beach, 31, 106
Parker, Chauncey, 116
Parkhurst, Lewis, 93
Partridge, Frank, 123, 124; and Vermont Flood Credit Corporation, 99–100, 106–7
Passumpsic River, 27, 145
Pavilion Hotel, Montpelier, 18, 21
Pawtucket, Rhode Island, 3
Payne, John Barton, 72, 103
Peach, Arthur, 155, 157
Peay, Governor Austin, 75
Pennsylvania, 5
Pennsylvania Railroad, 110
Perkins, Frances, 164
Perkins, Henry: and eugenics movement, 53–54, 152, 156–57, 163; and flood, 153–54; and Vermont Commission on Country Life, 152–55, 156–58, 159, 164; and Weeks, 153
Perry, Dean, 170
Philadelphia, 55
Pierce, Loren, 85
Pinneo Flats school, 27, 88–89, 92
planning, in Vermont, 150–51, 164
Plumley, Charles, 159
Plymouth, 14
Plymouth Notch, 46, 136
Pollard, Clark, 136–37
Pollard, Sarah, 9, 136
population growth, 33, 46, 47
Port Kent, New York, 60
Portland, Maine, 112
Portsmouth, New Hampshire, 82, 121
Post Office, U.S., 43
Potash Brook, Barre, 16
Powell, Max, 132, 134, 135

power companies, 97, 142, 144–45, 146–48
"power trust," 147, 149
Powers, Hiram, 158
Proctor, 12–13, 33, 60, 61, 96
Proctor, Emily, 13
Proctor family, 78, 96
Proctor, Governor Redfield (junior), 141; and Mountain Rule, 130; role in Weeks candidacy, 134
Proctor, Governor Redfield (senior), 52, 53
Proctorsville, 9
progress: and change, 50; and rurality, 57; and tradition, 56, 177
Progressive movement, 130, 152
Protestantism, 50–51
public health, 64, 159
Puerto Rico, 31, 136
Putney, 148

Quebec, 3, 4, 109
Quechee, 126–27

race issues, 55, 156
radio, use in flood, 21
railroads, 159, 162; flood damage in Mississippi, 32; flood damage in New England and Vermont, xiii, 9–10, 12, 32, 92; importance to Vermont, 37, 108–9; rebuilding, 108–18. *See also names of individual lines*
Ralston, Lieutenant-Colonel Robert, 143
Randall, Reverend Leon B., 169
Randolph, 60, 68, 114, 140
Randolph Herald, 153; on bond issue, 94; on *Rural Vermont,* 160; on Weeks candidacy, 132–33
Ransom, John Crowe, 55, 151
rationing, 63, 65
Ratshesky, A. C., 98, 105
reapportionment, legislative (1965), 48
reconstruction, xiii; press coverage, 166
recreational opportunities, rural, 159
Red Cross, xii, 3–4, 69, 72, 90, 167; designated official relief agency, 72, 90–91; farm relief, 100, 101–3; and flood relief, 76, 94–98, 108, 121, 175; fundraising, 91, 95, 106, 136; gratitude and public support, 94, 105, 175; Hearst press, 95; Honor

Flag, 106; local-national relations, 64, 71, 94–98, 101, 102–3, 105; Mississippi flood, 31, 75, 95; New England report, 105; policies, 95, 96, 99; professionalism, 95; and Vermont Flood Credit Corporation, 100–101, 106–7; work in Addison County, 96; work in Burlington, 66; work in Cavendish, 97; work in Gaysville, 93; work in Johnson, 66, 94, 98, 101; work in Lamoille County, 65; work in Montpelier, 72, 75, 80, 94, 96–9; work in Northfield, 27; work in Rutland, 11, 96; work in Waterbury, 68, 101–2. *See also* Baker, Henry M.; Fieser, James; Harris, William; Howland, Fred; Weeks, Governor John E.
Red Wing (train), 10, 125
regionalism, 151, 157
Reid, Congressman Frank, 143, 144
Republican Party, national convention (1928), 136
Republican Party (Vermont): and Mountain Rule, 130; primary (1928), 134–35; state convention (1928), 133
reservoirs, and flood control, 145
Reynolds family, 7
Rhode Island, 3, 31, 51
Rice, Howard, 131–32
Richford, xiii, 101
Richmond, 26, 68
Rita, Hurricane, 174
Robinson, Rowland, 156
Robsion, Congressman John, 123
Rochester, 13, 36, 63–64, 116, 146; resumption of rail traffic, 116; and White River Railroad, 109, 115–16
Rockefeller, Nelson, 68
Rockefeller Foundation, 98, 176
Rockefellers, 55
Rockingham, 166
Rockwell, Norman, 49
Rockwood, Edward, 84–86, 166; on Weeks candidacy and Mountain Rule, 132–34, 135
Rogers, Will, 90
Roosevelt, Eleanor, 164
Roosevelt, Franklin D., 80, 140, 164
Roosevelt, Colonel Theodore (son), 90
Roosevelt, President Theodore, 40, 50

Ross, Robert, 144
Rossiter, William, 52, 153
Rotary Club, 56, 71, 114
Roxbury, 2, 10
Royalton, 7, 14, 27
rural free delivery, 48
Rural Vermont, 149–50, 159, 161–64, 165. *See also* Vermont Commission on Country Life
Rutgers University, 84
Ruth, Babe, xi, 71
Rutland, 2, 36, 46, 54, 107; Coolidge visits, 136; Democratic Party, 140; and flood, xii–xiii, 6, 11–12, 63, 167; flood relief and recovery, 71, 96, 127; highways, 38, 125–26, 128; industry, 33–34; photograph, 11; resumption of rail service, 61, 109
Rutland County, 52
Rutland Herald, 54; anniversaries of flood, 73, 169, 171; 1929 legislative session, 141, 142; Mountain Rule and Weeks candidacy (1928), 131; railway loan, 93; *Rural Vermont*, 160; tourism, 127; Vermont independence, 44. *See also* Hindley, Howard
Rutland Railroad, 36, 37; damage, 9–10, 109; reconstruction, 109, 117

Sacco and Vanzetti, xii, 175
Saleeby, A. J., 14–15, 107
Saleeby, Mrs., 66, 71
Salem, Massachusetts, 91
Salisbury, 40
sanitation, 64
Santa Fe, 151
Saratoga, battle of, 43
Sargent family, 22
Sargent, Attorney-General John G., 79, 136
Savage, R. E., 93
Sawyer, Representative, on highway bill (1929), 142
Scandinavia, 52
Scotland, 52
Searls, Paul, 47–48, 57, 58
Sears, E. E., 12–13
"Second Vermont Republic," 177
Sénécal, André, 52
Sessions, Gene, 34

Shanghai, xii, 172
Shangraw family, 15
Shangri-la, 44
Sharon, 7, 14, 111, 142
Shawmut Bank, 91
Shelburne, 131, 140
Shepard, Andrew, 8
Sherbrooke, Quebec, 4, 10
Sherman, Michael, 44
Shoreham, 146
Shurtleff, Harry, 135
Simpson, W. A., 141
Slack, Estelle, 72
Slaight, Reuben, 79
Slip Hill, 25, 111–12; photograph, 112
Small, Frank, 17, 97
Smilie, Ellen Pinneo, 89
Smith, E. C., 113, 130
Smith, Governor Al, 76, 137, 140, 169
Smith, Levi, 142
Smith College, 3–4, 69
Smuggler's Notch, 74
Social Sciences Research Council, 154
Somerset, 6
South Barton, 10
South Dakota, 43, 129
South Royalton, 28
Southern Agrarians, 55, 151
Southwick, John, 56, 134; flood control and flood relief, 143; on Mississippi flood relief, 124; on outside aid, 82, 143; Pinneo Flats school, 88–89; on Weeks candidacy (1928), 134; on Weeks and legislature (1927), 41
Spargo, John, 42, 43, 133, 135, 140
Special Mississippi Flood Committee, 79
Spiero, Matthew, 97–98, 176
Spirit of St. Louis, 34, 172–73
Springfield, Massachusetts, 3, 4, 80
Springfield, Vermont, 34, 52, 170, 173
Squier, Lloyd: on flood in Waterbury, 8, 22–23, 170; on Hoover, 79; on winter (1927–1928), 126
St. Albans, 1, 6, 34, 60, 74; and Central Vermont Railway, 36, 112; resumption of rail traffic, 111–13
St. Albans Messenger, 89
St. Francis Dam, 31

St. Johnsbury, 1, 2, 10, 36; flood, 26, 86, 170; industry, 33–34; relief, 71; resumption of rail service, 109

St. Johnsbury & Lake Champlain Railroad, 36; damage to, 109; state loan to, 85, 93, 116; resumption of rail service, 109–10

St. Johnsbury Republican, 1, 118

St. Louis, 5

St. Michael's College, 68

Standard Oil, 116

Stanley, Dr. Eugene, 65

State Emergency Board, Vermont, 82

State Publicity Bureau, 57

Steele, Edwin, 20

Steinberg, Ted, 31, 173

Steiner, Michael, 55

sterilization, eugenic, 152, 159, 154–57, 159

Stevens Branch, 15

Stevens, Fred, 10

Stewart, John, 134

Stockbridge, 116

storage reservoirs, 144. *See also* flood control

Stowe, 6, 36, 113–14; aid to Waterbury, 24, 64, 65, 67

student relief work, 68–69, 71; photograph, 69. *See also* Dartmouth College; Middlebury College; Smith College; St. Michael's College; University of Vermont; Williams College

suffrage, 159–60

survivance, 54

Swanton, 36, 109

Taconics, 3

Taft, William Howard, 49, 57

Tamer, Shuffy, 6

Tammany Hall, 124

Tate, Allen, 55, 151

Taylor, Dexter, 114

Taylor, Henry, 154, 160

Tell, William, 44

Tennessee, 75

Texas, 43

Thomas, A. E., 54

Thomas, John, 46, 84, 162

Thomas family, 16

Thompson, Clara, 27–28, 88–89

Thompson, George, 60

Thompson, Zadock, 157

Thornton, Sir Henry; background, 110–11; and Central Vermont reconstruction, 110–11, 113–14; on highways, 37; on 1929 legislation, 141–42

Three Rivers, Quebec, 34

Tibet, and Vermont compared, 44

Tokyo, 82

tourism, 48, 164; effects of flood, 127–28; and *Rural Vermont*, 156, 159

Townsend, Artemus, 116

Tracy, William, 101, 176

tradition: and progress, 56; role in reconstruction, 163

Troy, 8

Tugwell, Rexford G., 164

Tuttle, Fred, 10

Underhill, 6

United States Congress, 93, 122–23; House Committee on Flood Control, 122, 143; House Roads Committee, 123. *See also* Brigham, Representative Elbert; Gibson, Representative Ernest; Greene, Senator Frank

United States Department of Agriculture, 122, 167

United States Geological Survey, 144

United States War Department, 74

United States Weather Bureau, 32

University of Vermont, 53, 61, 152, 158, 176; and student aid in recovery, 68

"uphill Vermont," 47–48

Urban, Arecca, 66

urbanism, 51

Vermont: "can take care of its own," 72–76, 125, 169, 171, 178; character and characteristics, xiii–xiv, 42, 45, 49, 50, 52, 54–55, 58, 78, 155, 163, 173; decline and degeneracy, 152–53; economy, 33, 107–8; exceptionalism, 43, 48–49, 57; and federal government, 120–24, 133; flood control in, 124, 143, 146, 149, 150; hydropower, 97, 145, 147–48; image of, xiii, 1, 42–45, 48, 49–50, 57–58, 76, 171–72, 176–77; importance to nation, 57–58, 171–72, 177; independence of, 43, 44, 56, 123; industry in, 15, 33, 34,

Vermont *(continued)*
  46, 161–62; population, 33, 37, 47–48, 168, 175; religious life, 51, 156; sesquicenten- nial (1927), xi–xii, 42, 43, 135; state plan- ning in, 150–51, 164; taxation, 141–42; tra- ditions, 48, 67, 124, 155. *See also* "Greater Vermont"; highways and bridges; Red Cross; Vermont State Government; Ver- mont State Legislature
Vermont (play), 54
Vermont Chamber of Commerce, 37, 45, 151, 167; and effects of flood on tourism, 127
Vermont Commission on Country Life, 150–65; and agriculture, 155–56; compo- sition of, 153–55, 175; and eugenics, 154, 155–56, 158; and immigration, 156; and New Deal, 164–65; origins of, 151, 152–53; religion, 51, 156; and tourism, 156; Ver- mont traditions, 155, 157–58, 162. *See also* Perkins, Henry; *Rural Vermont*
Vermont Farm Bureau, 162–63
Vermont flood (1927): as American history, xi, xiv, 58; anniversaries of, 169, 171; and change in Vermont, xi, xiv, 168–69, 171–72; damage, xii–xiv, 31–33, 59, 63, 122, 166–67; and other disasters, 30–31, 173; and historians, 170; loss of woodlands, 144; compared with Mississippi flooding, 5–6, 122
Vermont Flood Credit Corporation: forma- tion of, 99; farm relief, 100–101, 106–7; and Red Cross, 100, 106–7; summary of work, 107–8. *See also* Partridge, Frank
Vermont floods (other than 1927), 30, 125, 144
Vermont Free Public Library Department, 92
Vermont Historical Society, 160–61, 170
Vermont Marble Company, 33, 78, 90, 96, 99; damage to, 12; and White River Rail- road, 116
Vermont National Guard, 11, 16, 64, 74, 82
Vermont Review, 44, 135, 166; on Mountain Rule, 132
Vermont State Government, 40; relationship to towns, 82, 124, 142, 169, 175; restruc- turing after flood, 76–78. *See also* Mont- pelier; Weeks, Governor John E.

Vermont State Highway Board, 60, 127
Vermont State Legislature, 40, 48, 147; flood control measures, 145, 148; 1927 regular session, 40–41; 1927 special session, 82, 83–85, 93; 1929 session, 141–42; 1931 ses- sion, 147–49; small town interests, 142; and Vermont Commission on Country Life, 160
Vermont State Planning Commission, 164
Vermont State Public Service Commission, 32, 144, 147; and Advisory Committee of Engineers, 142
Vermont State Publicity Bureau, 57
Versteeg, Jennie, 44
Votey, J. W., 144–47

Waitsfield, 9
Wall Street Journal, 94
Walter, Charles, 1, 118, 170
Walton, Eda Lou, 158
Walton's Register, 167
Ward, John William, 172–73
Washington County, 135
Washington, D.C., 21, 90, 111. *See also* United States Congress
Washington Legal Foundation, 174
Washingtonian (train), 27, 114–15
Waterbury, 27, 36, 59, 61, 63, 79, 83, 107, 111, 126, 167; anniversaries of flood, 171; Con- gregational Church, 24, 64, 70, 86–87, 126, 171; and flood, xii, 6, 8, 21, 22–25, 61–62, 63, 74, 168, 170; photographs 24, 60, 70; and Red Cross, 68, 101–2, rescue and relief, 23–24, 63, 64–65, 66–67, 68, 69–70, 75, 86–87, 92; resumption of rail traffic, 112–13; State Hospital, 22, 23, 40, 65, 92
Waterbury Record, 22, 135
Webb, Watson, 131
Weeks, Governor John E., 93, 176; Advisory Committee of Engineers, 145, 147; on ag- riculture in Vermont, 36, 103, 151; alleged rejection of outside aid, 72–75, 93; back- ground, 39–40; compared to Coolidge, 86; compares Mississippi and Vermont damage, 122; Coolidge visit (1928), 135–36; effects of flood on tourism, 127; election of 1926, 37; flood relief funds,

91–92, 123; highways, 37, 85–86, 126, 141; Hoover, 73, 79, 80, 81, 169; hydropower, 147; leadership after flood, 72, 75, 76–78, 177; in Montpelier at time of flood, 18–20, 21, 72, 76; Mountain Rule and second term candidacy, 129, 131, 132–33, 134, 135, 140; 1927 regular legislative session, 40–41; 1927 special legislative session, 82, 83–86; 1929 legislative session, 141, 142; 1931 legislative session, 147; optimism after flood, 86, 92, 93, 166; photographs, 39, 104, 137; qualities of, xiii, 40, 51, 86; railroads, 113–14, 116; Red Cross, 72, 90, 96, 97, 101–3, 105, 106; requests for aid, 75, 76; sesquicentennial of 1927, 42; Vermont Commission on Country Life, 153, 159; on Vermont qualities, 56, 72–73, 128

Weeks, Hattie, 18–20, 72; photographs, 19, 137

Wells River, 10, 83

West River Railroad, 16, 141

Westerly, Rhode Island, 3, 31

Westfield, Massachusetts, 4

Weston, 6

White, William Allen, 49–50

White Mountains, 3, 4

White River, 7, 13, 29; flood control, 145–46

White River Junction, 13, 27, 36; flood, 2, 9; relief, 8, 68; resumption of rail traffic, 113–14

White River Railway, 36–37, 117; flood damage, 109; photographs, 115, 117; reconstruction, 115–16

White River Valley, 37, 116; flood and flood damage, 5, 15, 28, 107, 110–11, 115, 128

Whitehall, New York, 3, 36, 128

Whitney, Mary, 7, 27

Williams College, 3

Williamsburg, Virginia, 55

Williamstown, Massachusetts, 10

Willingdon, Lord George, 4

Williston, 111

Wilson, Foster, 60

Wilson, Harold, 47

Wilson, Governor Stanley, 134, 145; candidacy (1928), 131–34; on flood, 166; flood control, 147–48

Wilson, Woodrow, 50

Windsor, 107

Windsor county, 51

Winooski, 6; bridge to Burlington, 6–7, 61, 109, 128; Democratic Party, 140; industry, 34, 46; photograph, 62

Winooski River, 5, 21; flood and flood damage, 6–7, 83, 88, 111, 125, 144; flood control, 145–46, 150

Winooski Valley: flood and flood damage, 15, 62, 110; relief and reconstruction, 68, 75, 126; resumption of rail traffic, 111–13

"winter thesis," 47

Wisconsin, 135–36

Wolfe, Professor Alan, 183n

women: in emergency relief, 69, 71; and Vermont Commission on Country Life, 155

Woodstock, 30, 46, 106, 109

Woonsocket, Rhode Island, 3

yeast, 21, 63

Y.M.C.A., 91